Chords And Scales
For Guitarists

Printed and bound in the EU

Published by SMT, an imprint of Bobcat Books Limited
8/9 Frith Street, London W1D 3JB

www.musicsales.com

Copyright: © David Mead 2002

Music typesetting: Cambridge Notation

Cover image courtesy of Getty|Stone/Patrick Coughlin

Photography by Carol Farnworth

While the publishers have made every reasonable effort to trace the copyright
owners for any or all of the photographs in this book, there may be some
omissions of credits, for which we apologise.

ISBN: 1-86074-432-X
SMT1584R

Chords And Scales

For Guitarists

David Mead

BOOK CONTENTS

ACKNOWLEDGEMENTS

My thanks, as ever, to Carol, for her encouragement – and I will write that novel one day! To my sons Tim and Toby who delight my every waking moment and may have their own musical tales to tell.

To friends and family who endure my mood swings while writing, to Lilly the iBook who faithfully captured every word in her unfathomable insides...

To Phil H for a good time in the studio and much sonic wisdom and every pupil I have ever introduced to chords and scales in the past!

FOREWORD

In this excellent book, David Mead sets out to give guitarists the building blocks upon which to base a working knowledge of improvisation and accompaniment on the guitar. As David said when I quizzed him about it, 'It's loosely based on the principle that if a guy asks you for a fish and you give him one, it'll feed him for a day; show him how to catch fish and you'll feed him for life...except I'm doing it with chords and scales.'

Chords and scales are indeed the musician's twin staffs of life, for without a grounding in both it will be difficult to progress from beginner to the point where one can solo proficiently, or even work out the latest pop tune to play down the local pub. What you'll gain here is insider knowledge from both a fine teacher and working guitarist, not simply another meaningless list of shapes, or strings of notes with incomprehensible names.

In his typical down-to-earth style, David sets out the basics of how chords are built, so they become not just shapes under the fingers, but organic clusters of notes with real musical meaning. Scales are just as easily explained, and rather than simply list them by rote, David explains that really it's all about our old friend the major scale (or 'doh, re, me') and the changes you can make to it in order to create great music. If you can understand this much, then you're on the road to thinking like the professionals do, and the way they think is to relate everything back to the basics.

Feel like you're locked outside a door marked 'musical understanding', with no way in? Then look behind you, because David Mead is there with the key. Enjoy your tour!

Neville Marten
Editor, Guitarist *magazine*

INTRODUCTION

This book is the end result of a lifetime engaged in trying to work out what makes guitar music tick – and why it ticks in the first place.

I've always thought that music is made up from four basic elements: melody, harmony, rhythm and imagination, and that it's my duty to teach the first three whilst stimulating the fourth as far as possible.

My most successful pupils were the ones who questioned everything about what I was teaching them – Why does this work? Why can't I do that? – and it is to them that this book is dedicated.

During the course of the book, you will not only learn the 'what' but the 'why' regarding the subject of chords and scales, with a few words of guidance on the almost bottomless-pit subject of improvisation.

I also pass on to you something that I learned from the great guitarist Joe Pass: the CAGED idea of fretboard orientation – something that was definitely a catalyst in my own development as a player and a musician and something that has formed the basis of my teaching ever since.

My aim is simple: I want everyone to have as much fun with music as it has given me over the years. I also want to put across that information in as clear, uncluttered and jargon-free way that I can.

Music can be a tough nut to crack, and yet mastering so few of its principles and learning so few of its rules can bring so much enjoyment to your life.

Have fun looking at *Chords And Scales*, and I hope that what you find feeds the fire of your own creative enthusiasm for the guitar and music in general!

David Mead
Bath
Autumn 2002

1 GUIDE TO NOTATION

Throughout this book I've tried to keep all the illustrations and exercises as clear and as user-friendly as possible. But if you're not familiar with the contemporary systems of notation for guitar music, you'd do well to read this section without delay!

Tablature

Tablature (or 'tab' for short) is a system of dedicated notation for the guitar that goes way back. In fact there are examples of tab in museums dotted around the globe that go back to the 16th century, to give you some idea of how ancient an idea we're talking about.

Baroque lutenists would have relied on tab as the only means available with which to notate pieces, as opposed to the more universal system of music notation we have

available today. But it was tab's exclusivity that was to lead to its eventual downfall and general abandonment in favour of regular written music – principally because it was only guitarists who could read it. Standard notation took over and remained in favour until about 30 years ago, when, once again, the charm and simplicity of tablature took a grip on the current generation of guitarists. It became the norm for guitar parts to be written down in both tab and standard notation, and this provided guitar students everywhere with the perfect transcription package deal.

Now, you can't move for transcriptions of just about every famous song, riff or guitar solo ever played in tab, and this bulk of information and study material is open to you with only the simplest set of instructions and about 15 minutes of your time.

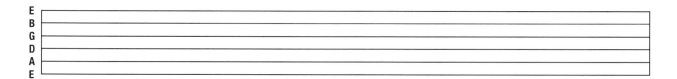

Unlike regular music's five-line stave, tab comprises a grid of six horizontal lines, each representing a string on the guitar. In the diagram above, the bass E string is shown at the bottom, with the A, D, G, B and E strings ascending in order.

Fret positions are shown by numbers written on the grid, like the diagram opposite.

In the last example, you play the sixth note on the guitar's B string. Taking this logically to the next step, if a scale passage or melody line is written down, it looks like this:

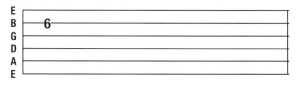

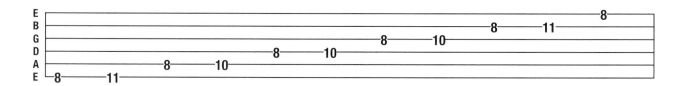

You read the numbers from left to right in series, but you'd probably worked that one out for yourself!

So much for melody lines – what about chords? If you're meant to play more than one note at a time, the numbers appear vertically in the tab, like this:

The chord above is C major – probably more familiar to you in this form:

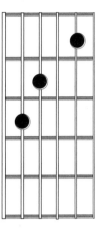

If you compare the two diagrams, you should be able to see exactly what's going on.

Now, believe it or not, that's about as complex as tab gets! Reading actual standard notation is an altogether more complex rite of passage, as far as coming to terms with written music is concerned. The next example should show you what I mean...

Look at the diagram below; a note in the middle of the music staff or 'stave', as the grid of five lines with the funny-looking squiggle at the beginning is known.

Because I have personally laboured long in the halls of learning, I know this note is an 'A' – but there's nothing there that tells you that, is there? No ingrained information at all. To make matters worse, even if you did the mental arithmetic and arrived at the answer 'A', you've still got another question ahead of you: where do I play it? That pitch of A is available to you at four locations on the guitar: here...

Here...

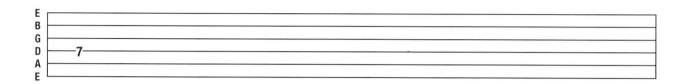

Here...

And here...

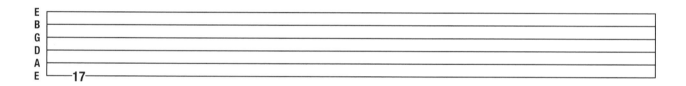

All of those notes are the same pitch (as I'm sure you've just found out if you've reached for a guitar to play through the previous examples) and so how do you know which one is the right one to play, in the context of standard notation?

The answer is that you've got to look ahead in the music and make a decision based on where it would be most practical to play the note, taking into account the location of the next series of upcoming notes. If that all sounds like an awful lot of unnecessary mental torment to you, you'd be absolutely right! Tab, however, solves the riddle in one...

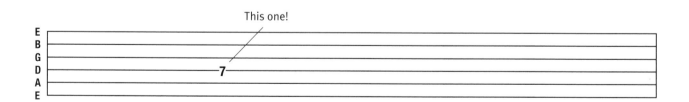

Couldn't be more precise, really, could it? And so you can probably see why tab was welcomed back with open arms when someone decided that it was a quick and easy way to teach the 'rock' generation a solo or two.

I Got Rhythm – Or Rather, I Haven't...

But, of course, you don't get away that easily. Tab's one major drawback is that it doesn't impart any rhythmic information and so you don't get to know how long a note is meant to last or whether the piece you're trying to play is a heavy-metal 4/4 or a waltz!

Back in the 16th century, rhythmic information was included along with the fret locations, but was considered unmanageable when tab was reborn. After all, if you impose rhythmic information on tab, you'd be better off using the system of standard notation already available and you'd be three-quarters of the way towards reading 'proper' music. This is why tab is more often seen accompanied by standard notation – as I've already said, it means you've got the best of both worlds.

Incidentally, if you're interested in learning the basic principles of rhythm without the unnecessary encumbrance of going the whole hog and learning how to read music *per se*, I've written a book called (funnily enough) *Rhythm: A Step-By-Step Guide To Understanding Rhythm For Guitar*, which is available through the same good people who printed, bound and delivered this book to your local bookstore!

Dots

I've tried to keep this book standard-notation free, as I believe tab serves a perfectly adequate purpose for getting across basic scale and chord information, but there's no harm in looking at the basics. And so, just for the sake of further orientation, here is a rough guide to what's where as far as the notes on the music staff are concerned.

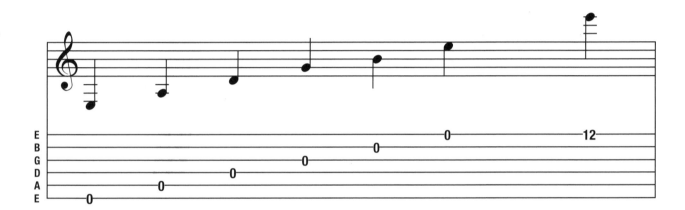

Fear not, the above examples will serve you well if you need to find a few notes on the guitar from tables of written music, but there is no need to go much further with it. People ask me all the time if it's necessary for them to learn to read music, and I generally reply that it depends on how you're eventually going to use it. If, for example, you wanted to get a job as a professional guitarist with the expectancy of doing recording sessions, pit work and so on, then yes – having the ability to read music would definitely be advantageous.

If, on the other hand, you want to play in a gigging band and go on-stage, anywhere from your local pub or club to the stage at Wembley Stadium (when it's rebuilt), then tablature will serve adequately. It's a fact that most guitarists in bands don't read music, so you're far from being alone.

Chord Boxes

I'm sure you've probably come across chord boxes already in your travels, but just in case you haven't, here's a rough guide to their ins and outs.

Chord boxes are effectively just another kind of tablature, but instead of using numbers on a horizontal grid to indicate what to play, here we're using a far more pictorial interpretation.

If you imagine a guitar standing up in the corner of the room, facing you, the top of the fretboard would look approximately like this:

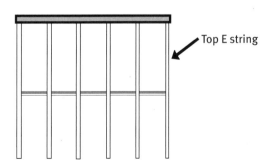

Top E string

That is, the bass E string would be on the left-hand side of the diagram, the treble E string on the right. Finger positions are shown on the diagram as blobs, like this:

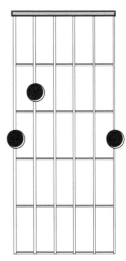

If you are expected to leave an open or 'unstopped' string unplayed, a little 'x' is shown at the top of the grid, like this:

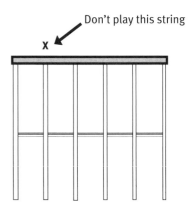

Don't play this string

X

On the other hand, if you are meant to include the open string in the chord somewhere, it will be shown with a little 'o' above it:

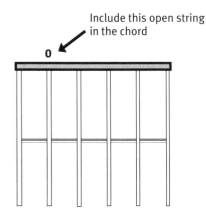

Include this open string in the chord

0

All well and good for playing chords down at the nut end of the guitar, but what about when you need to venture further up the neck? Well, we've got that event covered, too. In those instances, a little number appears at the side of the diagram, indicating at which fret you're expected to line everything up. The number at the left-hand side of the diagram shows that this chord should be played at the seventh fret:

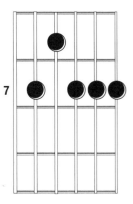

7

Fretboard Diagrams

An extension of the chord-box theme, fretboard diagrams offer you a sort of aerial view of a scale passage. If, for instance, I wanted you to play the tab at the top of the next page, it would complete the picture immeasurably if the whole scale was shown as a pattern on the fretboard, as shown directly underneath the tab. This way, you've got the best of both worlds: the tab showing you the basic fingering route map, and the fretboard diagram offering some idea of the overall pattern.

Don't forget, we learn chord diagrams by remembering patterns – it's possible (and advantageous) to learn scales this way, too.

Chord Charts

There is a long-standing tradition in music where guitarists are presented with chord charts, as opposed to the more formal 'dots' or standard notation. Chord charts do away with any references to melody, offering only the accompanying chords to any particular piece.

So, occasionally, you might come across something that looks like this:

‖ Cmaj / / / | Gmaj / / / | Cmaj / / / ‖

The example above tells you that you're expected to play the chord of C major for one bar, G major for bar 2 and C major again for bar 3. Each bar is divided by vertical lines, like this:

| Cmaj / / / |

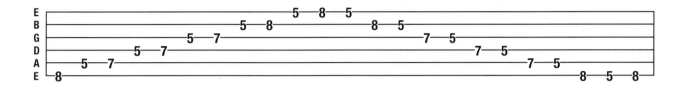

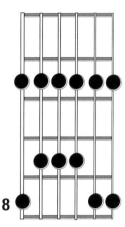

Reading tab and fretboard diagrams

The slash marks indicate that the chords should be played four times per bar.

If two chords occur in the same bar, it would be shown like this:

| Cmaj / Gmaj / |

This indicates that the first two beats of the bar are C major, and the final two beats belong to G. Be sure to check out the 'slash' marks, because sometimes a chord will last three beats, with another chord coming in on the final beat, like this:

| Cmaj / / Gmaj |

Obviously, if four chords are present in the same bar, they are all given their due space:

| Cmaj Fmaj Cmaj Fmaj |

If the pace implied by the above example looks too hot to handle, fear not – four-to-the-bar chord changes are fairly rare!

On occasion – usually at the end of a piece – a chord might be played only once. I usually notate that set of circumstances like this:

| Cmaj / / / | Cmaj ||

The final bar of a piece or section is traditionally indicated by using two vertical lines, as shown above.

This system of notation can, on occasion, get more involved than this – as would be necessary in complete scores, for instance – but the examples above cover everything you'll find in this book.

2 FRETBOARD ORIENTEERING

Are you good at jigsaw puzzles? Because I've got a real lulu for you that will arguably form the basis of how you continue to view the guitar fretboard from here on.

Way back in the 1960s, a system for orienting yourself on the guitar fretboard was formed and taught (as far as I can ascertain, anyway) principally by mouth – it's very rarely turned up in written form. I myself came across it at a guitar seminar I attended with the late jazz guitar virtuoso Joe Pass during the early 1980s and have literally never looked

back to this day. Since that time, it's formed the basis of how I teach the relationship between chords and scales in books and seminars.

Now, I believe that it's easier to absorb information if it's based on something that's already familiar to you, and the information here is so straightforward that you'll find you've been familiar with its basis since those early days of fumbling around with chords...

Take a look at these five chord shapes:

Track 3

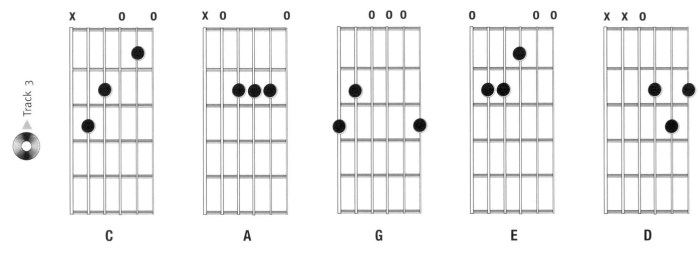

C   A   G   E   D

Exercise 1

I expect you'll agree that the chord shapes shown above are all pretty straightforward – but how would you react if I told you that *all* chord shapes are based on just these five shapes?

In order to prove that this rather grand statement is actually true, let's look at the fretboard from the point of view of a single key, C major. The first time we meet the chord of C major, it's usually down at the nut end of the fretboard – it's one of the first chords you usually come

across as a starting-out guitarist and a member of the set that I've dubbed 'campfire chords'. The finger positions for an open C major chord are shown in Diagram 1 over the page. It's simple enough and you're probably already familiar with it, so there's nothing too controversial there.

Moving up the fretboard, the next time we meet C major it's in the form of a barre chord located at the third fret, as shown in Diagram 2.

This barre shape certainly resembles a root-position A

chord, and so it commonly goes by the name of 'an A-shape barre'. But its shape has got absolutely nothing to do with the actual name of the chord – it's C major all the way. And so, if you ever hear this chord referred to as 'an A-shape barre for C major' you'll know exactly what's going on – go straight for third-fret gymnastics.

The next time we come across C major, it's as a barre on the fifth fret, as illustrated by Diagram 3. However, before you grab a guitar to try this chord out for yourself, let me add at this point that, yes, I know it's uncannily awkward to play and not one of the really practical barre alternatives on hand, but its position on the fretboard is very important to remember, so just go along with me for a while and persevere with it.

Of course, this shape closely resembles an open G major down at the nut – another one of my 'campfire chords', in fact – and so it goes by the name of 'a G-shape barre for C'. Once again, don't confuse 'shape' with 'name'. This might look like a G, but it's definitely a C in this context. Practising these harder-to-play barres will not only improve your understanding of where chords lie on the fretboard, but it will also improve your finger strength and

barre technique as well as boost confidence in your knowledge of the fretboard.

Using the same methodology by which we found C in the previous two exercises, at the eighth fret we find a barre shape for C, which is probably already familiar to you – as the A shape was a couple of paragraphs ago. The finger positions are shown in Diagram 4.

You don't need me to tell you that this chord shape looks like an open E played down at the nut, and so it's no surprise that this particular barre shape answers to the name of 'an E-shape barre for C'. Again, practising these E-shape barres will benefit more than one aspect of your playing.

Last – but by no means least – in line in the series of C-related chords checks in at the tenth fret, with another familiar face. You may well have worked it out for yourself, following the same routine as described in the previous exercises, but it's shown in Diagram 5. This particular one isn't so much a barre chord as one of the series of 'moveable' chord shapes. It really occupies only the top four strings, and so getting your hands around a full barre isn't really worth the effort. It wouldn't be too unreasonable to refer to it as a D-shape barre, however.

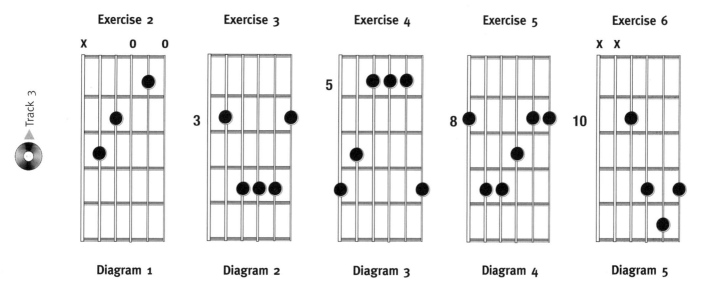

Track 3

| Exercise 2 | Exercise 3 | Exercise 4 | Exercise 5 | Exercise 6 |
| Diagram 1 | Diagram 2 | Diagram 3 | Diagram 4 | Diagram 5 |

And so, to recap, what we've seen so far looks like Exercise 7 over the page:

Exercise 7

Track 3

CAGED:
The various versions of the chord of C major, spelling 'CAGED' up the guitar fretboard. Notice how the shapes overlap and interlock with one another

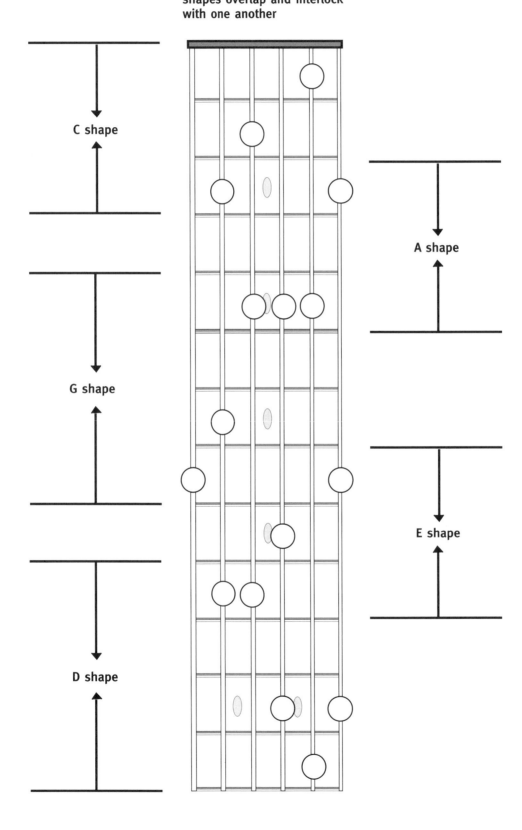

C shape

G shape

D shape

A shape

E shape

Obviously, if we went any further, we'd end up meeting the C shape again, this time as a barre at the 12th fret. From that point on, everything repeats.

So if we take all the barre chord shapes we've used in series, you'll notice that it spells out the word 'CAGED'. Let's look at another key, to cross check.

We'll take an 'awkward' key: E♭. (On an instrument like the guitar, where the same shapes move around to give similar chord and scale shapes across the spectrum, there shouldn't be any such thing as an 'awkward' key. But E♭, A♭, G♭ and so on just sound hard to contemplate.) Okay, then, in E♭ we first find this chord shape down at the bottom of the neck:

E♭ major

Exercise 8

A quick look tells us that this is the D shape. Next along the line, we find this:

E♭ major

Exercise 9

This is the barre C shape for E♭ on the third fret. Once again, it's not the easiest barre, but it does crop up, and so it's worth persevering with.

Moving up to the sixth fret, E♭ makes another appearance in the guise of an A-shape barre:

E♭ major

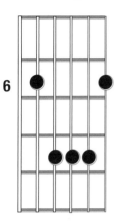

Exercise 10

Then, at the eighth fret, the G-shape barre:

E♭ major

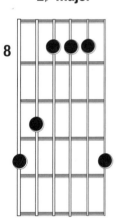

Exercise 11

Finally, for E♭, we come across the E-shape barre at the 11th fret:

E♭ major

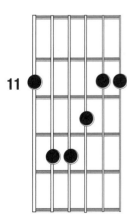

Exercise 12

So, this time, we've spelled out DCAGE, if we look at the chord shapes for E♭ in order, which is an anagram of CAGED. All this goes to prove that the various different barre shapes for any key progress up the guitar neck ALWAYS IN THE SAME ORDER.

It might be more helpful to think of it like this:

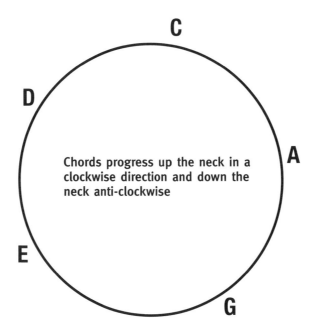

Despite the fact that this may be a lot of information to take in all at once, this should already be beginning to feel like quite a manageable system for organising things on the fretboard. And we're not finished yet...

The first steps towards fully understanding this system call for some practical work on your part. Fretboard orienteering is a little like moving house into a new area; your awareness of the new locality begins slowly and builds up over time. But this will depend on you exploring for yourself. You wouldn't dream of relying solely on maps – you'd pick up on things far more quickly if you were to get out there and put together the whole picture in your mind by assimilating the various landmarks and visual clues to your location. Becoming familiar with the fretboard is no different – and this is where the practical work has to come in.

The first thing to do is to make yourself a fretboard diagram with all the whole notes on it. By 'whole notes' I mean the basic musical alphabet comprising A, B, C, D, E, F and G without any of the sharps and flats. Because of the somewhat dubious naming convention in music, whereby B♭ can also be called A♯ and G♭ can be called F♯ and so on, plastering the neck with every note option would make the neighbourhood look very crowded indeed. So it's better to stick to the whole notes and tell yourself that you can fill in the gaps mentally by thinking that these 'in-between' notes are related to the notes on either side, like this:

The note in between G and A is called both G♯, to note its relationship to G, and A♭, to indicate its relationship to A

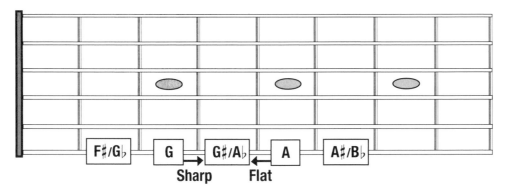

So your neck chart should look something like this:

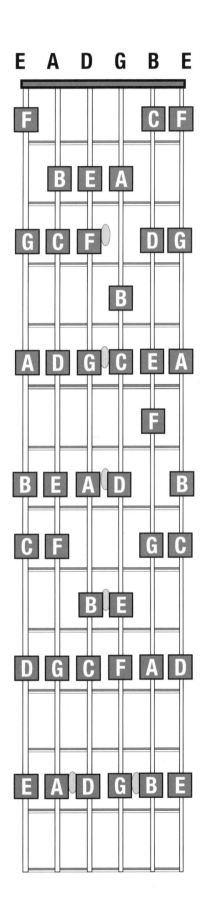

I would still advise you to copy out your own chart and not rely solely on this one for two very good reasons: one, yours needs to be bigger so that it's easily visible from a distance when you have a guitar in your hands (for example, you need to see it from either a music stand or the floor, wall or so on). The second reason is that by writing it out, you'll actually find that you begin to remember the location of a few notes – what we in the teaching biz call 'pen memory'. And, seeing as even the longest journey begins but with a single step, this is a very good move towards you having a complete idea of what goes and – most importantly – where it goes on the fretboard!

Your First Few Landmarks

The next thing to do is to pick a different key every time you practise and try to work out the CAGED series of chords in that particular key. In order to do this, you'll have to know where the 'root' notes of the five chord shapes are – and this really couldn't be simpler, because you're working only over the E, A and D strings.

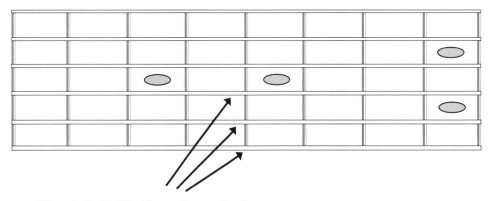

The whole CAGED idea relies on finding root notes on the three bass strings

The G-shape and E-shape barres have their roots on the sixth string, whereas the C-shape and A-shape have theirs on the fifth. The D-shape barre has its root on the fourth string. So, if you were trying to find the series in the key of A, your first root would be on the fifth fret on the bass E string.

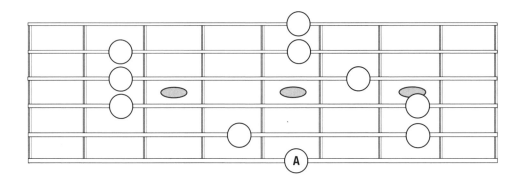

Exercise 17

Another way to remember this idea is that, for any given root on the low three strings, there's a chord going to the left and right along the fretboard visually, something like this:

Root on the sixth string: G shape on the left, E shape to the right

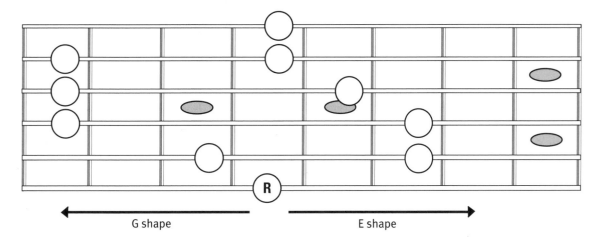

Root on the fifth string: C shape on the left, A shape to the right

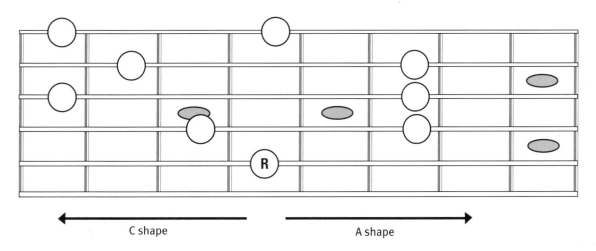

Root on the fourth string: top of E shape on the left, D shape to the right

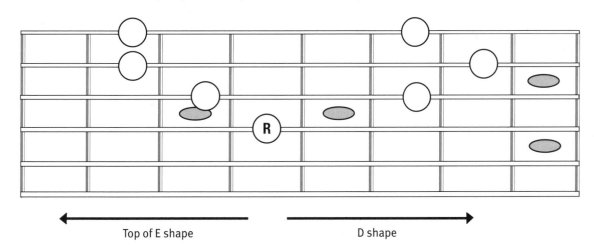

The D shape is the only exception here; from any root note on the fourth string, the D shape goes off to the right, but the shape to the left is really only the top of the E shape.

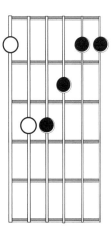

The F shape doesn't really exist in its own right in the CAGED idea, as it's really just the top four notes of the E shape

So, we've found our first root for A at the fifth fret of the sixth string. The next one is down on the fourth string, at the seventh fret, giving us the location for the D shape.

Track 3

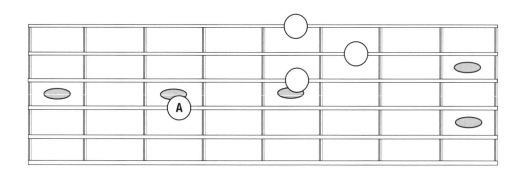

Exercise 20

Finally, there is an A at the 12th fret, fifth string – and this gives us the location for the C and A shapes:

Track 3

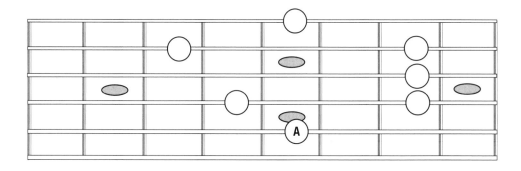

Exercise 21

Once you've found the CAGED series in any given key, leave it alone until the next time you sit down to practise, when you should pick another, different, key and work the whole thing out again.

Doing this slice of mental arithmetic regularly will mean that you'll soon become used to the 'feel' of how the different chords progress up the neck. Literally, your hand will learn the spaces between them and should be able to move between them quickly, pretty much by instinct. This will do a lot for your basic orienteering skills, as we will be putting the CAGED idea to the fullest possible use for the rest of this book.

3 LEARN TO BARRE

Over the next few pages, I'm going to introduce you to the various families of chords. I've grouped them together in this way because each basic type of chord has a predefined function to fulfil and, for now at least, it's convenient to believe that each family is mutually exclusive of the others.

It makes the job of learning chords far easier if you've got some sort of categorisation, and so our family tree is split into three main areas: major, minor and dominant, with a further sub-branch containing diminished and augmented chords. But before the introductions begin, there's one more task to contemplate.

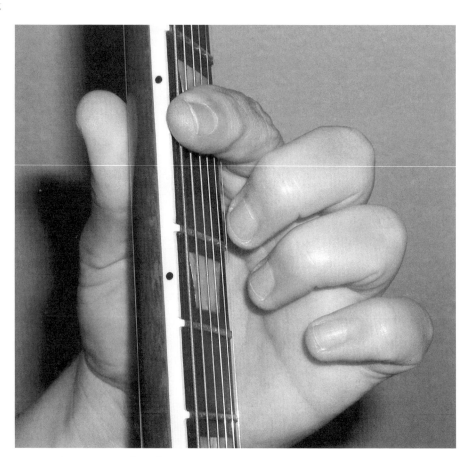

Mr Good Barre: the first finger lays practically over the fret to ensure a good cut-off point for the strings and to eliminate buzzes

Barre It All!

When we first begin to contemplate learning chords, it's not only our musical muscles that need developing; the physical side of playing requires both hands to execute some slightly unusual manoeuvres that simply aren't on the body's original blueprint. The necessary muscular acumen develops with time, but this doesn't stop the frustrating realisation that certain things seem impossible to begin with. Chief gremlin during those early days is the prospect of mastering barre chords. It's difficult, awkward and sometimes downright painful, especially while the little bit of muscular development that has to happen takes place.

I generally encourage students to begin wrestling with barre chords from fairly early on to ensure that development begins as soon as possible. Gently does it at first, of course – we don't want to encourage any repetitive-strain injuries.

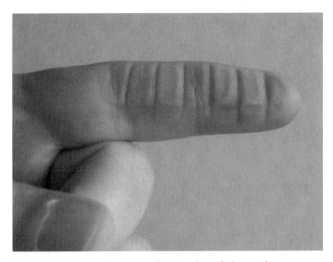

Art is pain: you can see the tracks of the guitar strings across my finger, clearly showing that the main barre pressure is actually on the 'side' of the finger rather than the 'flat'

First Step

If barre chords are still a problem for you, there are some simple steps to undertake to set you on the right path towards full proficiency. First of all, you need to position your left hand index finger across all six strings and make sure that each string still rings clear. Don't bother with an actual chord shape at first; the correct index-finger position is a key factor in getting things off to a good start.

The correct place for the strings to make contact with your index finger is slightly on the edge, nearer the thumb. Putting the finger down flat actually restricts the movement in your hand and makes the job of positioning the rest of your fingers much harder than it needs to be. The other thing to watch for is that you must lay your finger down just behind the fret, as shown in the pictures.

This is to ensure that the notes are 'cut off' effectively. Move the finger back towards the nut and you're making things harder for yourself.

Next, sound each string individually and listen to the results carefully. Are they all ringing clearly? If not, there could be another couple of adjustments you'll have to make to your playing position. Principal suspect is thumb position:

is your thumb providing proper support for your index finger? It should be directly behind it – take the guitar away and the two would touch. If your thumb has slipped to the left, your index finger will be pressing against nothing and therefore can't be expected to come up with a full house of clearly ringing strings. Just take a few minutes to adjust your thumb position as it can make all the difference (see 'Fingering Tips' on page 184).

If any of the strings still aren't ringing clearly, take another look at your index finger and alter its position slightly until everything is sounding good. Only when this happens every time are you ready to move on to the next stage.

I used to get asked by students going through their first ambling barre-chord steps if they were applying enough pressure with their index finger. I'd check their thumb and index-finger positions and, if all looked well, apply a simple test to see if actual pressure was still a problem. All you have to do is reach over with your right hand and use your right hand-index finger and thumb to 'pinch' their left-hand counterparts and apply some additional pressure. Sometimes, the barre cleans up immediately and we know that pressure is therefore the source of the problem and that maybe those muscles still need to develop some more – which they will, over time. Other times, everything would remain the same and we would direct our investigations into the Mystery Buzz elsewhere.

Second Step

Next, try playing a couple of simple barre chords like the ones shown below and carry out all the same checks outlined earlier:

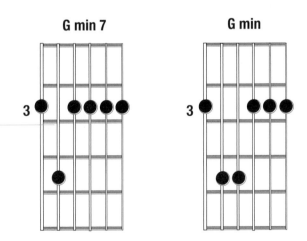

Everything loud and clear? If not, take a good look at what's happening and, if necessary, go back a step and check that your basic barre is still holding up.

Once you've graduated from the chord shapes above,

you can afford to become slightly more ambitious and try some fuller shapes like these:

G maj

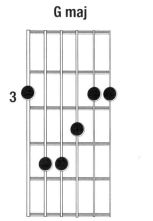

G7

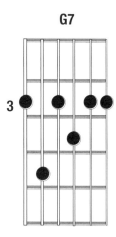

Each time you learn or experiment with a new barre chord, apply the one-string-at-a-time test to make sure everything is in order before striking it from your 'to-do' list. If it isn't – for example, if a string isn't sounding clearly – take a look at the things listed above – thumb position, basic barre integrity, individual fingers and so on – and work on them slowly and methodically.

By the way, it's perfectly normal for your hand to ache slightly while it takes on the burden of learning barre chords, but make sure you take things easy all the same. There's a big difference between that 'glow' you get from exercise and actual pain that is an indication that something's wrong.

Third Step

This step is arguably the easiest part of the whole barre-chord-preparation plan. Gradually introduce more and more barre chords into your everyday playing and, eventually, they'll become second nature. Experiment with different shapes of barre chord instead of using the same one each time – it'll certainly improve your knowledge of the fretboard and you'll be impressed by the variety of sounds you'll find on offer.

Barre Chords Versus Moveable Chords

The basic difference between barre chords and moveable chord shapes is that most moveable chord shapes don't call for the index finger to lie completely over the neck, as we have been seeing in the previous barre-chord examples. So, the difference between the two can be summed up like this:

A min 7

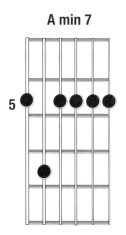

C maj 9

The Amin7 is a fully fledged barre shape calling for the first finger to be laid over all six strings, whereas the maj9 chord is a moveable four-string unit

Obviously, one of the immediate bonuses with both types of chord is that you have to learn only one basic shape, which you can then use all over the guitar neck in various keys as you require it. For instance, while this barre shape would be G major if played at the third fret...

G maj

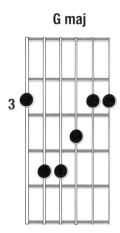

...if we repeat the exact same shape at the eighth fret, it becomes C major:

C maj

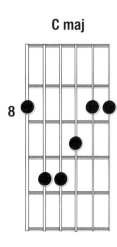

So you can play all 12 major chords from this one basic chord shape. Even better, you can expand this idea to include as many moveable chord shapes as possible, meaning that you can learn chords in multiples rather than individually.

The strategy here is to learn where a chord's root note is found. This is the note that gives the chord its name. In the examples above, the root note is on the sixth string, and so lining the shape up with the G on the bass string gave us G major, whereas moving it up to the eighth fret and lining it up with C produced C major.

There are literally hundreds of chords which can use this idea, meaning that expanding your knowledge of chords will be enhanced greatly if you're familiar with the two essential pieces of information to perform this chordal shortcut: learn where the root note is and learn the names of the notes on at least the lower three strings.

In this book I've included as many moveable chord shapes as possible and, for the sake of space, I've concentrated on chords in a single key, leaving the task of moving them to other keys to you. Don't worry, though, it really is easier than it sounds!

4 CHORDS

One of the main reasons that learning chords seems to present the average guitar player with a nightmare of bewilderment is the fact that there seems to be so many of the darned things to contemplate in the first place. Just browsing through the tutors in a typical music shop will throw up any number of books with titles along the lines of '*50,000 Essential Guitar Chords*', and this only adds fuel to the already raging blaze of disillusionment.

Many newcomers to the guitar look at the seemingly daunting task of learning, or at least assimilating, chords in entirely the wrong way. Sure, there are hundreds – or potentially thousands – of chords available in music's vast span, but there are hundreds of thousands of words in the average dictionary and yet most of us can manage to hold a perfectly decent conversation knowing only a comparatively small percentage of them.

This kind of thinking transfers to music, too: you can hold your own in almost all musical situations by knowing a selection of chords. The only remaining problems are which ones, and where to start.

In this section, I've laid out a system whereby you'll learn the chords you need to know, starting with the basics and moving towards a full understanding of where chords come from, what they do, what they sound like, and how to catalogue them for future use. What's more, we're going to make the journey with no unnecessary jargon bogging us down, no sidetracking and no impossible targets – just the quickest route to becoming a fully functional chordmonger.

What Are Chords?

It's a common misconception that guitar chords are somehow different from those found in the music mainstream, but in fact nothing could be further from the truth. Music is music. It doesn't matter what style or form of orchestration you throw at it, music functions because of a few pretty static sets of rules, and it doesn't matter if we call it country, rock, pop, nu metal, swing, bebop or whatever; it basically functions in exactly the same way from a chordal point of view.

If we examine harmony in its most basic form, there is actually very little difference between a classical orchestral piece, a string quartet and a pop song. They may sound very different, of course, but apart from that there are more similarities to be found than there are differences.

The defining factor here is simply that of orchestration – or, more basically, the actual instruments involved in the music. A pop song may use two guitars, bass, drums and keyboards, and it's mainly because of this factor alone that it sounds the way it does. An orchestra, on the other hand, has a vast number of instruments to call on, and all the various timbres and tonalities combine together to make things sound...well, bigger.

If we strip things down to the basics, though, we'll find that the fundamentals remain constant. In other words, a C major chord played by an orchestra is still the same chord – the same notes – played by a rock or pop band, in essence. It just sounds different, that's all.

Chords Up Close

At their most basic, chords contain only three notes – and once again, it doesn't matter whether they're being played on a guitar or by a symphony orchestra; three notes it is.

Consider the chord of C major. Down at the nut of the guitar, it looks like this:

Exercise 1

C major

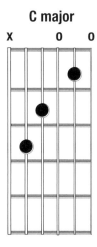

Owing to the way that music works, the chord above contains three notes excerpted from the C major scale. (Don't worry too much about exactly why this is and why these three notes were chosen to represent the sound of the scale; it's all down to hundreds of years of musical evolution. There are some clues in Chapter 8, 'The Origin Of The Species', later on in this book. If you find yourself unable to sleep out of curiosity and need a more detailed analysis of music history, there are loads of harmony books available that will help put your mind at rest. I promised to keep things basic and, hey, a deal's a deal.)

The three notes in question are these:

C E G

The chord above contains these notes:

C E G C E

And if you want me to prove it, here's the chord again with the notes written underneath:

C major

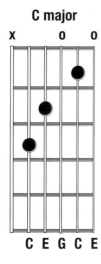

C E G C E

All that's happened is that we've repeated a couple of the notes. The above example is still a three-note chord. If you were a pianist, you might choose to play the notes in a different order, but the stark naked CEG part of the equation would remain consistent. What's more, if you were to add another note or two that was anything other than C, E or G, the resulting chord would have a completely different name.

All this should tell you that the science of chords is pretty exact, despite appearances to the contrary. In fact, music does its darndest to let us know what's going on, chordally speaking. All you've got to do is crack the naming convention code.

So Where Do Chords Come From?

There's little doubt that man's first experiments with music were monophonic – that is, they consisted of melody but no harmony as such – and certainly some of the earliest written music confirms this. Early religious music took the form of plainsong, and if you've ever come across modern-day recordings of original Gregorian chants you'll know that the order of the day was many voices singing the same melody with no supporting harmony either from other voices or accompanying instruments. Gradually, it was found that, very basically, certain notes sounded really good when sung together and others sounded excruciatingly bad. Musical evolution sorted out the good from the not so good and the harmonic system we have with us now is the result of literally hundreds of musicians and composers throwing their own interpretation of harmony into the ring throughout the centuries and good old convention has taught us to accept what we hear.

Put in very basic terms, our system of chords is based on harmonised scales – literally harmonising every note of a scale to produce a chord. Now, despite the fact that we're swerving very close to the edge of that ravine known as Formal Music Education, I'd encourage you to take a look at this next section before delving straight into the forthcoming few chapters.

What follows will help you understand more fully exactly what we're dealing with.

The Harmonised Major Scale

Firstly, let's look at the notes of a regular C major scale. Here it is:

C D E F G A B C

All this represents is the musical alphabet arranged in such a way that it spells out the 'code' for the C major scale. If you want, you can play it so that you can hear its effect:

Exercise 3

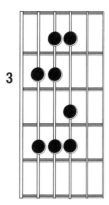

Nothing too controversial there, I think you'll agree. In fact, the major scale has spawned some of the greatest melodies ever written – everything from Bach and Beethoven to The Beatles, Blur and beyond – and they've all been harmonised using the same basic convention we're going to look at here.

The passage of time and various experiments done by musicians and composers over the years brought us the first of the harmonised C-scale chords – C major, which was constructed from the first, third and fifth notes of the C scale.

C	D	**E**	F	**G**	A	B	C
1	2	**3**	4	**5**	6	7	1

We'll be looking at this kind of idea later on, and so I'm not going to dwell on it here, but the notion was that, if other notes in the scale were harmonised using the C major chord as a template, we'd end up with seven chords, each based on a note of the scale.

So, if C major is constructed by using alternate notes from the scale, let's see what happens if we apply this kind of thinking to the note D:

C	**D**	E	**F**	G	**A**	B	C
1	**2**	3	**4**	5	**6**	7	1

The result, as you can see from above, is a chord comprising the notes D, F and A – known to its intimate chums as D minor. And just to prove that this basic maths actually works, here's the chord:

Track 4

Exercise 4   **D minor**

X X O

D A D F

So if this kind of template is applied to every other note in the scale, let's see what happens. We'll continue with the E:

C	D	**E**	F	**G**	A	**B**	C
1	2	**3**	4	**5**	6	**7**	1

Put together, this particular combination of notes results in an E minor chord. Check out the notes in this chord shape:

Exercise 5   **E minor**

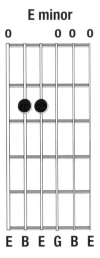

0   0 0 0

E B E G B E

Track 4

Exactly the same strategy can be applied to every other note:

C	D	E	**F**	G	**A**	B	**C**
1	2	3	**4**	5	**6**	7	**1**

This gives us an F major chord. Don't worry about all the theory that works out whether a chord is major or minor for the moment. Just take things at face value for now and everything will become a lot clearer with time.

Here's an F major chord with the notes detailed:

Exercise 6   **F major**

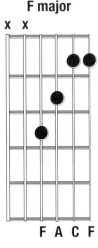

X X

F A C F

Track 4

Next, we move on to the G – and this calls for us to look at the C scale to be lengthened a bit (a two-octave scale, to be precise):

C	D	E	F	**G**	A	**B**	C	**D**	E	F	G	A	B	C
1	2	3	4	**5**	6	**7**	1	**2**	3	4	5	6	7	1

Music tells us that the notes G, B and D make a G major chord, like this:

Exercise 7

— C major
— D minor
— E minor
— F major
— G major
— A minor
— B diminished

Exercise 9

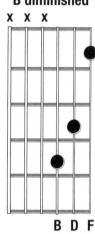

Next in line is the A:

C	D	E	F	G	**A**	B	**C**	D	**E**	F	G	A	B	C
1	2	3	4	5	**6**	7	**1**	2	**3**	4	5	6	7	1

This adds up to an A minor chord, as shown here:

Exercise 8

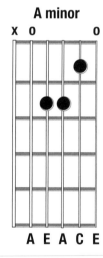

Finally, we come to the B:

C	D	E	F	G	A	**B**	C	**D**	E	**F**	G	A	B	C
1	2	3	4	5	6	**7**	1	**2**	3	**4**	5	6	7	1

The expression 'there's one in every crowd' definitely applies to the B, because instead of being either major or minor, it's a diminished chord. (More on these later.)

So now we have a complete set of chords which have all been built up using the same essential strategy, and so the whole scale looks like this:

As you can see, we're positively awash with major and minor chords, and it's possible to play these chords one after the other and hear the scale within them. Have a go at this:

Exercise 10

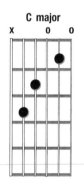

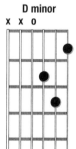

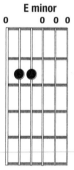

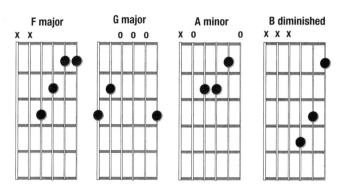

If you've mastered the art of playing barre and moveable chords and want to try playing the chords another way

that spells the scale out even more clearly, have a go at playing this:

Exercise 11

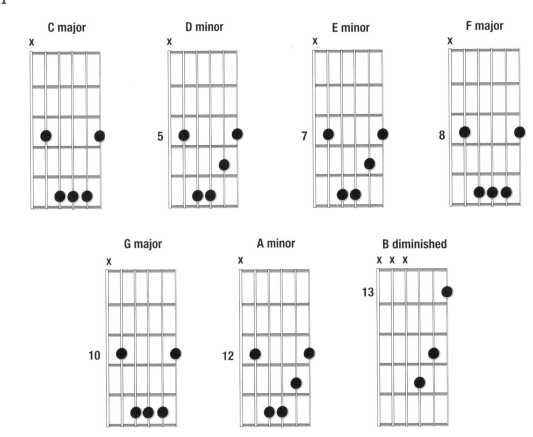

What we've ended up with, in effect, is a way to harmonise every note of a melody based on C major with a separate chord.

In practice, this actually turns out to be far too busy-sounding (and hard work for the guitarist), and so we take the far more sensible approach of letting one chord support several melody notes, which sounds a lot easier on the ear.

So chord arrangements tend to let one chord support several melody notes. I like to think of chords as being something like fence posts, whilst the melody is the horizontal beams between them. In this way, you only need chords spread out at regular intervals to take the 'weight' of the overlying melody.

It's fair to say that the last few paragraphs might make music sound a bit too much like maths to you, and indeed you might find yourself better off returning to this section after we've spent some time having a look at the various chord families later on in the chord part of this book. But at least you have a very basic idea about where chords come from, even if the picture isn't 100 per cent clear as yet.

Guitar Pioneers, The '60s And The Three-Chord Trick

Back in days of yore, when I was still a comparatively young man, there was a legend amongst the guitar pioneers of the day. It was known as the 'three-chord trick' and was as closely guarded a secret as anything held sacred by the Magic Circle today. But before I reveal all, let me just add a few lines of colourful detail, just to give you some sort of idea about what the guitar scene was like back in the early days.

If you wanted to learn guitar back in the early '60s (when I was actually at nursery school) and it didn't happen to be classical guitar, you were just about screwed. Music convention saw to it that this new beast, the electric guitar, and, worse still, pop music, were segregated from 'proper' music and given very little or, preferably, no regard whatsoever.

Tales of trying to learn during this period are rife. During my days as a guitar-magazine journalist the question 'How did you start playing?' was popped into every interview I carried out, and the answers from the '50s/'60s generation of players were always pretty much the same. A lot of the time it was straightforward word of mouth. A pack of youthful guitar enthusiasts would gather together with their instruments and exchange ideas and songs they'd learned since the last assembly. Eventually, an alpha male would establish himself as being a much better player than his peers, and it was he who would go forward to the next stage alone – which was usually another group of suitably advanced enthusiasts who would sit around and show each other things!

One thing was for sure: there were no books around to show you the way; no teachers, either. It was all a very weird science that relied on the ability to pick things up by ear from the blues and rock 'n' roll records imported from the USA. If you could put something together that sounded close enough, you could be king.

Looking back at the early '60s, Eric Clapton once told me, 'Anybody that had any idea of how to play any instrument could just about hold their own because there was no competition; there was no one around... If you could play anything in a halfway convincing fashion, you were the boss, and there were so few of us. And if you were pretty good, you could work all the time and get fairly well paid; you were successful.'

The point here is that musicians of this particular generation (and several generations before them, it has to be said) were forced unknowingly to develop a set of musical reflexes that perhaps go undeveloped in many of today's generation – that of playing 'by ear'.

Today, the market is flooded with tutors, magazines and so on which fill in a lot of the blanks using transcriptions, chord boxes and tablature. Music schools dedicated to learning electric guitar positively flourish across the country and each has a library of tabbed-out solos for their students to study. But while all this information is being ingested by the student, what exactly is happening to their musical senses, reflexes, instincts and so on?

I believe that there is a danger that playing music 'by numbers' should be moderated with continuous doses of ear training. We take a far broader look at training the musical senses in Chapter 11, 'Improvisation', so I won't waste any further time on it here.

The Three-Chord Trick

So, back to the '60s and the unfolding story of electric-guitar playing's evolution. Given that the early generation of electric guitarists (and, for that matter, their forefathers from the jazz generation) had to seek some sort of enlightenment by developing some musical instincts, they were obviously happy with any time-saving similarities that they found to be ongoing between songs.

One thing was definitely the standard blues 'I-IV-V' progression. (The Roman numerals merely refer to the position of the chords in the scale. A I-IV-V progression in C would be C – I, or first note – F, the fourth note, and G the fifth.) The other was that just about every song they came across was possible to play using only three chords...

Now obviously this is a bit of a sweeping statement; not every song is possible this way around, but an awful lot of pop and rock 'n' roll seemed to share very similar chord arrangements. It was found, for instance, that a great deal of music could be played over the chords C, F and G. Transposed to other keys, this meant that similar musical excursions could be guaranteed fruitful if the chords concerned were G, C and D, or E, A and B and so on. And here's why...

Remember when I said that chords are kinda like fence posts in the way they support a melody? It was just before I started reminiscing about the good old days when men were men and a 1958 Les Paul was just a 'second-hand guitar' (and cost about 100 quid).

The fence-post analogy means that it's not necessary to support each and every melody note with a chord – that would make the harmony part far too busy to be practical and would sound lumpy, jagged and thoroughly unmusical. Instead we settle for a single chord supporting a bit of melody, before a chord change comes along to support the next melodic 'crossbeam'. So how and why does this work, exactly?

In order to understand it fully, we'll have to go back to looking at exactly what notes go to make up chords, and once again we'll head for the convenient foothills of C major to do so.

```
C major     = C   E   G
D minor     = D   F   A
E minor     = E   G   B
F major     = F   A   C
G major     = G   B   D
A minor     = A   C   E
B diminished = B   D   F
```

Remember, all of the chords above are related to the scale of C major and are the predominant chords we would use to harmonise or accompany a melody in C.

In C major, the 'three-chord trick' is made up from C, F and G, and so let's have a look at those chords by themselves:

```
C major = C   E   G
F major = F   A   C
G major = G   B   D
```

Between them, these chords contain the following notes:

C   E   G,   F   A   C,   G   B   D

Put them into alphabetical order (starting on C) and we have this:

C   D   E   F   G   A   B   C

In other words, just those three chords contain all the notes of the C major scale and therefore are capable of supporting any melody drawn from it.

You can probably imagine how a lot of pop music in particular remains faithful to single keys and so probably get the idea of how useful the three-chord trick actually was. Applied with due caution, it would fit most songs – sometimes snugly, sometimes provoking the feeling that the melody would have to grow to fit the accompaniment – but, as a rule of thumb, it was immensely useful and inspired an almost 'instant repertoire' for many musicians from that era (and beyond – needless to say that the same rule applies today). Songs such as 'Twist And Shout' and 'La Bamba' stuck faithfully to the basic three-chord ambit, and many musicians of that time found that they didn't need to look any further at harmony in order to put a complete set together!

Case History

I had a pupil once who came to me because he wanted to expand his knowledge of chords and harmony. It turned out that he was pretty much a professional musician already, playing solo four or five nights a week in various pubs and clubs with a set list comprising popular songs – pop and folk – from the previous three decades.

He told me that he knew he could make most things fit around the three-chord trick, but he wanted to take things further and get into more involved arrangements, and so I started to teach him the basics of harmony.

It was obvious to me, after only a short while, that he was finding it hard to come to terms with all the new information. The problem was that he already had something that worked well enough for him to be out gigging practically non-stop, and so for once I took the attitude that what he had wasn't broken and so there was no need for me to fix it. I recommended that he carried on the way he was, assuring him that, in his case, ignorance was lucratively blissful!

Of course, the example above is contrary to my basic ethic as far as teaching is concerned. In general, learning about music's inner workings is a good thing and can only be of benefit, but sometimes you come across a musician whose evolution is so singularly and idiosyncratically well formed around the basics that it's best to leave things be.

5 MAJOR AND MINOR

The first thing to do in our quest to understand more about chords and their uses is to try to put together some sort of order or categorisation. At present, it may seem that there are just chords and more chords, and just when you think you've found a use for all the ones you know inside-out, there are still some left at the back of the chord book that will have you scratching your head in bewilderment.

Learning chords by rote can be an intimidating business unless you get the idea that there is some sense of order in amongst the chordal chaos. And, of course, there is...

I often ask people at guitar clinics how many different types of chord they think exist, and the replies I receive range from a couple of dozen to a few hundred. In fact, if we strip things down to the absolute bare essentials, chords begin as being one of two things: either major or minor.

This is an important distinction to make, as there isn't a more vital difference to comprehend in music – either intellectually or purely by ear. I liken it to fundamental gender differences, and we all know how important they are!

Understanding the difference in sound between major and minor couldn't be easier. All you need is a guitar and a diagram like this one:

Exercise 1

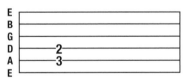

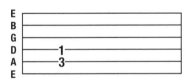

On the left-hand side, you have a major third – that is, it's a root and the third note of the scale, as illustrated here:

```
C   D   E   F   G   A   B   C
1   2   3   4   5   6   7   1
```

The notes we're concerned with are C and E, the first and third notes from the scale shown above.

Play these two notes together and the resulting sound is happy and positive-sounding, but feel free to interpret the sound as you wish. It helps enormously if you define the things you hear at a personal level. This way, you're building up a catalogue of different sounds that your ear can call upon when you're improvising or just playing in general.

In any case, the thing to do here is to listen to the sound made by this interval (as we call the distance between two notes from a scale in music).

Next, have a go at playing the example below, the minor third. This should sound very different, and you'll probably agree that it sounds far more sullen – melancholy, even – than the major third. The main difference between the two examples is that the major third resides in the major scale and the minor third in the minor scale. All chords contain one or the other (and some have both, but let's leave the lunatic fringe until later on).

```
Major: C   D   E   F   G   A   B   C
       1   2   3   4   5   6   7   1

Minor: C   D   Eb  F   G   Ab  Bb  C
       1   2   3   4   5   6   7   1
```

Both are the third notes of their respective scales, but their importance goes beyond that of any other note relationship in music.

Taking things further still, look at the neck diagrams below: you can see straight away that the major third is

further away from the root note on the fretboard than the minor third – one fret, in fact. It's this one fret's distance that acts as the crucial factor. Now, let's listen to the difference between the two different types of third when they play out their roles in chords.

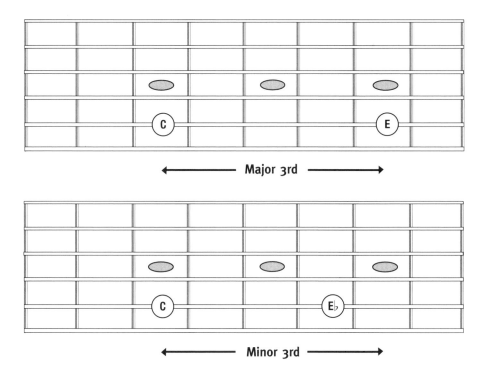

◄——————— **Major 3rd** ———————►

◄——————— **Minor 3rd** ———————►

The neck diagrams below show the finger positions for the chords of C major and C minor. Play them one after the other and their differences are even more pronounced. If I told you that this interval – a major or minor third – is present in 99.9 per cent of all chords, you may begin to

understand their significance, both technically and musically.

So it's possible to put chords into two main categories: those with a major third – major, dominant 7th and augmented chords – and those with a minor third – minor, minor 7th and diminished chords. I feel a diagram coming on...

▲ Track 5

Exercise 3

C major
X 0 0

C E G C E

C minor
X 0 X

C E♭ G C

Major Third	Minor Third
Major	Minor
Dominant 7	Minor 7
Augmented	Diminished

That makes things a lot neater, but I don't think we've yet reached a workable system. I believe it's far more useful to look at chords as being members of one of three distinct family groups: major, minor, and 7ths – two groups containing the major-third relationship and one the minor.

This makes everything defined by its musical usage, as the way in which each of the family groups is implemented musically is very different.

The reason for this is based upon the fact that each of the chord types comes from a different scale – and obviously we're going to be looking at scales later in this book, so you'll gain a much fuller understanding of the whys and wherefores in this area after reading both sections.

Major

C	D	E	F	G	A	B	C
1	2	3	4	5	6	7	1

Minor

C	D	E♭	F	G	A♭	B♭	C
1	2	3	4	5	6	7	1

7th

C	D	E	F	G	A	B♭	C
1	2	3	4	5	6	7	1

As you can see immediately, the different scales contain only a very slightly different array of notes, but this is enough to make a crucial distinction between them.

Remember earlier, when we looked at how chords were put together and found that basic majors and minors contain only three notes apiece? If we apply the same logic to the scales above, we find these three basic types of chord. But, for reasons that will become apparent in a paragraph or so, we'll start by looking at the major and minor scales, as these are your basic building blocks.

Major: 1 3 5 = C E G

Minor: 1 3 5 = C E♭ G

Take another look at the chord examples we saw a moment ago to remind you of the difference between these two types.

When it comes to 7ths, however, the rules change a little. If we took only the first, third and fifth notes of the 7th (or dominant) scale, we'd be able to see immediately that it is, in fact, identical to the major chord – or triad, if you want to use the correct musical term.

7th: 1 3 5 = C E G

As we will see, though, 7th chords have a very specific musical function, and in order for them to perform their allotted task correctly we need to add another note to the basic three.

It probably won't come as much of a surprise to you when I say that the extra note we're going to add to the 1, 3 and 5 we already have is the 7th. After all, these blighters got their name from somewhere. So the chord of C7 would, in fact, look like this...

7th: 1 3 5 7 = C E G B♭

...which, in turn, gives us this chord shape:

Exercise 4

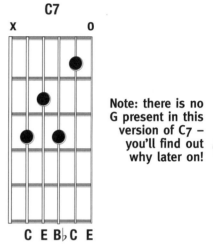

Note: there is no G present in this version of C7 – you'll find out why later on!

So now it's time to meet the families:

Exercise 5

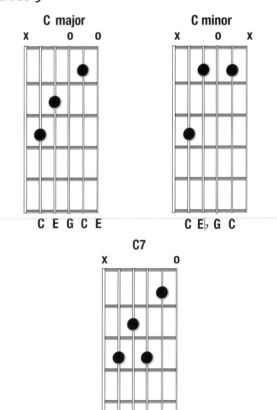

You should be able to hear distinct differences between these chords when you play them – and it's vital for your developing sense of music that you do. It's a good idea, at least at this stage, to play the three chord types daily, as part of your practice routine. Listen to each one carefully because we are going to build just about every other chord in the book on these three examples.

The Families Close Up

In order to take the next step in understanding chords, we need to take a thorough look at each of the chordal family groups in turn. We'll start with the most common chord type found in music: the major family.

We've already considered the major chord in its basic form and found that all basic major chords contain only

three notes: the first, third and fifth notes of their respective major scales. As vital revision, here are some major scales and their respective major chords.

D major: D E F♯ G A B C♯ D
         1 2 3 4 5 6 7 1

G major: G A B C D E F♯ G
         1 2 3 4 5 6 7 1

E major: E F♯ G♯ A B C♯ D♯ E
         1 2 3 4 5 6 7 1

A major: A B C♯ D E F♯ G♯ A
         1 2 3 4 5 6 7 1

Exercise 6

Track 5

D major   **D A D F♯**

G major   **G B D G B G**

E major   **E B E G♯ B E**

A major   **A E A C♯ E**

Hopefully, this proves that the system holds up in every key. But, obviously, there are more major-type chords than just the straightforward triads...

As you'll have realised, music is full of different textures and tonalities, and very often this is expressed by adding notes to the basic triad to bring out a different hue or flavour.

As an example, let's take the chord C6 and compare it to a basic C major:

Exercise 7

Track 5

C major   **C G C E G**

C6   **C G C E A**

You should be able to hear the difference between the two chords. It's a subtle difference – just like there are plenty of different shades of the colour red on a paint company's colour chart – but it's there.

So what's going on, from a musical point of view? Let's look at the major scale once again:

       C D E F G A B C
       1 2 3 4 5 6 7 1

Now, given that C major looks like this...

       C E G
       1 3 5

...any ideas what a chord that calls itself C6 might have in its ranks?

       C E G A
       1 3 5 6

All we've done is added the sixth note from the scale to the basic triad, giving us a four-note chord with a slightly different musical hue.

Of course, the trick works in every key, too, and as a failsafe we'll look at D6:

Basic triad: D   F♯   A
                1   3   5

D6: D F♯ A B
       1   3   5   6

And here are the two chord shapes as neck diagrams to play with:

Exercise 8

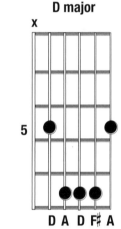 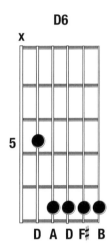

D major   **D6**

D A D F♯ A   D A D F♯ B

Once again, if you sit down with your guitar and have a go at playing both chords one after the other, you should be able to hear clearly the subtle difference that the simple addition of another member of the scale has made to the basic triad.

Let's take another example, back in the now-familiar key of C. This time, we'll add the seventh note of the major scale and see what happens to the chord we know so well.

C   E   G   B
1   3   5   7

And Exercise 9 provides a neck diagram showing the chord shape of the resulting Cmajor7. This time, the difference is arguably more pronounced; the result is a very sweet-sounding chord. At the risk of sounding very soppy indeed, I'd even go so far as to say that it sounds 'romantic'.

But, however you want to categorise the change that

Exercise 9

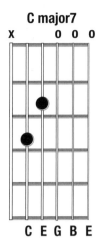

C major7

C E G B E

the addition of this particular scale member has made to the chord, the most important thing is to recognise that this is all that has happened. We haven't applied any rocket science here to turn a basic major chord into a major 7th. We've added the 7th note of the scale and made up a shorthand chord symbol – Cmaj7 – to let everyone know exactly what's going on.

In fact, you'll soon begin to realise more and more that most chord symbols are just that: shorthand. And, once you crack the code, you'll be able to understand how you can build a chord right there on the fretboard, without the need to refer to a chord book. But that comes later; for now, let's continue adding scale tones to see what happens.

Incidentally, if you want me to prove that the major-7th trick still works in other keys, not just the one we've mentioned so far (and this is the last time I'm going to do this, I promise), here's Emaj7 broken down into its component parts. The chord box is shown at the top of the next page.

E major scale

E F♯ G♯ A B C♯ D♯ E
1   2   3   4   5   6   7   1

E major triad

E G♯ B
1   3   5

Emaj7 chord

E G♯ B D♯
1   3   5   7

Before we go on adding any other scale members, let me

Track 5

Track 5

Exercise 10

E major7

E B D♯ G♯ B E

introduce you to a bit more of music's stranger conventions. Look at this string of letters:

C D E F G A B C D E F G A B C

This is two C scales stuck together, that's all. But check out the numbering convention:

C	D	E	F	G	A	B	C	D	E	F	G	A	B	C
1	2	3	4	5	6	7	1	9	3	11	5	13	7	1

Completely loony, isn't it? This is the point where I usually end up telling people at seminars, workshops and so on, 'I don't make the rules, I only work here!' Honestly, this system was in place before I came along and tried to make sense of it.

In fact, all that's happened is that we've numbered two octaves of the scale but kept the important members of the scale teamed up with their original numerical positions. The root (1), third (3), fifth (5) and 7th (7) are present in both octaves, so the only newcomers are the 9th, 11th and 13th.

You wouldn't be the first person to tell me how daft all this sounds, let me assure you, but like I said, it's been a part of music's inner workings for so long now that we're well and truly stuck with it, and so we might as well just grin and bear it.

If ever you're faced with a number attached to a chord symbol that's higher than seven, remember this: just deduct seven from it and you'll find out its original position in the scale. For instance:

$$13 - 7 = 6$$
$$11 - 7 = 4$$
$$9 - 7 = 2$$

It's simple maths, but it might shed some light in the darkness occasionally.

So, to get back to our chord manufacturing, let's take another example. How about a Cmaj9? If you check out the two-octave diagram for C major shown earlier, you'll be able to see that C's 'ninth' is, in fact, the note D, and so all we've got to do is add a D to the basic triad and *voilà*, surely? Well, heck no. Nearly right, but we've one more musical chasm to cross together. Hold tight…

Chord construction takes a couple of things for granted and one of them is this: 9ths, 11ths and 13ths are usually built up this way:

Cmaj7 = 1 3 5 7 = C E G B
Cmaj9 = 1 3 5 7 9 = C E G B D
Cmaj11 = 1 3 5 7 9 11 = C E G B D F
Cmaj13 = 1 3 5 7 9 11 13 = C E G B D F A

Now, those of you that noticed that a Cmaj13 contains seven notes and we've got only six strings (unless you're into nu metal and have a seven-string guitar), form an orderly queue and I'll talk to you in a moment. The rest of you can stare in disbelief for a while longer.

As crazy as this all sounds, I must point out that these are The Rules; I didn't make them (like I said, I'm the caretaker, not the inventor), but the funny thing about rules is that you need to know them before you can break them and, thankfully, music's rules are broken all the time (for instance, every time you play a maj13th on a six-string guitar).

So, a Cmaj9 looks and sounds like this:

Exercise 11

C maj 9

C E B D G

This chord shape presents a bit of a loopy fingering proposition, but it's important to hear all the various members of the chord together at this point. You'll learn about chord editing a little later on!

▲ Track 5

To me, this chord sounds very sweet and dense, and the reason for this is easy to understand: the chord contains five notes out of a possible seven scale tones. In some ways, we're lucky that chords like this don't sound like someone has sat down at a piano keyboard.

Out of interest, if we'd taken the logical route and merely added the D to the C major triad, we'd have arrived at this:

C E G D

1 3 5 9

Exercise 12

C add 9

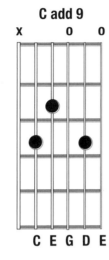

This is, in fact, another chord you may have run across, called Cadd9. Once again, musical shorthand leaps in and tries to sort things out. The 'add9' tells us that all that has happened is that we've merely added the ninth to the basic triad.

Compare the two chords together and see what your ear makes of the difference between them. To me, the add9 has lost some of the cloying quality that was very much present in the major-ninth example. It's a little like one teaspoon of sugar in your tea as opposed to three.

Try playing the following three chords slowly, one after the other, and try to pick out the difference between them:

Exercise 13

As for the other 'extended' major chords I mentioned above – the 11th and 13th variants – you won't often run up against them. We're concerned with popular use, not the more rarefied musical forms. Having said that, the Cmaj11 would technically look like this:

C E G B D F

1 3 5 7 9 11

And this would be a plausible chord shape:

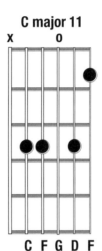

Exercise 14

A difficult chord to put together because it starts to sound like a G7 if you're not careful (which is why I've left out the B here). This should give you a flavour, however

I say 'plausible' because it's not exactly textbook-perfect in terms of its construction. It's not a particularly nice-sounding chord, either, although it has its place. You'll see later on how it's wise not to disregard chord shapes which are 'highly flavoured' or 'a bit ugly sounding'; rather, think of them as colours that you'll use occasionally – in some instances, very occasionally – but you couldn't stand the idea of painting a whole wall using them. That, after all, isn't their purpose.

The major 11 is a case in point here. A few chord books will deny its existence altogether, although, as you can see, it's got to exist, at very least from a technical point of view.

The main problem with this kind of 11th chord is that its constituent parts tend to fight with each other. If you look at the major scale...

C D E F G A B C

1 2 3 4 5 6 7 1

...you'll see how the 4th (aka the 11th) sits right next door to the 3rd – one of the principal players in the triad, as well as being the 'gender-defining' interval, don't forget. To make matters worse, musically these two intervals are only a semitone (one fret) apart, which doesn't tend to 'work' too often from a harmonic point of view.

Try the following simple test: play your open E string at the same time as playing the fourth fret on your B string, like this:

 Track 5

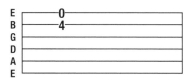

Not a particularly pleasant noise, is it? (Although, if you're interested, this was quite a popular interval in music's Baroque era.) Even if we split them up and place them an octave apart, like this...

 Track 5

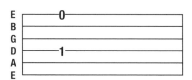

...it's still not easy on the ear, by any means. So the fact is that the 4th – or 11th – which should play a leading role in the chord that's named after it, clashes with one of the members of the basic triad – and, as we have seen, a pretty important member at that. So what do we do? Take the third out altogether? By doing so, you'd be removing the signpost to the chord's gender, and it wouldn't technically be a 'major' 11th any more. You see the problem?

So, this chord has to exist – and it has its uses; even the most highly scented herb has its place in the kitchen (that sounds very Zen, but I did in fact just make it up!) – and so we shouldn't leave it out of our basic understanding of where chords come from and how they fit into a musical landscape.

The last in line, as far as our current game of adding chord tones to the basic 1, 3 and 5 is concerned, is the major 13th. Once again, it's not a particularly common chord and, as we've seen, it's got too many notes for us to play on a six-string guitar anyway.

The major 13th's construction would look like this:

C E G B D F A
1 3 5 7 9 11 13

After a quick rummage through the bit box, we come up with another 'plausible' chord shape, which would look like this:

C major 13

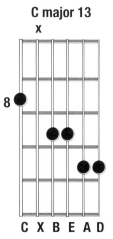

Exercise 15

A cut-down version of the major 13 with no 'bad boy F' to mess things up and no G, either. You'll be learning about chord editing soon...

 Track 5

Now, I happen to like the sound of this chord, and I do tend to use it, but people tell me I'm odd and so don't take any notice. As always, it's best to take a listen for yourself and make your own decisions as to whether you think it's a useful addition to your chord retinue.

When you do take a listen to it, you'll see why, once again, it's one of those highly specific chord voicings that you'd use once in a blue moon, perhaps, but certainly not every day. But blue moons are not unknown, and so it's best to have at least a passing knowledge of the major 13th's sound.

Following on from what we said about the 11th, you can see that the same dissonance is going to occur once again in this chord, so be prepared to edit down the voicings you find in books in order to relieve some of the natural inner tensions that would otherwise be present.

There are really no rules for editing chords. There are times when intervals are omitted purely on the basis that fingering them on the fretboard is too much of a technical challenge – large stretches, for instance. Sometimes only the basic 'flavour' of the chord need be present and so a couple of a chord's basic parts fall naturally redundant.

The important thing here is not to become phased by all the different versions you find in various chord books. Some will have as many notes in them as is feasible, while others will have been edited quite dramatically. The point is, they're all useful, all viable, given the circumstances. By understanding this, you attain more flexibility as a musician.

Odd Men Out

Whilst we're on the subject of 'trimming' chord voicings – that is, those that technically contain more notes than it is physically possible or musically appropriate to play – we might as well take a closer look at how this process works out in the field.

Chord editing – meaning that you've obviously got to

miss notes out of chords occasionally to make them possible to finger on the fretboard – is, as I've mentioned above, not an exact science.

The most common questions I get asked here are 'which ones?' and 'why?'. In answer, I usually ask people to think of a time when they're packing to go away somewhere and want to try to get three suitcases of stuff into one. (For some reason, this analogy seems to resonate more with my female pupils...)

The 'editing' process – deciding what to take and what to leave behind – starts by including essentials first. There are some things that you couldn't do without under any circumstances. I don't want to go into details, but these usually centre on underwear and toiletries for the most of us (not always 100 per cent true, I know, but we'll be talking a bit about jazz later...if you see what I mean).

As far as chords are concerned, the 'essentials' tend to be the notes that will define enough of the chord's character for its true personality to come through. After all, if the music you're playing is calling for an E major chord, even if you need to cut a few things out, you'll still need enough left to spell out E MAJOR for anyone listening. Chords are there for a purpose, and it's very unwise to mess with them too much unless you really know what you're doing.

So, what notes of a chord qualify as being essentials? The answer is surprising, because even some of the star players become expendable once we start extending chord voicings.

As an example, take the chord of E major – it's easier to consider this process when we're still dealing with chords at a fairly basic level.

You might automatically play a chord shape like this one for E:

E major

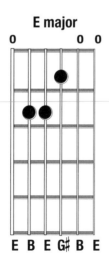

E B E G♯ B E

E major triad = E   G♯   B

Notes in the previous shape = E   B   E   G♯   B   E

First of all, you'll notice that we've 'doubled up' on our three basic notes, and there's really no mystical or otherwise good reason why this is the case. There are no specific rules in music that say that it's either advisable or desirable to have two of everything (well, most things at any rate). So, for a start, we could pare our basic E major chord shape down to something like this:

Exercise 17

E major

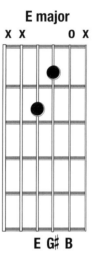

E G♯ B

Track 5

We have only one of everything in this example, and yet you'll agree that the essential character or 'thumbprint' sound of E major still remains in the above example.

In fact, if you play one after the other and let your ears do the deciding...

Exercise 18

E major

E B E G♯ B E

E major

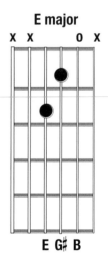

E G♯ B

Track 5

Firstly, if we take a quick look at what notes we've got against which ones we need, we get something like this:

...you'll hear how, although we might have lost a little of the chord's original 'big sound', we've managed to retain its core personality, the flavour that tells us that it's a major chord.

If, on the other hand, we wanted to retain some of the larger chord shape's undoubted grandeur, we could always wield the editing blade a little differently. One example of such a pruning exercise might look like this:

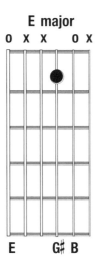

E major

O X X O X

E G♯ B

Here, we've kept some of the important characteristics of the original – the deep bass note, for instance – but trimmed the rest to fit accordingly.

The important thing to note here is that, in both instances, we've freed up three strings, allowing us to build bigger chords with all the essentials intact.

Adding a 6th, therefore, is straightforward:

Exercise 20

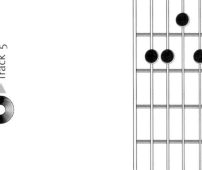

E major 6

X X

B E G♯ C♯

Track 5

And we've still got two free strings to play with, quite literally.

But what about times of real chordal famine? If we were to come over all draconian, which notes would get the chop?

The answer to this question is not as straightforward as it might seem, I'm afraid to say, because it really depends on the circumstances involved. Just bear in mind that there can be only one basic rule: everything that you do to a chord alters its sound somewhat and therefore redefines its musical role to some extent, however small.

So, given the understanding that we are proceeding with due caution, let's take hold of the scalpel and start hacking away.

1   If you're playing with a bass player or keyboard instrument, you'll find that you can quite often omit the root note of a chord

Why? Well, bass is very important, that's true, but if there's another instrument in your ensemble playing it anyway, you don't really need to. Here, we're evoking the same rule that we applied when we cut out the 'repeated notes' from the E major chord previously. If it's there already, it doesn't need to be there twice. This rule doesn't necessarily apply to soloists, though. Bass notes help sort out the character of a chord pretty quickly – the 'there's a low E and so it must be an E chord' type of logical thought. It is not necessary for a soloist to play every single bass note to every single chord, according to the rule of the listening audience that says, 'Enough, already; we get the picture!'

2   Occasionally, you'll find that you can quite safely omit a chord's 5th

This will come as another major shock for those of you who thought that the basic triad was sacred and that we shouldn't mess with it. But it's true all the same, although this rule tends to be called upon more when the going gets really tough and you've got a real handful of chord tones and you're looking for voluntary redundancies.

The relationship between a chord root and its 5th is very strong. Way back in more unenlightened times, the note relationships of a triad used to be tied in with gender. The relationship between a root and its third used to be referred to as being 'feminine' because it was thought to be somehow 'weaker' (before anyone from the PC police starts hunting me down, let me remind you, I didn't invent this terminology!). Play the chord shown in Example 1 on your guitar and see what it says to you.

The interval relationship between a root and its 5th, however, was deemed to be 'masculine' because it was much stronger. Play Example 2 on your instrument and see what you think.

Play both of them after the other – does one sound musically stronger than the other?

As a real litmus test, play the two chords shown in Examples 3 and 3a.

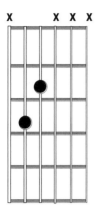

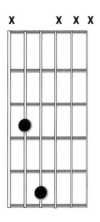

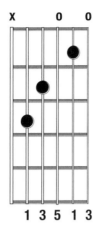

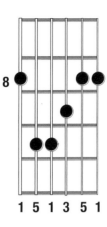

Example 1:
A 'feminine' 3rd

Example 2:
A 'masculine' 5th

1 3 5 1 3

Example 3:
C major with
two 3rds

1 5 1 3 5 1

Example 3a:
C major with
two 5ths

Example 3a has more 5ths than 3rds, whereas the opposite is true for Example 3.

If you agree that the 5th-heavy version sounds a bit more butch than the '3rds', it will probably seem even more amazing that the 5th can end up on the cutting-room floor every so often, but it's true. As to *when* to leave it out, you'll have to wait until we look at some of the more extreme chord extensions later on for the best examples. But we have to cover a bit more ground beforehand, otherwise nothing you find there will make any sense.

3   The 3rd is cut occasionally, but less frequently than the root or 5th

Having established that the 3rd is the 'weaker' interval, when being compared to the 5th, how is it that the 3rd generally survives the reaper's administrations? The answer is because of its ranking, musically. Remember that the 3rd defines a chord's basic gender – major or minor – and, as we've already seen, this is one of the most important distinctions you can make in music.

So, as a signpost to whether a chord has major or minor tendencies, the 3rd is more often reprieved and gets to stay in place.

As an example of how well a third can spell out 'major' or 'minor', try this test: play both of the chords shown on the right. One is very obviously major, the other equally obviously minor – and yet you're playing only two notes each time. This obviously wouldn't work with 5ths – they have no gender-determining power whatsoever.

So the 3rd usually gets the chop as a last resort or when the actual context of the music leaves no doubt whether the particular chord is major or minor. There are

a couple of chords that don't feature a 3rd on quite a regular basis – and we're going to meet them in a moment – but, as far as the other members of the chordal pack are concerned, whether we leave them in or chuck them out is down to individual cases.

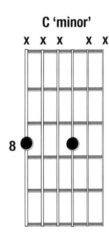

C 'minor'

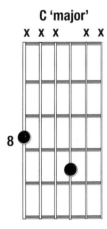

C 'major'

As a really irritatingly obvious example, if the chord desired was a Cmajor9, it would be severely unwise to leave out the D (Cmaj9 = CEGBD) because you would lose the basic colour of the chord in an instant. Also, as we saw earlier, leaving out the B would redefine the chord and change its name to Cadd9.

However, it's possible to leave out the C or G and still have enough of the chord to retain most of its important 'Cmaj9' personality, especially if you were playing with other musicians at the time.

My personal favourite Cmaj9 chord shape is this particular one. There's no 5th in there, but it's still a very sweet-sounding, useful major 9th sound:

Exercise 25

C major 9

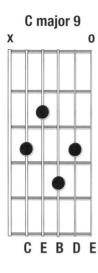

C E B D E

C major 6/9

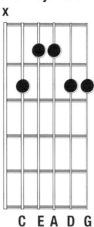

C EA D G

C add 9

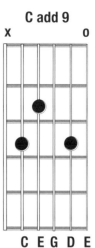

C EG D E

Mix And Match

We'll be returning to the concept of 'chord editing' later on, but for now we have a little more building work to attend to.

There are a couple more members of the major chord family that will no doubt crop up in your everyday playing. One is the major 6/9 chord, and it looks like this:

C E G A D
1 3 5 6 9

It has to be said, however, that a few major 6/9 chords tend to omit the root to make the fingering easier – I've included it here so you can hear the full effect...

Exercise 26

C major 6/9

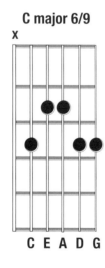

C E A D G

They also have a distinct character and tend to crop up in jazz, bossa nova and occasionally pop music. If you compare a 6/9 with both a 6th and an add 9th, you get an idea of the exact musical refinements of this chord:

Consider the chord shapes above, once again, to be like slight variations in colour on a colour chart that you'd find in a paint shop. We're well used to the idea that there might be 17 different shades of blue available to us and that each variation has its purpose, and so it's not a huge mental leap to turn that kind of thinking around to music.

Sometimes, you'll find that a 6/9 is dead right; sometimes, it will need tweaking – literally taking down a shade or two – and, by knowing that the add 9 and major 6th are very much in the same part of the musical spectrum, you'll have alternatives at hand.

If you thought that having five members of the scale present in the same chord was pushing things a little, then there's still one more alternative at hand which sounds like it shouldn't work, but, surprisingly, it does.

The chord concerned goes by the rather long-winded name 'maj6/9(maj7)' and it looks like this:

C E G A B D
1 3 5 6 7 9

I know of only one chord shape that has the full complement of notes in it, and it looks like this:

Exercise 28

C maj6/9 (maj 7)

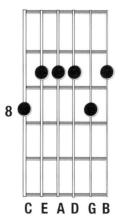

8

C E A D G B

You'll probably be quite surprised at the sound it makes – it's not at all unpleasant, and yet we've used six notes from the seven available in the scale.

This chord, although quite nice-sounding, isn't particularly useful as an everyday type of chord. As a simple experiment, try playing an ordinary C major chord four to the bar for about four bars, and then try exactly the same thing with our new friend, and you'll see what I mean.

▲ Track 5

|| Cmaj / / / | Cmaj / / / |
| Cmaj / / / | Cmaj / / / ||

|| Cmaj6/9(maj7) / / / | Cmaj6/9(maj7) / / / |
| Cmaj6/9(maj7) / / / | Cmaj6/9(maj7) / / / ||

You couldn't possibly play the Cmaj6/9(maj7) chord for that long; it's harmonically saturated, when compared to the ordinary, back-to-basics C major.

In fact, taking this example further, you could make something of a rule yourself and say that the more you do to a chord – the more scale tones you add to it – the more rarefied becomes the use of that chord.

As another example, we have proved that an ordinary C major chord can be played four to the bar for quite a considerable length of time. But arguably the most common use for a Cmaj6/9(maj7) is as a final, sweet-sounding chord with which to end a piece. So, while the ordinary C major chord could crop up as many as 50 times or more during the course of a song, the Cmaj6/9(maj7) chord would possibly feature only once.

Special Cases: The Sus4 Chord

When you're going through the labours of getting your chords down on the guitar, it's generally not long before you run across a 'sus' 4 chord or two. In order to fully understand where this particular type of chord comes from, it's actually quite useful to consider it as not being a chord at all. I don't; I consider it as being a musical device – and only half of one at that. To explain why and how in more detail, let's first break a 'sus' chord down into its component parts:

Csus4: C F G
         1 4 5

And here's a chord shape. You can see straight away that a 'sus' chord is different in that it contains no third – and so the three notes it does contain can hardly be considered to be a triad, in the technical sense. And when I say that a 'sus' chord is immediately followed by a major chord of

Exercise 29

C sus4

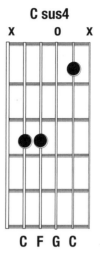

C F G C

▲ Track 5

the same root (Dsus4 to D major, for example) nearly 100 per cent of the time, you'll get the idea why I consider it to be only half a musical device, rather than a chord in its own right. For example, try this:

Exercise 30

C sus4

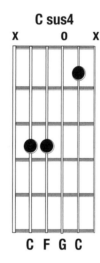

C F G C

C major

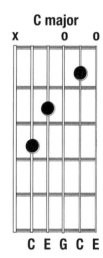

C E G C E

▲ Track 5

After playing the example above, it will probably come as no surprise to find that 'sus' is short for 'suspended'. Play the example above again and you'll hear how the first chord sounds incomplete; it needs the resolution provided by its other half, otherwise it would simply be left 'suspended' in space.

In order to see more closely what's going on, let's look at what happens when a sus4 chord is resolved by a major:

Sus4 = 1 4 5
Major = 1 3 5

There's only one note different – but it's an important one: the 3rd. We saw a few paragraphs ago how the 4th and the 3rd make strange bedfellows and tend to misbehave when in the same chord together. The sus4 chord actually splits them up into two separate entities and takes advantage of their incompatibility by exploiting it.

The 4th note of the scale has been suspended over the third, totally eclipsing it, in fact. But the resolution of one chord into the next is very pleasant-sounding and often used in songwriting – the most prominent example being 'Pinball Wizard' by The Who.

The sus4 chord is not the only sus chord in existence. You might occasionally run up against the sus2 chord as well. In actual fact, the sus2 chord is very similar to the add9, although, from a technical point of view, there's one important difference. Look at the diagram below:

$$Csus2 = C \quad D \quad E \quad G$$
$$Cadd9 = C \quad E \quad G \quad D$$

Now, bear in mind that this is the drawing board, these are the blueprints, and that a lot can happen between here and the real world.

We've already seen how chord voicings can be a hit-or-miss affair in that the guitar isn't exactly laid out as laterally as the piano and so, quite a lot of the time, these two types of chord are interchangeable. But remember that, technically speaking, in a Csus2 chord (for example), the D should be next to the root of the chord. Check out and play through the following example, if it's still unclear – but don't get worried about it! There's no such thing as the Music Police who are going to prosecute if you get the name of a chord wrong.

Exercise 31

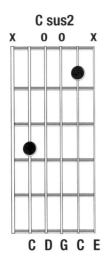

C sus2

C D G C E

To Infinity...

You might think that we've surely exhausted the number of notes that we can cram in to a major chord. After all, we've used every single one of them...haven't we?

Track 5

Well, no. I'm afraid there's still a little bit further to go. It's a somewhat strange convention (although among the jazz fraternity, it's positively commonplace), but, when it comes to chords, seven notes are not nearly enough.

Sometimes we need to look further afield, and the only place to go is amongst the non-scale tones – daunting though that may sound!

To illustrate exactly what I mean, here's the C major scale once again...

C	D	E	F	G	A	B	C
1	2	3	4	5	6	7	1

...and here's the chromatic scale – every note in the musical alphabet:

C	C♯/D♭	D	D♯/E♭	E	F	F♯/G♭	G	G♯/A♭	A	A♯/B♭	B	C
1	2	3	4	5	6	7	8	9	10	11	12	1

Don't worry about why certain notes have got two names; all will be revealed on that score in the section on scales.

So, out of the 12 notes available in the full musical alphabet, we use only seven in a major scale. (That's any major scale, incidentally; I just give C major as an example because it's by far the easiest one to write out!)

If we subtract seven from 12, it leaves us five – that's elementary maths. But these five so-called 'extra' notes – all of which live perfectly happily and virtually invisibly, too, as far as the major scale is concerned – do in fact enjoy a relationship with the scale nonetheless.

If we take a look once again at the C major scale but this time with all the so-called 'extra notes' included (these, incidentally, would be the 'black notes' on a piano keyboard) and add a numbering system that relates all of them to C, let's see what turns up:

C	C♯/D♭	D	D♯/E♭	E	F	F♯/G♭	G	G♯/A♭	A	A♯/B♭	B	C
1	♭2/♭9	2	♯9/♭3	3	4	♯4/♭5	5	♯5/♭6	6	♭7	7	1

It looks a real mess, doesn't it? Also, you'll notice that music's naming convention dictates that terms like '♯2', '♯1' or '♯6' are rarely, if ever, used. And, of course, where certain notes have been allocated two symbols apiece – C♯ and D♭, for instance, are in fact the same note with two different identities – they get to have two numerical locations, too. Similes like ♯9 and ♭3 are the same note, but their names imply different functions, as we will see a little later on in the book.

If we now return to our basic major chord and start adding these new non-scale tones arbitrarily, the result would be nothing short of catastrophic. When non-scale tones are added to a chord, it's generally to introduce a little dissonance – none of them will end up making a major chord sound sweeter. Once again, there's a comparison here to cooking, where you would be right to add a bitter ingredient in very small amounts to introduce piquancy to a sauce, for example. Very few of us would enjoy a garlic sandwich particularly – although garlic bread is fine, of course – and so the keyword here is 'restraint'.

It's time, then, to separate out the good from the bad. So, which non-scale tones are the heroes, and which are the villains?

For a start, look at this chord:

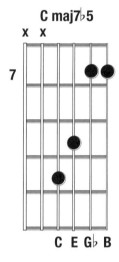

C maj7♭5

C E G♭ B

This is actually a Cmaj7♭5, and you have every right to think that you'll probably never use it. But, as with any dissonant-sounding chord, resolving it somehow brings out the necessary contrast and, in so doing, gives you a much better idea about how the particular chord type may fit in and play a worthy role. So let's try resolving the Cmaj7♭5 chord into a straight Cmajor7 and listen to what happens. Here's what we'll be doing if you look at it from a chord-formula point of view:

$$Cmaj7♭5 = 1 \quad 3 \quad ♭5 \quad 7$$
$$Cmaj7 = 1 \quad 3 \quad 5 \quad 7$$

And Exercise 33 shows a couple of chord diagrams.

Doesn't sound quite so bad now, does it? You may be sitting there thinking that you could use a chord like that somewhere in your own field of music after all.

A lot of the time, if you place a chord in its context, you'll hear more effectively what it's capable of. It's a little like looking an unknown word up in a dictionary; it's always better if some kind of example of the word in use is included, rather than just a straight definition.

Exercise 33

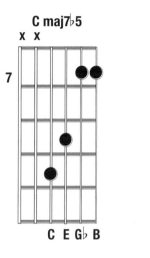

C maj7♭5

C E G♭ B

C maj7

C E G B

▲ Track 5

You might run across a major 7 chord with a sharpened fifth – maj7♯5, for short. If so, expect to hear something like this:

$$Cmaj7♯5 = C \quad E \quad G♯ \quad B$$
$$1 \quad 3 \quad ♯5 \quad 7$$

Exercise 34

C major 7 ♯5

C E G♯ B

▲ Track 5

But play a Gmaj7♯5 with an E bass, like this...

G major 7 ♯5

E G B D♯ F♯

Exercise 35

Playing this chord with an E on the bass actually makes it into an Emin9(maj 7) chord – sometimes chords can have two or three names apiece. See the section on 'Chord Similes' in Chapter 7.

▲ Track 5

...and it might sound more familiar. No? How about if I tell you that it's that mysterious-sounding chord at the end of the James Bond theme?

Once again, now that you've an idea of its context, perhaps the chord doesn't sound so unusable after all. Oh, and do try to bring it back in one piece, 007...

We could include a ♭5th in a major 9th chord and come up with this formula:

$$Cmaj9♭5 = C \quad E \quad G♭ \quad B \quad D$$
$$1 \quad 3 \quad ♭5 \quad 7 \quad 9$$

And this chord shape:

To my ears, at least, this chord doesn't sound too bad in any case. It's still got that 'mysterious' element about it and hopefully, just like the 'James Bond chord' we met a moment ago, you can imagine it fitting in somewhere.

Obviously, the variations, in terms of what can be done with the major chord family, are almost endless. You could, in theory, go on adding non-scale tones to the basic chord and come up with all kinds of weird and wonderful variations that would almost certainly have a place somewhere in music's vast realm, and a little later on I'm going to be showing you how to construct chords using the CAGED idea. But I think it's time we met another of the chord families now: the dominants.

C major 9 ♭5

X

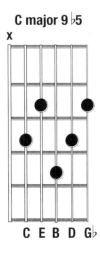

C E B D G♭

Exercise 36

This chord is easier to finger
if you omit the C root

▲ Track 5

54

6 THE DOMINANT FAMILY

You can probably imagine that constructing dominant chords is a very similar job to the one we've just been doing. And it is, save for the fact that we start with slightly different materials...

Dominant chords start their lives as basic major triads and take on their full identities only when we add a crucial fourth note. But here's the distinction: we're no longer talking about constructing chords by using the major scale. Instead, we're using the dominant scale, or the Mixolydian mode, if you want a long word to play with.

First of all, let's take a look at the difference between the two scales:

C Major

C	D	E	F	G	A	B	C
1	2	3	4	5	6	7	1

C Dominant 7

C	D	E	F	G	A	B♭	C
1	2	3	4	5	6	7	1

If you study the diagrams above, you'll see that there is, in fact, only one note different between them; in C, this is the B. But in *any* key, it's always the seventh note that marks the vital difference between straightforward major and dominant varieties.

We'll learn more about the derivation of the dominant scale in the section on scales, and so your curiosity on this subject will be sated at another point in the book. For now, we're concerned with building a reserve of dominant chords from the ground up – so we'd better get on with it.

To begin with, you'll remember that chordal titles – or shorthand – nearly always tell the story of exactly what's going on with a chord, and the dominant 7th is no exception. Its basic construction looks like this:

$$C7 = C \quad E \quad G \quad B♭$$
$$1 \quad 3 \quad 5 \quad 7$$

Now, I want to make sure that it's completely understood that this is where all dominant-family chords begin – they don't start as triads like the major family; they come into the world as full-blown, four-note chords.

Dominant chords all have a musical function to perform, too, and that function is probably best appreciated by hearing the dominant next to an ordinary major chord.

Exercise 37

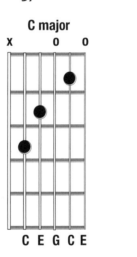

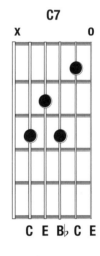

Track 6

If you play both of the chords above, you'll probably agree that the major chord sounds 'rested': you could happily end a piece of music or a song with a major chord and everything would sound properly punctuated.

The dominant chord, on the other hand, sounds 'unfinished'. It sounds restless and incomplete, as if something is missing. At the risk of being heavy-handed in stressing this point – and it is an incredibly important point, believe me – play these two examples:

‖ Cmaj / / / ‖ Gmaj / / / ‖ Cmaj / / / ‖ Fmaj / / / ‖
‖ Cmaj / / / ‖ Gmaj / / / ‖ Cmaj / / / ‖ Cmaj ‖

‖ Cmaj / / / ‖ Gmaj / / / ‖ Cmaj / / / ‖ Fmaj / / / ‖
‖ Cmaj / / / ‖ Gmaj / / / ‖ C7   / / / ‖ C7 ‖

The second of the two examples doesn't really work, does it? As far as musical punctuation is concerned, it sounded like the example ended with a comma instead of a full stop. The reason for this is that dominant chords are, simply put, signposts home. Their role is to help the ear find a key's tonic chord, but they are also used to convey 'unfinished business', 'restlessness' or 'movement', musically speaking, as a contrast to the more restful and 'finished' qualities of the major chords.

Every key has a dominant chord falling naturally within it. Remember when we looked at how we can harmonise a scale and come up with triads for every note? If we take that idea a step further, you'll see where the dominant 7th lives.

If we extend all the harmonised scale chords one step further and turn them all into 7ths of some kind, it's the G (in C major) that becomes a natural dominant:

$$
\begin{aligned}
&C = C \quad E \quad G \quad B - Cmaj7 \\
&D = D \quad F \quad A \quad C - Dmin7 \\
&E = E \quad G \quad B \quad D - Emin7 \\
&F = F \quad A \quad C \quad E - Fmaj7 \\
&G = G \quad B \quad D \quad F - G7
\end{aligned}
$$

$$
\begin{aligned}
&A = A \quad C \quad E \quad G - Amin7 \\
&B = B \quad D \quad F \quad A - Bmin7\flat5 \\
&C = C \quad E \quad G \quad B - Cmaj7
\end{aligned}
$$

If we remember also that G is the fifth note of the C major scale – and that anything which applies to one key applies to all others – we can come up with a rule: the dominant chord is always formed on the fifth note of any major scale. We can prove this in every key:

D	E	F♯	G	A	B	C♯	D
1	2	3	4	5	6	7	1

F	G	A	B♭	C	D	E	F
1	2	3	4	5	6	7	1

A	B	C♯	D	E	F♯	G♯	A
1	2	3	4	5	6	7	1

The scales above are D, F, and A major. If you look at the numbers and find five, you'll have the dominant chord. So, D's dominant chord is A7, F's is C7 and A's is E7. To hear this signposting for yourself, try this next example:

Exercise 38

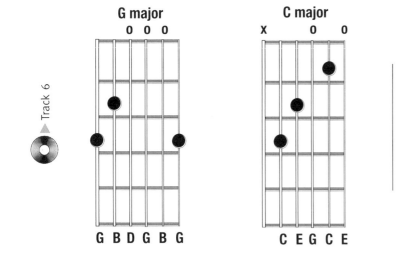
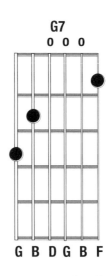
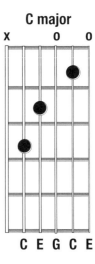

G major – C major: good   G7 – C major: better

Hopefully you can hear how the dominant chords lead directly to the 'home' chord. If you want one further, and slightly more ridiculous, example, you need look no further:

Exercise 39

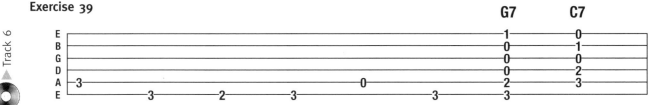

This is a fine way of remembering the function of a dominant chord. It's a musical cliché and absolutely perfect for ramming the point home.

Of course, that's not the only thing a dominant chord does. Dominant chords can lead into each other as well. Try this:

| Emaj / E7 / | Amaj / A7 / | Dmaj / D7 / |
| Gmaj / G7 / | Cmaj / C7 / | etc

Here, you have a cascade of 7th chords which all appear to be leading 'home' to straight major chords, but then set off again in another direction when those major chords are transformed into 7ths themselves.

What I've done here is linked the keys of E, A, D, G and C together to form something of a musical daisy chain. Be aware that this sort of trick doesn't work particularly well if you're trying to link any random series of keys together. If you were to take out your musical slide rule, you'd see that all the keys in the example above are the same distance apart.

In mentioning this fact, I'm veering very close to hardcore music theory that goes way beyond the study and basic understanding of chords and scales. But I will introduce you to a thing called the 'cycle of keys' (sometimes referred to as the 'cycle of fourths' or the 'cycle of fifths' – hardly anything in music has just one name!). Have a look at the diagram below:

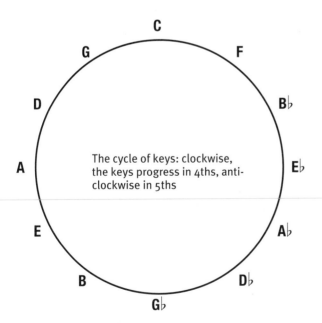

The cycle of keys: clockwise, the keys progress in 4ths, anticlockwise in 5ths

This is used almost like a compass by composers to sail the somewhat choppy waters of music's domain. You'll see how the daisy-chain key-change example I gave earlier follows it around one side almost like a clock.

Dominant Chord Construction

So, now that we've seen what dominant chords actually do – the role they play in the greater musical scheme of things – let's take a closer look at how they're built and what variations are available to us.

In order to establish ourselves on the dominant construction site, to begin with we'll take a look at a two-octave dominant scale:

C	D	E	F	G	A	B♭	C	D	E	F	G	A	B♭	C
1	2	3	4	5	6	7	1	9	3	11	5	13	7	1

And, once again, the formula for the basic dominant chord:

$$C7 = C \quad E \quad G \quad B♭$$
$$1 \quad 3 \quad 5 \quad 7$$

And a convenient chord shape:

Exercise 41

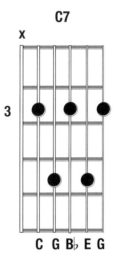

C7

X

3

C G B♭ E G

▲ Track 6

The reason why we look at the two-octave scale straight away is that all dominant chords are followed by a number higher than seven to start with. The chord formula says we've already 'gone up to seven', so most additions come from the second octave. So the first dominant chord we'll look at is the 9th...

$$C9 = C \quad E \quad G \quad B♭ \quad D$$
$$1 \quad 3 \quad 5 \quad 7 \quad 9$$

Be prepared for the fact that many of the dominant chord shapes you'll come across in books will appear in an 'edited' form. For instance, a popular 9th shape would look like this:

Exercise 42

As you can see, there is no 5th in the chord, although adding it isn't too much of a stretch:

Exercise 43

The 'editing' rules are the same as before, but remember that the 7th sound itself should always remain intact. This unfinished sound is really down to two notes within the 7th chord: the 3rd and 7th. These notes played together form a 'tritone' or 'diminished 5th' (we'll talk about intervals later), and it's here that lies the heart of the dominant chord's power.

We've already experienced the difference in sound between the major triad and the basic 7th chord, and so it's obvious that we can't do without the 7th in the chord. But, even if we remove the root and 5th from the 7th chord and leave ourselves only two notes – the 3rd and 7th – the essential 'dominant sound' survives, as shown in Exercise 44. Listen to the chords here and you should be able to hear what I mean. The 'stripped-down' shape on the right is a nice, economic way of accompanying a blues, on occasion. In fact, you can play an entire blues using this idea and the effect of the restless 7th is not diminished.

Exercise 44

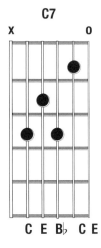  

Of course, that's not to say that you won't find any 7th chord shapes anywhere that omit the 3rd – I expect you will. The relationship between the root and 7th is still reasonably strong, and sometimes it will be strong enough.

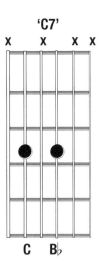

It's just not as satisfying a resolution as it would be if the 3rd and 7th resolved into a tonic chord – C7 to F, for instance:

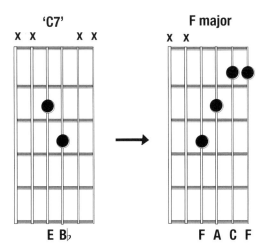

Hopefully, the point has got across by now, and so we'll proceed to the next dominant chord in line: the 11th.

Remember when we looked at the major 11th chord and found that it was a bit of a difficult one to use because the 4th and 3rd in the same chord made a dissonant clash? The same really applies to the dominant variety, too. So most dom11th chords tend to omit the 3rd, meaning that they are similar in sound to the basic sus4, except for the fact that both the dominant 7th and 9th are present.

This means, too, that we've lost that all-important relationship between the 3rd and 7th, and so the overall identity of a dom11th is a little schizophrenic, to say the least.

In any case, here's the basic formula for a C11th:

$$C_{11} = C \quad (E) \quad G \quad B\flat \quad D \quad F$$
$$\phantom{C_{11} = } 1 \quad (3) \quad 5 \quad 7 \quad 9 \quad 11$$

And here are a couple of chord shapes:

Exercise 47

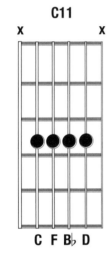

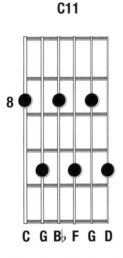

C F B♭ D   C G B♭ F G D

Be prepared to see 11th chords referred to as 'dominant sus' chords because of the way they tend to omit the 3rd

As you'll hear, the predominant voice here is still that 'sus' sound – although, I think, the 9th being present does a lot to pretty things up.

Following on from the 11th, we come to the 13th. Once again, this is, technically speaking, a seven-note chord, and so a little judicious editing is always necessary in order to give some functional chord shapes. The first note to go, in almost 100 per cent of cases, is that troublesome 11th, so that the all-important 3rd and 7th tritone relationship can push through and make sure that this chord performs its prime objective.

The basic 13th chord formula would look like this:

$$C_{13} = C \quad E \quad G \quad B\flat \quad D \quad (F) \quad A$$
$$\phantom{C_{13} = } 1 \quad 3 \quad 5 \quad 7 \quad 9 \quad 11 \quad 13$$

And my own personal favourite 13th chord shape would look like this:

Exercise 48   **C13**

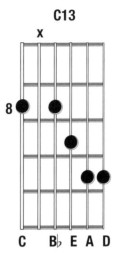

C   B♭ E A D

As you can see, this particular chord form has been trimmed back so that the 9th is missing (as well as the 11th), but its role as a fully functioning dominant becomes even more obvious when you resolve it into the appropriate major chord.

Exercise 49

C13   F major

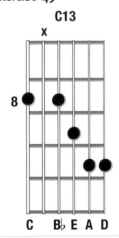

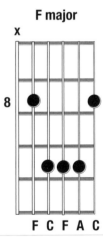

C   B♭ E A D   F C F A C

You might find yourself asking, 'How do I choose between the various dominant chords? How do I know which one fits?'. Remember that we are talking about different hues or flavours all the time when we're considering individual chord voicings. The four dominant chords we've looked at so far all sound slightly different from one another, and each would suit a different musical occasion perfectly. Listen to them side by side and try to hear their individual personalities. By performing this sort of exercise, you are increasing your musical vocabulary – or adding a couple more colours to your paint box!

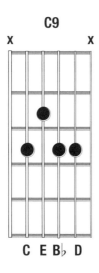

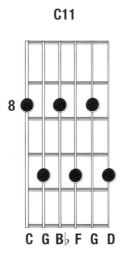

The most important job is to understand basically where these different types of chord come from, how they are constructed and what they sound like. The actual realisation of how and when to use each voicing will come later on when your ear has developed more.

Non-Scale Tones – The Altered 7ths

As we saw when we looked at major chords, when we run out of actual scale tones, there are always some non scale tones that can be added to the basic chord, just to spice things up a bit more.

The dominant chord is tense, unlike the resolved major chords, so by adding the dissonant non-scale tones to the basic dominant formula, we are reaching migraine-inducing levels of musical tension.

Just as opposites occur through life and its various philosophies – night and day, black and white – so too in music there exists a world of contrast. Tension and release, dissonance and consonance predominate, as far as harmony is concerned. And 'altered' dominant chords provide much of the necessary tension.

We usually talk of a dominant chord being 'altered' when non-scale tones are present within the basic dominant structure. To review again where those 'altered' notes occur, let's look at a the chromatic scale:

C C#/D♭ D D#/E♭ E F F#/G♭ G G#/A♭ A A#/B♭ B C
1 ♭2/♭9 2 #9/♭3 3 4 #4/♭5 5 #5/♭6 6 ♭7 nat7 1

The only thing different from last time is the 'nat7'. This is to distinguish the two 7ths present in the chromatic version of the scale. The nat – or, in full, 'natural' – 7th belongs to the major scale, whereas the ♭7 resides in the dominant scale.

Major scale = C D E F G A B C
                  1 2 3 4 5 6 7 1

Dominant scale = C D E F G A B♭ C
                     1 2 3 4 5 6 7   1

Both notes are in the same position – 7th – in their scales, so some distinction must be made. Sometimes you'll see the dominant 7th written as '♭7', but it's important to have some sort of uniformity and indicate that, in both cases, we're dealing with the seventh note of the two respective scales.

So, summing up the potential non-scale-tone 'visitors' that we can invite into the dominant domain, we would end up choosing between the following:

♭9 #9 ♭5 #5 nat 7

We can pretty much dismiss the 'nat7' as being a viable contender for two reasons: firstly, having both types of 7th present in the same space would confuse the aural identity of the chord, and, secondly, it would sound ghastly! Imagine having the root, natural 7 and dominant 7 lined up; on the fretboard, it would look like this...

Dominant 7th

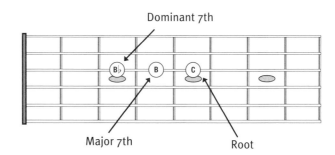

Major 7th   Root

...and sound like this:

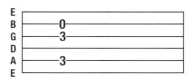

Point proved? I think so. After all, I know I said that dominant chords can be used to introduce some contrasting dissonance into a piece, but sometimes you can take things too far.

So, realistically speaking, we're left with four non-scale tones that we can use to spice up a basic dominant 7th chord.

The first, and arguably most common, interloper is the ♭5th – pronounced 'flat fifth' or sometimes 'flat five'. The flat 5th has a story to tell, too, in that it has achieved a certain notoriety in music because of its association with...wait for it...the Devil.

The reasons behind this rather remarkable fact are typically drenched in superstitious twaddle emanating from erudite churchmen of the Middle Ages. But it makes a pretty good story nonetheless, so get yourself comfortable...

Diabolus In Musica

The flat 5th was condemned, somewhat unfairly to my mind, to one of the circles of Hell merely because of its position in the chromatic scale. This musical equivalent of being in the wrong place at the wrong time is easy to demonstrate if we summon up the chromatic scale once again, this time with a slightly easier-to-read numbering system:

C	C♯/D♭	D	D♯/E♭	E	F	F♯/G♭	G	G♯/A♭	A	A♯/B♭	B	C
1		2		3	4		5		6		7	1

Exactly halfway along the scale between the two Cs we find F♯, the flat 5th in the key of C. Now, by itself, F♯ is harmless enough – after all, it's merely another note. But when you play it together with its root, C, what do you think happens?

Exercise 53

Track 6

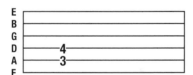

```
E |------------------|
B |------------------|
G |------------------|
D |----4-------------|
A |----3-------------|
E |------------------|
```

Doesn't sound particularly pleasant, does it? But wait, there's more to come. Every other note in the chromatic scale enjoys a dual relationship with its root. In other words, if we were to take the note D, for instance, we'd see that it's two scale tones from the bottom of the scale:

C	C♯/D♭	D
1		2

But it's seven notes away from the C at the other end of the scale:

D	D♯/E♭	E	F	F♯/G♭	G	G♯/A♭	A	A♯/B♭	B	C
7		6	5		4		3		2	1

This game we're playing here, incidentally, is called 'inversions', and we're going to be looking at them in more detail in another chapter. For now, just take my word for it.

Every note has two positions relative to its root, and this has a musical significance that we'll understand more about later on. Every note, that is, except the diabolically minded flat 5th. Observe:

$$C \longrightarrow G♭ = 7 \text{ semitones inclusive}$$

And then again:

$$G♭ \longrightarrow C = 7 \text{ semitones inclusive}$$

The flat 5th, you see, inverts to itself and – even more teeth-gnashingly obvious an indication of its devilish attitude – it's the only interval that does so.

So let's sum up the Inquisition's case against the flat 5th. It occupies an unique position in the chromatic scale, it magically 'inverts to itself' and yet it sounds absolutely awful. So, back in the unenlightened times of the Middle Ages, where pretty much all coincidences were thought to be the result of either heavenly or diabolical intervention, the poor old flat 5th was exiled from all music concerned with the Church.

When you stop and think about it, this wouldn't have been too hard on the face of it, because musically it's a bit of a stinker and not really much of a contender, melodically speaking. But, as we've seen, the flat 5th (or 'tritone') is a natural inhabitant of the dominant 7th chord, and they crop up in music all the time.

In order to get around this particular inconvenience, the Church took some extreme measures (they really did take this seriously – a musical entity that was meant to represent the Devil). Today, we might expect a piece of music to have an ending like this:

| G7 / Cmaj / ||

Track 6

To put it in other words, a dominant 7th chord doing its day job is signposting the 'home' or 'tonic' chord. The Middle Ages churchmen, however, had to settle for this...

| Fmaj / Cmaj / ||

...thereby neatly avoiding the dreaded Diabolus in Musica. This last example still occurs in hymns and some other types of religious music today and is known as the 'plagal cadence' ('plagal' means 'of the Church' and 'cadence' is just a fancy word for 'ending'). If you play it, you will probably be able to hear why it's also sometimes referred to as the 'Amen cadence'.

Meanwhile, of course, the flat 5th has found a new life for itself as *the* chord change in the darker side of heavy metal...

| E5 / / / | B♭5 / / / ||

Hey, perhaps they were right after all!

Meanwhile, back on the dominant-chord building site, the flat 5th sits in an ordinary 7th chord like this...

$$C7♭5 = C \quad E \quad G♭ \quad B♭$$
$$1 \quad 3 \quad ♭5 \quad 7$$

...and sounds like this:

Track 6

Exercise 56

C7♭5

X   X

C G♭ B♭ E

As before, when we've met chords that sound dissonant and unfriendly, you've really got to hear the 7♭5 in context before it really begins to make any sense. So here goes:

Exercise 57

Track 6

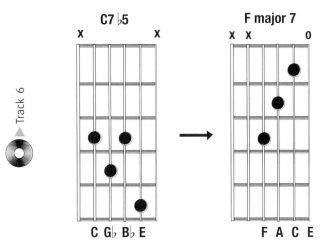

C7♭5 → F major 7

C G♭ B♭ E   F A C E

This particular chord enjoys a sort of 'double dissonance', in a way, because it contains both the normal flat-5th relationship between the 3rd and the 7th and another between the root and ♭5. But, as you can see from the previous example, in its proper setting, you'd hardly know it was there at all.

Before we leave the subject of flat 5ths for a moment, they're pretty easy to spot on the guitar fretboard because they tend to look like this:

Flat fifths look like this on all but the second and third strings...

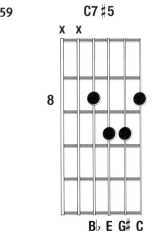

...when they look like this

Where would rock 'n' roll be without the intro to Jimi Hendrix's 'Voodoo Chile (Slight Return)', eh?

Sharp 5ths

Moving on, but staying with how the 5th can be altered within a dominant chord, we find the flat 5th's counterpart, the sharp 5th. In some circles, this interval is known as the 'augmented 5th' and has a sound all of its own. It doesn't have the notoriety of its colleague, the flat 5th, and neither does it sound particularly great on first hearing, but here's the basic formula:

$$C7♯5 = C \quad E \quad G♯ \quad B♭$$
$$1 \quad 3 \quad ♯5 \quad 7$$

Exercise 59

C7♯5

X X

8

B♭ E G♯ C

Track 6

If you're thinking that you'll never find a use for this chord, think of the beginning to Chuck Berry's 'No Particular Place

To Go' or the first chord of many rock 'n' roll ballads from that era. It's just one example of how this chord finds its natural place in the world.

Having altered the 5th in all ways that are possible, we can now turn our attention to the other two non-scale tones that turn up in dominant chords – the 9ths.

First of all, we'll take a look at the flat 9th:

$$C7\flat9 = \begin{matrix} C & E & G & B\flat & D\flat \\ 1 & 3 & 5 & 7 & \flat9 \end{matrix}$$

And the chord shape:

Exercise 60

C 7♭9

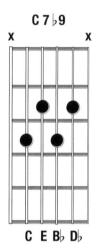

C E B♭ D♭

Sounds a real misery, doesn't it? So let's put it in some kind of context so you can hear how it works. We know that C7 resolves into Fmajor, so here's a way we can use C7♭9 instead of the basic chord.

Originally:

‖ C7 / / / ‖ Fmaj / / / ‖

Using the C7♭9:

‖ C7♭9 / / / ‖ Fmaj / / / ‖

Exercise 61

C7 ♭9   F major

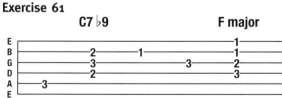

As you can hear, the dissonance of the C7♭9 chord is offset by the resolution back into F major. In some way, the fact that the C7♭9 is more dissonant than the original C7 chord

helps this contrast become even more pronounced. The other thing we can do to the 9th is sharpen it, giving us the basic recipe below:

$$C7\sharp9 = \begin{matrix} C & E & G & B\flat & D\sharp \\ 1 & 3 & 5 & 7 & \sharp9 \end{matrix}$$

And here's by far the most common shape for it:

Exercise 62   **C7 ♯9**

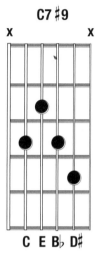

C E B♭ D♯

This chord makes an appearance in blues all the time – especially electric blues. Once upon a time, when guitar lore used to be handed down by word of mouth, this little item was known colloquially as the 'Hendrix chord', because of its seeming inclusion in so many of Jimi Hendrix's songs.

Played with a healthy dollop of distortion on an electric guitar, it assumes a pretty powerful identity; one that has been exploited by many electric blues players over the last few decades.

There is a reason why the 7♯9 chord is so at home with the blues. If you review the ♯9's alternate identity, you'll see that it can also be thought of as being the flat 3rd – or minor third. Now, we've already seen that the determining factor concerning musical gender is down to whether the 3rd of a particular chord or scale is major or minor. I also told you that this characteristic is one of music's most important. So howcome we have a chord that contains both major and minor thirds, technically speaking?

I believe that this chord thrives in the blues for a very good reason. As we shall see when we examine the blues scale later on, part of that music idiom's nature is that minor scales can be played over major chords, in order to achieve that slightly dissonant, plaintive quality that the blues most definitely has.

It's a fact that a music style's home-grown qualities are reflected in both its melody and harmony, and so it's only really a short leap of the imagination to see that the 7♯9 is in exactly the right place when heard in the blues. Major and minor are fighting it out right at the heart of the chord, enhancing the same kind of melodic conflict going on over the top.

Having said all that, it's really just another fine example of how placing an apparently dissonant and not particularly useful chord in its natural environment brings out the best in it.

Adding The Other Altered Tones

So we've looked at how the four non-scale tones can be inserted into a basic dominant 7th chord to bring their own indigenous form of added tension along to the party. So is that it, as far as altered dominants are concerned? Nope, we've only scratched the surface, because we can go on extending dominant chords a lot further.

Just as we started putting as many scale tones as possible into major chords – remember the Cmaj6/9(maj7)? – we can do a fair amount of mixing and matching here.

In fact it's the dominant chord family that enjoys, arguably, the largest tonal palette of all. You've already heard what happens to the dominant chord when we add one altered tone to it. How about adding two?

When we start down the path of 'doubling up' on additional non-scale tones, one of the first chords we meet is the 7♭5♭9. Here's the basic recipe:

$$C7\flat5\flat9 = C \quad E \quad G\flat \quad B\flat \quad D\flat$$
$$ 1 \quad 3 \quad \flat5 \quad 7 \quad \flat9$$

And here, as usual, is a sample chord shape:

Track 6

Exercise 63   **C7♭5♭9**

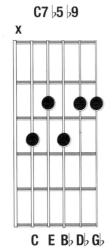

C E B♭ D♭ G♭

And you thought some of the earlier altered 7ths were ugly critters... But, using the analogy of colour tints and tonal variations, all that's really happening with the 7♭5♭9 chord is proof of the rule I mentioned earlier: the more you do to a chord, the more specific its use.

We're entering an area of more rarefied harmony – some people disregard altered 7ths by claiming that 'they're jazz chords, aren't they?'. In fact, they crop up all over, but yes, in jazz in particular, I guess.

So, given that we're entering this highly rarefied harmonic area, what kind of context can we dream up for the 7♭5♭9? Try this:

Exercise 64

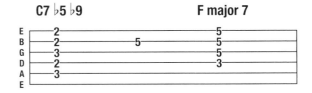

Track 6

Now, I don't expect you to love it particularly or even think that you'll be using it again and again, but you'll have to admit that the 7♭5♭9 chord is absolutely at home in that last example.

What's more, it wasn't being used any differently from how we'd use a basic dominant 7th. It was playing the same role, but playing it differently, if you like.

Musical categorisation like this is as personal as an individual appreciation of colour, food, wine, clothes or even holiday destination. Some would listen to the last example and condemn it outright as being unlistenable; others might say that it sounded 'dark' or 'foreboding'. Some would like it, at least being able to appreciate its special place in the musical colour chart, and therefore not disregard or write it off.

So it's advisable, when trying to gain an overall impression of chords and their natural habitats, to keep an open mind – or, more importantly, open ears.

The next few variations are fairly obvious and predictable in a kind of mathematical way. By this time, you've probably got the basic idea of adding chromatic, non-scale tones to a dominant 7th chord and have a fairly good idea about how they are going to sound, so we'll deal with the next few examples a little more swiftly than the ones we looked at earlier.

Obviously, when determining our choices when combining the sharp or flat 5ths and 9ths together, we come up with a set of static variations. Here they are:

$$C7\flat5\sharp9 = C \quad E \quad G\flat \quad B\flat \quad E\flat$$
$$ 1 \quad 3 \quad \flat5 \quad 7 \quad \sharp9$$

▲ Track 6

Exercise 65

C7♭5♯9

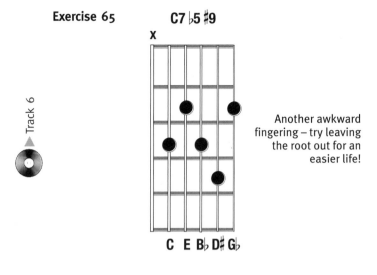

Another awkward fingering – try leaving the root out for an easier life!

C E B♭ D♯ G♭

C7♯5♭9 = C   E   G♯   B♭   D♭
         1   3   ♯5   7   ♭9

Exercise 66

C7♯5♭9

▲ Track 6

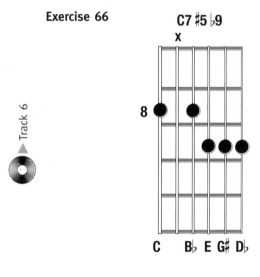

C   B♭ E G♯ D♭

C7♯5♯9 = C   E   G♯   B♭   D♯
         1   3   ♯5   7   ♯9

Exercise 67

C7♯5♯9

▲ Track 6

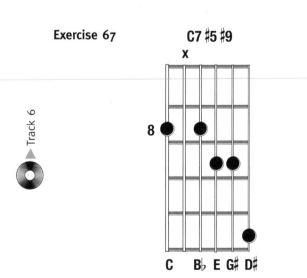

C   B♭ E G♯ D♯

When we get to this point, we've really exhausted all the possibilities available to us as far as basic 7ths are concerned. (I know it's a lot to take in, but I promise we're moving on quickly, so bear with me!) Other feasible variations that you could arrive at by looking at things logically would imply that chords such as C7♯5♭5♯9♭9 should exist, but in practice they don't. A look at the formula for that chord will tell you why:

C7♯5♭5♯9♭9 = C   E   G♭   G♯   B♭   D♭   D♯
             1   3   ♭5   ♯5   7   ♭9   ♯9

I can't possibly find a way of playing all of those notes without running out of available fingers in the very early stages. But even getting halfway is probably enough to prove that the resulting dissonance that results from this tangled mess is getting back to the 'garlic sandwich' idea. So, from a drawing-board point of view, it exists, but it's just too intense to let out into the real world.

In order to progress on our altered-7th safari, we actually have to start adding scale tones once again; in other words, we enter the realm of altered 9ths, 11ths and 13ths.

Altered 9ths

To begin with, when considering altered, 9ths one thing will become immediately clear: if you're dealing with a chord the principal tonality of which involves the 9th in some way or other, you don't want to start messing with it by including sharp or flat 9ths to cloud the proceedings.

In other words, although from a technical point of view such chords as C9♭9 ought to exist, they don't, simply because there's no point. And so, we only really have to consider two different types of altered 9th chord: one with a sharp 5th and one where the 5th is flat.

C9♭5 = C   E   G♭   B♭   D
       1   3   ♭5   7   9

And here's a chord shape to listen to:

Exercise 68

C9♭5

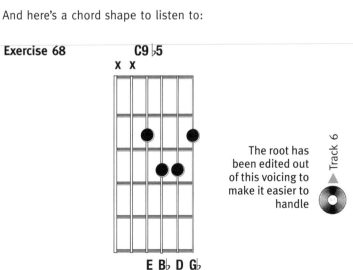

The root has been edited out of this voicing to make it easier to handle

▲ Track 6

E B♭ D G♭

One thing we have to consider is the comparatively rare occasion where both the flat and natural 5ths are included in the altered 9th chord. Having two different types of 5th doesn't affect the sound as much as it would if we used altered 9ths; there's no tonal confusion here, just another heaped teaspoon of dissonance to deal with.

In the instances where this happens, you're likely to see the chord referred to as a '9♯11' and the revamped formula would look like this:

$$C9\sharp11 = C \quad E \quad G \quad B\flat \quad D \quad F\sharp$$
$$ 1 \quad 3 \quad 5 \quad 7 \quad 9 \quad \sharp11$$

As with many six-note chords, though, you're more likely to find these particular examples edited down to their bare essentials:

Track 6

Exercise 69   C9♭5

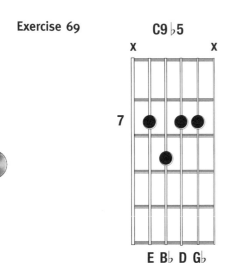

E B♭ D G♭

The result is an extremely tense, doom-laden chord which I would categorise as being one of the 'special effects' chords. In other words, its sound is so particular that it is literally only brought out on very special occasions, in times of dire need. Don't forget the rule: the more you do to a chord, the more specific its use.

Having flattened the 5th in a 9th chord, the only other way to go is to try sharpening it. And so…

$$C9\sharp5 = C \quad E \quad G\sharp \quad B\flat \quad D$$
$$ 1 \quad 3 \quad \sharp5 \quad 7 \quad 9$$

A representative chord shape would look like the one in Exercise 70. To my mind, this isn't such an ugly sounding chord; try resolving it into F maj or F maj 7 in order to offset the dissonance. This is definitely a chord used often in jazz, but not particularly in rock 'n' roll or folk (I felt it was time for an understatement!).

Exercise 70   C9♯5

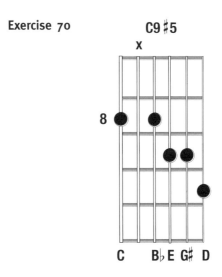

C   B♭ E G♯ D

Track 6

Altered 11ths

Moving on, we've seen before that 11ths can represent nothing but trouble on the chord-construction lot. That dodgy relationship with the important 3rd of the chord has upset things in the past, and so you can imagine what might happen if we start our look at altered 11ths by fooling with the 5th. We've seen that chords that include the 4th/11th often do so at the cost of losing their 3rds along the way; if we started destabilising things even further by altering the 5th, you'd possibly lose too much of the chord's intended identity. In other words, it wouldn't perform its intended function at all because it would start sounding like something else.

So, an 11th with a flat 5th is all very well in theory, but you're not very likely to find one out there in the real world.

Another interval that loses out with altered 11ths is the ♯9th. If you think about it, we've lost the third from the chord (in all probability) and so, by inserting what is essentially a minor third (remember ♯9th = ♭3rd) we immediately turn the chord into a minor. (This normally doesn't happen in ♯9th chords because the major 3rd is also present, giving that unique major/minor type of schizophrenic dissonance.)

So the altered 11th commonly enjoys only the presence on the ♭9th:

$$C11\flat9 = C \quad G \quad B\flat \quad D\flat \quad F$$
$$ 1 \quad 5 \quad 7 \quad \flat9 \quad 11$$

Exercise 71 shows the accompanying chord shape. It's mysterious, almost Spanish-sounding, to these tired old ears, but it's better, as always, for you to make your own mind up about how you think it sounds.

Just continue to think of all these exotic and rare chords as being more colours in your chordal paint box!

Exercise 71   **C11♭9**

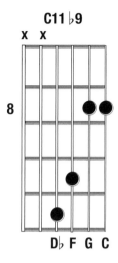

X   X

8

D♭ F G C

Altered 13ths

The final stop on our tour around the world of altered dominant-family chords is the 13th; and, unlike the 11th, this chord will take just about any alterations we care to throw at it.

We'll start by flattening the 5th. Once again, in some formulae for this chord, you'll see both the natural and flattened 5ths present, and the chord title should make it clear which is which ('13♭5' means no natural 5th, '13♯11' means both natural and flat 5ths present).

$$\text{C13♯11} = \begin{array}{cccccccc} C & E & G & B♭ & D & F♯ & A \\ 1 & 3 & 5 & 7 & 9 & ♯11 & 13 \end{array}$$

Obviously, this is an absolute whopper of a chord and will call for some serious editing before it becomes practical on the guitar fretboard. Expect to see chord shapes like this one:

Exercise 72   **C13♯11**

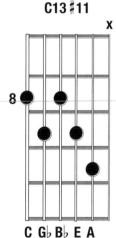

X

8

C G♭ B♭ E A

It's a very highly coloured and individual-sounding chord – and definitely one for the mystery-movie soundtrack category, to my way of thinking.

The other kind of 5th – the sharpened variety – is going to present problems within this type of chord; although, once again, simple maths tells us that it should exist. The reason why it's not so common is because of the clash that would be present between the 6th/13th and the sharp 5th: there's only a semitone's distance between these two intervals and the result tends to be overpoweringly dissonant, obscuring the basic personality of the altered 13th sound. (Incidentally, there are no rules that say you can't experiment with some of these chordal outcasts yourself; you never know, you might just come up with something unique.)

But, having said all that and just for good measure, here's the formula for a 13♯5:

$$\text{C13♯5} = \begin{array}{cccccc} C & E & G♯ & B♭ & D & A \\ 1 & 3 & ♯5 & 7 & 9 & 13 \end{array}$$

And a seriously dissonant-sounding chord shape:

Exercise 73   **C13♯5**

X

5

A   G♯ C E B♭

We've really come close to that garlic sandwich with this one, I feel!

The 13♭9 chord comes as something of a relief after the monster we've just looked at. Here's the recipe ingredients, as usual:

$$\text{C13♭9} = \begin{array}{cccccc} C & E & G & B♭ & D♭ & A \\ 1 & 3 & 5 & 7 & ♭9 & 13 \end{array}$$

And now take a look at the accompanying chord shape:

Track 6

Exercise 74

C13♭9

C B♭ E A D♭

Sharpening the 9th provides yet another interesting tonal variation...

$$C13\sharp9 = C \quad E \quad G \quad B\flat \quad D\sharp$$
$$ 1 \quad 3 \quad 5 \quad 7 \quad \sharp9$$

...which sounds like this:

Track 6

Exercise 75

C 13 ♯9

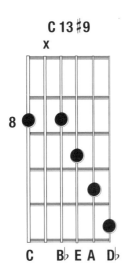

C B♭ E A D♭

Now, having exhausted the four non-scale tones, our absolutely final resort is to mix and match a couple of them. We really have reached the chamber of horrors now, as far as chord voicings are concerned.

$$C13\flat9\sharp11 = C \quad E \quad G \quad B\flat \quad D\flat \quad F\sharp \quad A$$
$$ 1 \quad 3 \quad 5 \quad 7 \quad \flat9 \quad \sharp11 \quad 13$$

A seven-note chord can only have a theoretical existence for us guitarists, as we've seen before; and I don't think I've ever seen one of these chords played in an unedited fashion. Normally, they will be summed up like this:

C13♭9♯11

Exercise 76

It's almost impossible to combine all of this chord's inner voicings. This version contains the vital stuff, but it's really only for use in an emergency!

Track 6

F♯ B♭ D♭ A

And finally, everything's suddenly gone sharp...

$$C13\sharp5\sharp9 = C \quad E \quad G\sharp \quad B\flat \quad D\sharp \quad A$$
$$ 1 \quad 3 \quad \sharp5 \quad 7 \quad \sharp9 \quad 13$$

...resulting in this sample chord shape:

C13 ♯5 ♯9

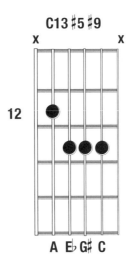

Exercise 77

Track 6

A E♭ G♯ C

At these levels of dissonance and 'alteration', chords become severely cut down to the bare essentials. Priorities have changed a little and we tend to give the altered intervals precedence, allowing the context in which the chord is found to provide some sort of sufficient harmonic continuity.

After that tour around music's dark and haunted back alleys, looking at the third and final chordal family is going to feel like a holiday in the sun!

The Minor Family

You might think that we're about to go through the whole process again – that is, merely adding scale and then non-scale tones to a basic minor triad. Well, sort of, but here we have the additional problem of there being not just one but three minor scales to choose from when we come to look for additional tones.

The reason why the minor family is in such a sorry state is down to several factors. Some say one is easier to sing while the other is better to extract harmonic information from, but I like to think that it's just never been formally sorted out in the way that the major and dominant scales have been.

Nevertheless three minor scales remain, all vying for the job of adding that essential dash of colour to the minor triad, and so we'll begin by considering the differences between them.

In actual fact, on paper it doesn't look like much of a difference at all. To really oversimplify matters, you could say that they all start off the same and then something goes seriously wrong when we get up to around the 6ths and 7ths. Look at this:

Harmonic minor

C D E♭ F G A♭ B C
1 2 3 4 5 6 7 1

Melodic minor (ascending)

C D E♭ F G A B C
1 2 3 4 5 6 7 1

Melodic minor (descending) – also known as the 'natural minor'

C D E♭ F G A♭ B♭ C
1 2 3 4 5 6 7 1

Realistically speaking, the only thing these three scales share in common – and it's quite useful common ground for us to have – is that the root, 3rd and 5th of each scale is the same in each case. And so the minor triad, by consensus, is as follows:

C minor = C E♭ G
1 3 5

It has to be said that, at this point, most harmony texts available will offer up a sort of ambiguous approach in answer to the question, 'Which of the three minor scales do we use for constructing minor chords?', and so I think it's wise for us to get some sort of rule in place from the offset. The facts of the matter are these:

1 All minor chords are based on the same triad – the root, 3rd and 5th of the scale, in exactly the same way that

we've seen previously with the major and dominant varieties.

2 All of the minor chords that are in use in popular music (and that's painting with broad strokes, if ever I heard it) use the natural 6th degree of the scale, if indeed it's used at all. The flat 6th – a native of both the harmonic and natural minor scales – produces a dissonant clash with the minor triad's 5th and, for this reason, is not particularly useful from a chord-construction point of view.

3 All extended minor chords (except a very few) use the flattened 7th.

Which means that, for our purposes, we're actually dealing with a scale that exists outside of the three I've already mentioned. It's known to its friends as the Dorian minor and it looks like this:

C D E♭ F G A B♭ C
1 2 3 4 5 6 7 1

One of the reasons why the subject of minor harmony seems so confusing (and changeable, depending on circumstance) is that, a lot of the time, we're not really playing in minor keys at all, but modal minor keys. The Dorian minor scale is one of the seven modes that are drawn from the major scale (see page 119 for an exploration of modes).

In other words, most of the uses that 'popular music' has for minor harmony tend to diverge somewhat from those of our classical counterparts, and so the 'official' text books on the subject tend to look at the way classical composers might brandish the minor scales, whereas we have something of a more comfortable ride.

Because of this, it's not a simple job to break down the minor scale – as we did with the major – and build triads on every note in order to give us some sense of 'colloquial' or 'local' harmony.

The more classically inclined texts, of course, have to perform this task, but I've never seen it turn out as anything other than a muddle, and so, if you'll forgive me, I'll spare you the confusion and we'll get straight down to the task of building the chords we need to use in a way that suits our purpose.

To begin with, we'll have a look at the very basic minor triad:

C minor = C E♭ G
1 3 5

Exercise 78

C minor

C E♭ G C

And, while we're here, let's consider the all-important musical differences between the minor chord and the other two we've been looking at:

Exercise 79

C major

C E B♭ C E

C E G C E

C minor

C B♭ G C

Play these three chords one after the other and try to define the difference between them to yourself. I would use words like 'happy' to describe the sound of the major, 'sad' for the

minor, and 'unfinished' for the dominant. However you want to sum them up yourself, be aware that the differences between these three chords are very important – vital, in fact, to a full understanding of chords and their function in music.

Moving on, one of the first variations on the minor chord we come across is the minor 6th. As we saw with the major chord, all that's happening here is that we're adding the sixth note of our agreed minor scale to the basic minor triad:

$$Cminor6 = C \quad E♭ \quad G \quad A$$
$$\quad\quad\quad\quad 1 \quad 3 \quad 5 \quad 6$$

Exercise 80

C minor 6

No 5th, but quite a representative minor 6th sound

C E♭ A C

Even the relatively sweet-sounding 6th cannot help this chord from sounding sombre, somehow. Compare its sound to that of the basic minor triad to hear the added colour that the 6th has brought to the overall tonal picture. As an aside, you're welcome to try the flat 6th with the minor triad and hear that clash between the flat 6 (aka ♯5th, remember) and the 5th. You'd be looking at a formula like this:

$$1 \quad 3 \quad 5 \quad ♭6$$

And it would sound like this:

C minor 6

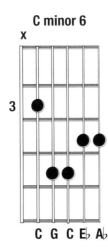

C G C E♭ A♭

An alternate minor 6 using the sixth note of the natural minor scale – a flat 6th. It clashes horribly with the 5th and confuses the sound of the chord

After the 6th, we find the 7th:

Cminor 7 = C Eb G Bb
1 3 5 7

And here's what it sounds like:

Track 7

Exercise 81

C minor 7

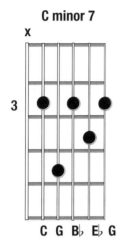

C G Bb Eb G

This chord has some extra significance because it's a member of the '7th clan'. We've looked at the major and dominant 7ths already; the minor 7th completes the picture. Once again, it's a good exercise to play each of them slowly, side by side, and try to pick out the difference between them.

C7

C major 7

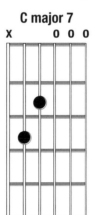

C minor 7

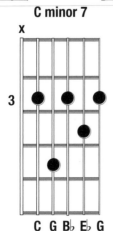

C G Bb Eb G

Remember that each chord represents its own family and that, on the whole, these chords are not interchangeable.

Not surprisingly, the next scale member to be added to the basic triad is the 9th.

Cminor 9 = C Eb G Bb D
1 3 5 7 9

Here's the chord shape:

Exercise 83

C minor 9

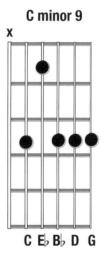

C Eb Bb D G

Track 7

As before, the minor 9th contains the 7th as well, making it a five-note chord. It won't be too long before we have to start thinking about editing the minor series to accommodate the fact that we have only a limited number of fingers – as we've done before with the other two families.

When it comes to the job of adding the normally troublesome 11th to the chord, we actually find a slightly subtle difference from what we've seen in previous examples.

The reason for this is that we are now dealing with a minor triad. With the third a semitone (one fret on the guitar neck) lower than in the major or dominant varieties, the conflict between the two notes is no longer pronounced.

Cminor 11 = C Eb G Bb D F
1 3 5 7 9 11

And if you quickly grab your guitar and have a play through the following neck diagram, you'll find that it sounds like this:

▲ Track 7

Exercise 84

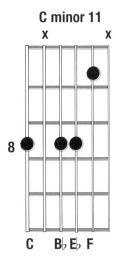

C minor 11

C B♭ E♭ F

Remember that a major 11 chord without a third is actually genderless – neither major nor minor – and so you will sometimes see that particular chord form cropping up from time to time in place of the true minor 11.

Compare the two by playing them one after another, listening out for the way the sound of the two chords is affected.

C minor 11

C B♭ E♭ F

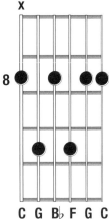

C minor 11 (no 3rd)

C G B♭ F G C

The true minor variation has a character all its own, that minor 3rd adding the right amount of gloom amongst the normally quite buoyant 'sus' sound of the 11th.

Another interesting point about the minor 11 chord is that, if you take another look at the chord formula above, you might be able to see how the open strings of the guitar can be referred to as an Eminor11.

Here's E Dorian minor (ie the chord-construction-friendly version of the E minor scale):

E	F♯	G	A	B	C♯	D	E
1	2	3	4	5	6	7	1

And the guitar's open strings:

E	A	D	G	B	E
1	11	7	3	5	1

Seeing as you've probably never thought of the sound that your guitar's idly strummed open strings make as sounding particularly musical, you'll appreciate how this particular chord has to be handled with care.

Of course, another thing to consider is that, once again, we're dealing with a six-note chord and it's inevitable that a certain amount of pruning will be present in the more 'popular' versions that you'll end up playing. Be prepared to see rootless minor 11ths – but remember that the minor 3rd must be present for it to be categorised as being a true minor 11th chord.

Minor 13ths are rare, because of that destructive semitone clash that has brought so many chord forms to their knees in the past. On this occasion, the clash occurs between the 6th and 7th degrees of the scale, producing an agonising amount of dissonance. The simple answer, of course, is to remove the troublesome 7th altogether, but this would change the character of the chord completely. Without the 7th (and, as is customary, the 11th which would otherwise dominate the chord too much), the chord becomes a minor 6/9:

Cminor 6/9 = C	E♭	G	A	D
1	3	5	6	9

Which sounds like this:

Exercise 86

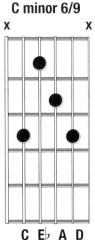

C minor 6/9

C E♭ A D

▲ Track 7

I think that the minor 6/9 is a nice, useful chord. Compare it to the sound of the original, basic minor chord and hear how full and characterful a picture it paints!

Now that we've added all the scale tones from the Dorian minor, you'd assume that we'd start adding non-scale tones as we have in the past, but the minor scale has a more fragile sound than the dominant. That scale can take almost anything you care to add to it in terms of chromatic, non-scale-tone visitors. But the minor, like the major before it, can take only so much before the fundamental flavour is affected too much and the original minor characteristic is lost.

One minor chord that includes a non-scale tone crops up quite a lot of the time, however: the minor 7♭5...

$$\text{Cmin7♭5} = \quad C \quad E♭ \quad G♭ \quad B♭$$
$$\qquad\qquad\quad 1 \quad 3 \quad ♭5 \quad 7$$

...which sounds like this:

Track 7

Exercise 87   **C minor 7♭5**

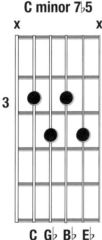
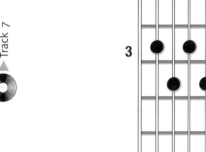

C G♭ B♭ E♭

If you think back to how we started with the minor-chord-building part of the operation, you'll recall how minor harmony is a bit of an inexact science, merely because there are so many minor scales to choose from.

The two intervals that are responsible for the irregularities are the 6th and 7th. Refresh your memory:

Harmonic minor (flat 6th, natural 7th)
C   D   E♭   F   G   A♭   B   C
1   2   3   4   5   6   7   1

Melodic minor (ascending) (natural 6th and 7th)
C   D   E♭   F   G   A   B   C
1   2   3   4   5   6   7   1

Melodic minor (descending – flat 6th and 7th)
C   D   E♭   F   G   A♭   B♭   C
1   2   3   4   5   6   7   1

By consensus, we've seen how the natural 6th is used in chords, generally speaking, in preference to the more dissonant flat 6th. The other interval we could consider is the natural 7th, which supplies surprising dissonance when inserted into a minor chord:

$$\text{Cminor (nat 7th)} = \quad C \quad E♭ \quad G \quad B$$
$$\qquad\qquad\qquad\qquad\quad 1 \quad 3 \quad 5 \quad \text{nat7}$$

Take a listen to this:

Exercise 88   **C minor (major 7)**

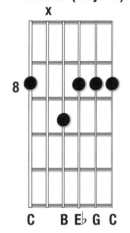

C   B E♭ G C

Track 7

Not pretty, is it? But it has its uses. If you think about this chord progression using the chord shapes below...

| Cmin / Cmin (nat7) / | Cmin7 / Cmin6 / ||

Exercise 89   C minor   C minor (nat 7)

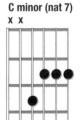

C E♭ G C   B E♭ G C

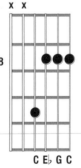

C minor 7   C minor 6

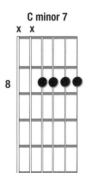
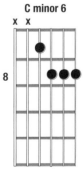

B♭ E♭ G C   A E♭ G C

...then your ear might be on familiar ground. This type of progression has cropped up in loads of songs, notably 'Michelle' by The Beatles and 'Stairway To Heaven' by Led Zeppelin, both of which make full use of the min (nat7) chord in this way.

So limited and so specific is its use, in fact, that this particular chord is almost always heard in this way and very rarely as a 'stand-alone' entity.

Believe it or not, this brings us to the end of our look at chord construction within the three family groups. Remember that we're still dealing with three basic types of chord and the variations available within their family units. Getting to grips with how the essential 'colour' or 'flavour' of a chord may be enhanced by the simple addition of a scale tone is one of the most fundamental ways in which to understand how chords work.

Armed with this knowledge, it's easy to see why a Cminor6 chord might be used instead of a straightforward C minor in a piece of music. The two chords have different tonal characteristics but, being from the same chordal family, function in exactly the same way.

Diminished And Augmented Chords

We couldn't possibly conclude our look at chord families without mentioning the diminished and augmented varieties. The idea that I'm going to try to sell you here is that both these chords tend to be considered as being offshoots of the dominant family. But, before we consider their actual parentage, let's take a look at how they're made up.

The diminished triad crops up quite naturally in the harmonised major scale. Remember when we looked at what chords we could find if we harmonised each note individually? If not, and to save you turning back pages (and because cut-and-paste makes it easy for me to help out here), here's a reminder:

Scale Tone	Triad	Chord Type
C	CEG	C major
D	DFA	D minor
E	EGB	E minor
F	FAC	F major
G	GBD	G major
A	ACE	A minor
B	BDF	B diminished

So you can see that the diminished triad appears when we harmonise the seventh note of the C major scale – or, indeed, any major scale.

As far as the diminished chord's parent scale is concerned, I'm afraid that it's one of music's not-quite-so-straightforward stories. The diminished scale is essentially

a man-made scale; it was 'manufactured' to be symmetrical, so that its intervals repeat in a predictable tone–semitone–tone–semitone fashion throughout. Take a look at the following notes:

$$C \quad D \quad E\flat \quad F \quad G\flat \quad A\flat \quad A \quad B \quad C$$
$$1 \quad 2 \quad 3 \quad 4 \quad 5 \quad 6 \quad 7 \quad 8 \quad 1$$

We'll be examining this scale in considerably more detail a little later on in the book, but for now it's enough to observe that the C diminished triad is made up of the first, third and fifth notes of this particular scale in just the same way as every other triad we've considered.

$$Cdim = C \quad E\flat \quad G\flat$$
$$1 \quad 3 \quad 5$$

And in case you're curious, it sounds like this:

Exercise 90

C diminished

X X X

C E♭ G♭

Track 7

The combination of the minor 3rd and the flat 5th mean that this chord isn't pretty. But in use it's not always the basic triad version of the diminished chord that we meet; we're more likely to meet its brother, the diminished 7:

$$Cdim7 = C \quad E\flat \quad G\flat \quad A$$
$$1 \quad 3 \quad 5 \quad 7$$

You'll notice that the note A – before now clocking in as C's 6th in major, minor and dominant chord forms – has now turned up in the guise of a 7th. This is because the diminished scale is eight notes long, and so the formula doesn't change, but when it's applied here, the content is less predictable. Even after the normally benign A has been added to a C chord, it doesn't cheer the diminished up too much...

Exercise 91

C dim7

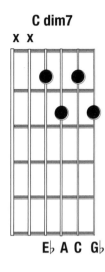

E♭ A C G♭

My own cataloguing of this chord has dubbed it the 'haunted-house' chord – especially when played like this:

Exercise 92

C dim 7

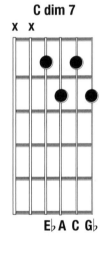

E♭ A C G♭

C dim 7

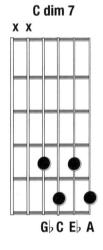

G♭ C E♭ A

C dim 7

A E♭ G♭ C

C dim 7

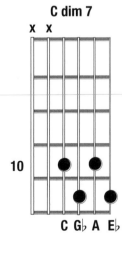

C G♭ A E♭

However, the diminished chord still has a few surprises left in store for us. For a start, it must be one of the most easily remembered of all chords, because there are only three diminished chords that you'll ever find yourself having to worry about.

This surprisingly convenient turn of events is down to the wonders of mathematics once again. Given that the make-up of its parent scale is symmetrical, it means that the notes contained in the chord are spaced evenly apart. Watch:

C	D	E♭	F	G♭	A♭	A	B	C
1	2	3	4	5	6	7	8	1

In each case, the notes that make up the chord are exactly one and a half tones apart in the scale. This means that the chord title can be taken from any of the notes contained in the scale:

$$Cdim7 = C \quad E♭ \quad G♭ \quad A$$
$$E♭dim7 = E♭ \quad G♭ \quad A \quad C$$
$$G♭dim = G♭ \quad A \quad C \quad E♭$$
$$Adim7 = A \quad C \quad E♭ \quad G♭$$

So, if we extend that trick a bit, look at how this relates to the chromatic scale:

C	C#/D♭	D	D#/E♭	E	F	F#/G♭	G	G#/A♭	A	A#/B♭	B
1	2	3	4	5	6	7	8	9	10	11	12

Looking at things this way, it's arguably easier to witness the symmetry of the notes within the diminished chord: it's pretty much a case of 'use one, miss two' in terms of spacing along the chromatic scale.

However, we have to perform this only another two times and we've covered all the diminished-chord options available.

Take a look at the following:

C	C#/D♭	D	D#/E♭	E	F	F#/G♭	G	G#/A♭	A	A#/B♭	B
1	2	3	4	5	6	7	8	9	10	11	12

This gives us another four diminished chords to play with:

$$C#dim7 = C# \quad E \quad G \quad B♭$$
$$Edim7 = E \quad G \quad B♭ \quad C#$$
$$Gdim7 = G \quad B♭ \quad C# \quad E$$
$$B♭dim7 = B♭ \quad C# \quad E \quad G$$

The final four diminished chords come from this particular configuration:

C	C#/D♭	D	D#/E♭	E	F	F#/G♭	G	G#/A♭	A	A#/B♭	B
1	2	3	4	5	6	7	8	9	10	11	12

Ddim7 = D   F   A♭   B
Fdim7 = F   A♭   B   D
A♭dim7 = A♭   B   D   F
Bdim7 = B   D   F   A♭

C – G♭ = flat 5th
G♭ – C = flat 5th
E♭ – A = flat 5th
A – E♭ = flat 5th

So there we have available to us a diminished 7th chord for every note of the chromatic scale contained in just three chord shapes. If you keep this formula in mind, deriving them from the chromatic scale becomes a relatively easy task.

As I've already said, I tend to think of the diminished 7th chord as being a member of the dominant family, as its musical role is nearly always that of signposting, in very much the same way as the rest of that particular family.

If we break the chord down even further, we'll find that it is positively rife with those urgent, 'unfinished' flat 5ths:

Cdim7 = C   E♭   G♭   A

It's this interval that powers a dominant chord, urging it to resolve. But the diminished contains two, increasing its potential in this area by 100 per cent. However, each of the flat 5ths it contains can be inverted, like this:

C – G♭ would appear naturally within the chord A♭7

A♭7 = A♭   C   E♭   G♭
       1   3   5   7

A♭7 would resolve comfortably into either D♭ major or D♭ minor. Play through the examples below to hear it for yourself.

Exercise 93

or

G♭ (aka F♯) – C would appear within D7

D7 = D   F♯   A   C
     1   3   5   7

D7 would resolve into G major or G minor, as shown below:

Exercise 94

or

So, by taking this idea forwards and relating it specifically to the diminished chord, you can see that this single dim7 chord could signpost no fewer than eight keys – four major and four minor – all at once! This kind of aural turbulence is a great wild card to play in the midst of a chord arrangement, making the diminished a very useful chord when some none-too-specific directions are called for.

Augmented Chords

Just like its partner, the diminished chord, the augmented chord suffers from a sort of dual-identity crisis, too.

Its basic character is a three-note chord, which belongs to the six-note whole-tone scale:

C D E F♯ G♯ A♯ C
1 2 3 4   5   6   1

It also crops up in the six-note augmented scale, as we can see:

C D♯ E G G♯ B C
1 2   3 4 5   6 1

Caug = C E G♯
       1 3 5

Exercise 95

▲ Track 7

C aug

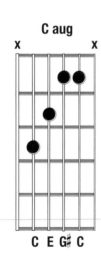

C E G♯ C

Once again, the augmented chord is symmetrical in that there is the same distance between its three constituent parts:

C – E = a major 3rd
E – G♯ = a major 3rd
G♯ – C = a major 3rd

And so the chord above has three identities:

Caug = C E G♯
Eaug = E G♯ C
G♯aug = G♯ C E

If we consider this from the point of view of the chromatic scale, we'll see that only four augmented chord shapes are required in order to make up the full augmented database:

C C♯/D♭ D D♯/E♭ **E** F F♯/G♭ G **G♯/A♭** A A♯/B♭ B
1 2 3 4 5 6 7 8 9 10 11 12

Caug = C E G♯
Eaug = E G♯ C
G♯aug = G♯ C E

C **C♯/D♭** D D♯/E♭ E **F** F♯/G♭ G G♯/A♭ **A** A♯/B♭ B
1 2 3 4 5 6 7 8 9 10 11 12

C♯aug = C♯ F A
Faug = F A C♯
Aaug = A C♯ F

C C♯/D♭ **D** D♯/E♭ E F **F♯/G♭** G G♯/A♭ A **A♯/B♭** B
1 2 3 4 5 6 7 8 9 10 11 12

Daug = D F♯ A♯
F♯aug = F♯ A♯ D
Daug = D F♯ A♯

C C♯/D♭ D **D♯/E♭** E F F♯/G♭ **G** G♯/A♭ A A♯/B♭ **B**
1 2 3 4 5 6 7 8 9 10 11 12

D♯aug = D♯ G B
Gaug = G B D♯
Baug = B D♯ G

Actual use of the plain augmented triad is comparatively rare; it's far more likely that you'll come across the augmented personality in the form of a 7♯5 chord, which, as we can see once again, earmarks the augmented as being a member of the dominant family.

Even the basic triad seems to perform the role of a 'signpost' in pretty much exactly the same way as we already know a dominant chord does. To clarify that idea a little, compare the two examples shown over the page.

Interestingly enough, it's not possible to say that the 'augmented 7th' is a mere extension of the basic triad made up from its parent scale, as both the augmented and whole-tone scales contain only six notes apiece. In other words, there are no 7ths present in either case. If anything, this

Exercise 96

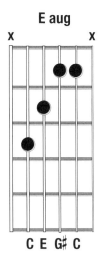

E aug

C E G♯ C

A major

A E A C♯ E

E7♯5

D G♯ C E

A major

A E A C♯ E

only strengthens the case for the augmented 7th chord – or 7♯5 – to be treated as an 'altered 7th'.

That concludes our look at just about every chord form in popular use. You can now see just how many 'voicings' or variations are available and why chord books always seem to look brimful with alternatives!

7 CHORDS IN CONTEXT

Now you have in your possession a guide to just about every type of chord you're ever going to meet – and shortly we'll be seeing how the formulae we've looked at can be applied in everyday terms, using the CAGED idea.

There are, however, a few more things for us to consider in order to complete the picture of guitar chords in the context of their actual use, and the first of these would be to look at the guitar's musical role more closely.

As far as musical instruments go, the guitar occupies a rare position in the instrumental world, in that it's capable of playing chords in the first place. When you sit and think about it, there are only keyboards and guitar where this is possible – in the mainstream, at least. Certainly violins, basses, saxes, cellos and so on are known for a single-note approach to both harmony and melody. So, in terms of being able to accompany other instruments by providing some sort of chordal backdrop, we can compare the guitar to a piano (as nominated keyboard representative) and use the results to understand more fully the guitar's special place in the world of harmony.

Instrumental Ranges

To begin with, we'll consider both instruments' range – that being the lowest to the highest notes possible on each.

A piano has a musical range of approximately eight octaves, whereas the guitar has, on average, just under four.

A comparison of the ranges of the two instruments would look like this:

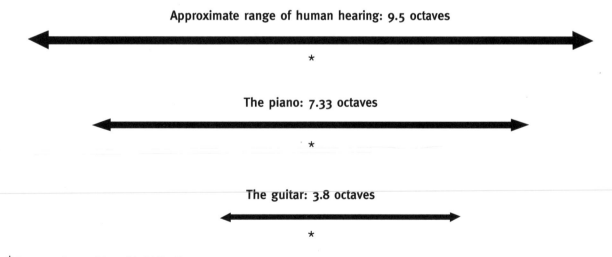

Approximate range of human hearing: 9.5 octaves

*

The piano: 7.33 octaves

*

The guitar: 3.8 octaves

*

* Denotes the position of 'middle C'

You can see that the range in common between the two instruments means that, very loosely speaking, the guitar begins roughly left of centre and runs out while the piano is still going strong.

The next things to consider are the physical limitations of both, from a player's point of view. The piano is played using both hands, meaning that ten notes at once would the obvious limit (although, in fact, more are possible by playing two notes with a single finger, etc), and chords can be spread in two clusters of five notes anywhere throughout the entire range. Typically, though, this would probably encompass a span of around three to four octaves.

The guitar, on the other hand, has half the range, a six-note limit and a musical working area of only two-and-a-bit octaves:

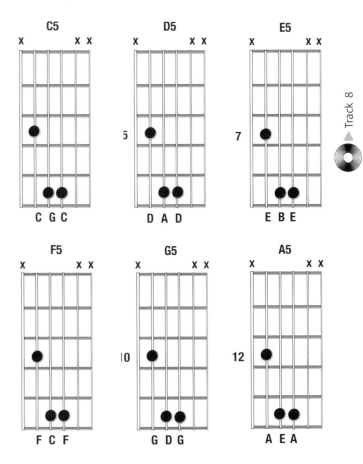

A natural handspan on the guitar fretboard covers around four frets, meaning that you've got around two-and-a-quarter octaves under your hand

Not surprising, then, that the guitar has often been referred to as the 'one-handed piano' in the past.

What I'm saying here is that, given its extended range, chord voicings on the piano tend to be easier to work with than on the guitar. By comparison, our two-octave 'handspan' narrows things down considerably; six notes over two octaves is going to be a very dense-sounding affair, whereas ten notes over four octaves would probably pass for a tolerable listening experience!

To give you one further example – and by now you should know my propensity for ramming points home – imagine a chord spread across the musical range of an orchestra, from the deepest double-bass note to the highest piccolo. In this scenario, you'd be painting on the broadest musical canvas available to you and a two-octave range would appear to be very meagre indeed.

All this adds up to a very strong case for chord editing, and so your next consideration, after 'What is a so-and-so chord?', would be, 'How can I voice this chord appropriately?'

Here, you'd be considering how to sum up the character of a chord in the most appropriate way to suit the context you're playing in.

As an extreme example, you wouldn't necessarily think of playing a series of sweet-sounding major 7ths or major

9ths in a heavy-metal band – but you might want to get across the basic 'major' sound somehow.

In rock circles, possibly the most extreme example of chord editing to suit circumstances is the 5th chord.

Exercise 3

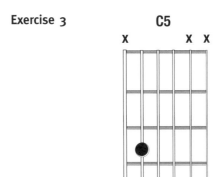

Here, you have a root note and its 5th, nothing more. In other words, this chord could stand in successfully for either major or minor. You can play a 5th on six out of seven roots in a major scale and still come up with something musical.

Exercise 4

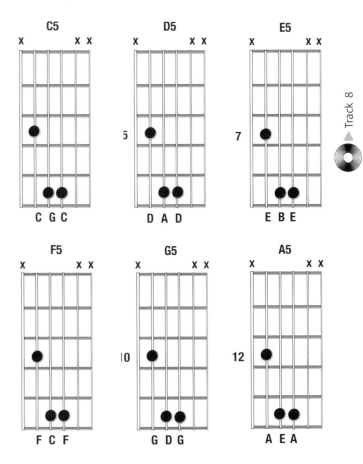

The reason why the seventh note – the B in this case – doesn't work properly is because it would have to be diminished. In other words, it would naturally contain a flat 5th, and so the normal 5th chord wouldn't sound quite right.

One of the reasons why the 5th chord came into being is that it holds together when moderate to extreme amounts of distortion are added to an amplifier. Thus it became pretty much the staple chord voicing of choice for a lot of heavy-rock bands during the '70s and '80s. Eventually, things got a lot more sensible in the rock world, distortion levels dropped a bit (in the main, at least) and amplifier technology leapt forward, meaning that the actual distortion itself lent itself more to the playing of fuller chords.

As an example of this, if you compare chord voicings in use during the late '60s (Cream, Zeppelin, Purple) to some that were prevalent during the '90s (Extreme, Satriani, Vai), you should be able to see what I mean.

So, after digesting the basic formulae for the chords you're likely to meet and working out some usable shapes, you'd still need to consider the context you're playing in before settling on something that fits or suits the musical arrangement at hand.

Remember how the relationship between the 3rd and 7th in a dominant chord can be used as a stand-alone to sum up the essence of the dominant sound? (See page 58.) This is the sort of thing I'm talking about.

Your choice of chord voicings would be different if you were playing in a duo with a bass player from the ones you'd choose if you were playing in a band with a keyboard player, for instance. In theory, you'd choose fuller voicings in a duo context than you would need to with the keyboard player – or even a horn section.

In this way, you can see that a fully rounded education as a chord wrangler doesn't stop with knowing a few shapes; it doesn't even stop with knowing the basic formulae. It has to go further – and this is exactly what we're going to do when we tie everything you've learned so far together with the CAGED idea for fretboard management.

Before that, there are a few loose ends to tie up...

Family Resemblances

I would trust that, by this stage, you're used to the idea that the three main chord families – major, minor and dominant – all perform set functions and that the type of major, minor or dominant chord in use merely varies the hue or texture within the set musical spectrum.

As an example, a C9 sounds slightly different from a C13, but they are still performing a similar function, musically speaking: that of being a dominant chord, usually signposting a chord change back towards the root of the key.

If we look at this concept the other way around, you can learn something – a trick, if you like – that might be of great use to you when 'out in the field'. It's something I've used many times to stop myself from tripping up on-stage – musically speaking, in any case.

Let's face it, even someone with a photographic memory is still going to be caught short for a chord shape occasionally. Most of the time, it won't matter – a few moments' thought and your memory will probably serve up something appropriate.

Then, of course, there's that time when you're playing on-stage and you experience a complete white-out. Playing on-stage carries with it a host of additional pressures. Even if you know a guitar part or song really well, it's still possible to have a very inconvenient lapse of memory, and this can be highly destructive to both the music at hand and your self-confidence.

As an example, from my own experience, I was once asked to play a concert in a large public school in Suffolk. It was meant to be an illustrated lecture on the development of the guitar. I chose to start with classical guitar pieces and work up to the electric guitar and good old rock 'n' roll over the course of an hour. At the time, I was having classical guitar lessons to improve my reading and fingerstyle, and my teacher asked me what pieces I was going to play. When I told him, he said that, although I was capable of playing both pieces, I wasn't ready to perform them. I didn't see what he meant: surely, if I was capable of playing them in the practice room, I was capable of sitting in front of 500 people and doing the exact same thing.

You might say that this particular concert was one of those 'life-lesson' experiences. When I began playing the Prelude to Robert de Visée's 'Suite In D Minor' – a piece I could play blindfold under any other circumstances – I blanked out completely. Luckily, I'd taken the music with me and had it on a stand where I could see it if necessary and I was told afterwards (one of my pupils was in the audience) that the brief pause while I found the next note on the music in front of me just seemed 'dramatic' rather than 'clumsy'. In short, I got away with it. But it taught me that, no matter how well prepared you think you are in the comfort of the practice room, playing live can still trip you up.

On-Stage Amnesia

So how can our knowledge of chords be called upon to help out in these times of on-stage amnesia? It's simple: if ever you're caught out in a playing situation and you can't remember the chord you need, look at what family it's from. Is it a major chord? Minor? Or a dominant? The clues will be there. Once you've sorted out which family this particular *bête noire* belongs to, play another chord from the same family instead. Under normal circumstances, it's wise to play a simpler version: for instance, if you can't remember what a C13 looks like, play C7 instead. Don't play a more complex voicing, like C13♭9, because the chances are that the music wouldn't call for anything more complex, but something a little less colourful will do just fine in most situations.

So remember that any major or minor chord voicing can be reduced to a simple basic triad will no ill effects on the music and, similarly, any dominant chord can be reduced to the basic four-note version without too much concern. All that would be happening is that you would not be playing the exact tonal hue being called for, but you'd be making a plausible substitution.

$$C13 = C \quad E \quad G \quad B♭ \quad D \quad A$$
$$1 \quad 3 \quad 5 \quad 7 \quad 9 \quad 13$$

$$C7 = C \quad E \quad G \quad B♭$$
$$1 \quad 3 \quad 5 \quad 7$$

It would make a difference to the sound of the chord, but not something that could be termed an actual mistake. After all, it's better than playing nothing!

Inversions

Another term that you might have heard bandied about is 'chord inversions', which cause grave concern amongst students of the guitar. I've spent many hours putting minds at rest on the subject, I can assure you.

If you'll bear with me, I'll quote some textbook harmony to you. Don't worry, I'll keep it brief...

This sort of thing is far easier to understand on a piano, but if you take one of our chord formulae, you'll notice how it's set out in order along the different degrees of the scale.

$$Cmaj = C \quad E \quad G$$
$$1 \quad 3 \quad 5$$

So we know that we're using the first, third and fifth notes of the scale – in that order. But what happens if we rewrite the formula like this?

$$Cmaj = E \quad G \quad C$$
$$3 \quad 5 \quad 1$$

For a start, we get another chord shape:

Exercise 5

C major

X X 0 0

E G C E

Track 8

Only slightly different from the one we all know and love, I'll grant you, but take a listen to it: don't you think it sounds somehow less definite and maybe just a tad sweeter? The chord is still C major, it's just that now we're hearing it in what's known as the 'first inversion'.

To steer a little bit further down the same path, look at the next example:

$$Cmaj = G \quad C \quad E$$
$$5 \quad 1 \quad 3$$

Once again, what we have here is another chord of C major, but this time there is a G on the bottom. Take a listen:

Exercise 6

C major

0 0

G C E G C E

Track 8

It still sounds like C major, but that G is taking our ears somewhere else, creating a little aural twist in a once-familiar story. This chord is known as a 'second inversion' of C major.

The most important thing to realise here is that we're not talking about chord similes; we're still dealing with a

C major chord functioning in almost exactly the way that a C major chord should. Consider it as another hue that it's possible to derive from a single chord, making it clearer that the harmonic palette we paint from is almost totally inexhaustible.

As I said earlier, this all makes so much more sense on the piano. When you're looking at a keyboard, with everything laid out before you in order, it's far easier to see that you've merely taken the C from the bass and added it to the top of the chord, exposing the E – the next note in line – a bit like this:

C   E   G
    E   G   C
        G   C   E

But, on the guitar, a lot of the notes in the chords we play aren't in the order the textbooks would prefer; it's not that kind of instrument. We've seen how sometimes it's necessary to omit the root, the fifth or whatever because of the need to be economic with space. And it is in this way that we can allow ourselves to make a sweeping statement which says that most guitar chords are inversions before we begin to mess with them.

Once again, the best way for you to 'deal' with the subject of chord inversions is to be aware of what they are, the minor differences they make to chords – and then not to worry about them and get on with the rest of your guitar-playing life.

Slash Chords

If anything, the way you'll see a chord inversion presented to you in guitar music is by way of 'slash' chords – and by that I mean chord symbols that look like this:

Dmajor/F♯ (or Dmaj/F♯ bass)

I used to get asked all the time by students, 'Which chord am I meant to play, the D or the F♯?'. The fact is that, if you're in any doubt, it's correct to play a straightforward Dmaj chord. It would certainly ruin your evening (and everyone listening) if you tried to play an F♯ chord. And here's why:

Dmaj = D   F♯   A

F♯maj = F♯   A♯   C♯

It's going to sound very bad indeed! What the chord symbol is asking you to do is put the F♯ on the bass of the chord, like this:

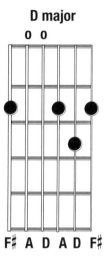

D major

F♯ A D A D F♯

And, if you play the chord shape above, you'll be playing a first inversion of D major.

It's in this way that you're far more likely to encounter inversions on the guitar. Occasionally, once you've familiarised yourself with the way a first inversion sounds, you might choose to play it instead of the root-position chord. In doing so, you'll have made a decision based on your familiarity with a certain sound: you'll have used a slightly different shade of the same colour the music was calling for.

Chord Similes

Something else worth considering – albeit briefly, because I don't want to cloud issues – is the concept of 'chord similes'. This is when two chords contain the same notes as each other but bear different names. How is this possible?

Well, when you think about it, there are 12 notes in the chromatic scale and we've already had a look at around 46 different varieties. When you spread those varieties across all the 12 keys available, you end up with the following sum:

$$46 \times 12 = 552$$

So, with only 12 notes to choose from and the contents of at least 552 chords to satisfy, it's no surprise that several chords are going to contain the same – or nearly the same – notes.

As an example of how this works in practice, let's have a look at a couple of examples. In order to see the inner workings of chord similes, it's probably best that we start on a fairly simple level before moving on to the more advanced stuff. Have a look at the two chords at the top of the next page:

83

Exercise 8

C major 6

X   0

C E A C E

A minor 7

X   0   0   0

A E G C E

Track 8

Now let's look at the formulae and break the chords down into their component notes:

$$C6 = C \quad E \quad G \quad A$$
$$ 1 \quad 3 \quad 5 \quad 7$$

$$Amin7 = A \quad C \quad E \quad G$$
$$ 1 \quad 3 \quad 5 \quad 7$$

As you can see straight away from the example above, each chord has all four notes in common with the other, only they're assembled in a different order depending on whether it's C6 you're playing or A minor. This idea can be taken even further, so now let's have a look at another example:

$$G6 = G \quad B \quad D \quad E$$
$$ 1 \quad 3 \quad 5 \quad 6$$

$$Emin7 = E \quad G \quad B \quad D$$
$$ 1 \quad 3 \quad 5 \quad 7$$

One more for luck...

$$F6 = F \quad A \quad C \quad D$$
$$ 1 \quad 3 \quad 5 \quad 6$$

$$Dmin7 = D \quad F \quad A \quad C$$
$$ 1 \quad 3 \quad 5 \quad 7$$

As you can probably gather from the above, every major 6th chord is also a minor 7th belonging to an entirely different root. (We could come up with a whole series of chord-simile formulae here, but forgive me if I don't. All will be revealed later on.)

There are other similes to consider along the way, too.

$$Emin7\flat5 = E \quad G \quad B\flat \quad D$$
$$ 1 \quad 3 \quad \flat5 \quad 7$$

$$C9 = C \quad E \quad G \quad B\flat \quad D$$
$$ 1 \quad 3 \quad 5 \quad 7 \quad 9$$

$$Gmin6 = G \quad B\flat \quad D \quad E$$
$$ 1 \quad 3 \quad 5 \quad 6$$

So what actually determines a chord's true identity, if it is seemingly capable of playing so may roles at once? The answer is, at least in part, one of context. Each of the chords above can reveal themselves only at the proper time and in the correct position: a C9 will carry out an entirely different function from a Gmin6 in such a way that the two chords are not, in a true sense, alternatives to each other.

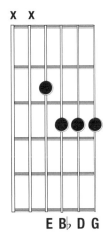

X   X

These notes are common to Gmin6, C9, and Emin7♭5 – but the contexts in which they are used are very different...

E B♭ D G

Try playing the above chord against the three different root notes (for example, E, C and G) and you should be able to hear how they sound functionally very different, despite their apparent similarity.

I could go on, giving many different examples of how chords with similar notes can acquire different names, but I hope you'll excuse me if I don't. My reasoning here is that I believe that being taught to think this way merely adds an awful lot of confusion to the subject of chords, especially in the early stages. Add to that the fact that, an awful lot of the time, music-theory pundits who put a lot of emphasis on chord similes (and, as we'll see, chord substitution) aren't really in the right area. A lot of the time, they're really talking about different inversions of a chord that have probably been named wrongly in the first place.

So my advice here is to be aware that similar-looking chords (in terms of content) can have very different identities and understand why. I've shown you the maths. Just tell yourself that it's no big surprise and that it's due to a shortage of raw materials at the chord foundry!

Chord Substitution

▲ Track 9

Another little item of guitar voodoo that you'll doubtless come across somewhere or other in your guitar-related reading matter concerns the black art of chord substitution. Now, this is another subject that receives far too much attention from the guitar theorists – in my opinion, of course. I know that it's another subject that comes up continually at guitar clinics and seminars and seems to worry people way too much.

I'm not out to make myself unpopular with the guitar academic literati, but I do find that the subject of chord substitution is overstated, in terms of its importance to the standard guitar student. What's more, out of all the amazingly competent guitarists I've interviewed in the past, not one has told me that they rely upon it in any shape or form. Music should never be reduced to a series of rules or formulae – it's far too spiritual for that. Giving people a method that relies on 'music maths' is like teaching someone in an art class how to draw a landscape using a ruler.

But chord substitution is definitely something you're going to hear about from somewhere, and so I might as well try to clear things up for you from the start.

The whole purpose of chords is to support and harmonise a melody line. If you remember, I compared the relationship between melody and harmony as being a little like a fence, with the upright supports representing the chords and the horizontal beams playing the part of the melody. Thus you are able to see the role of harmony being supportive to that of melody. It's a loose kind of comparison, but it works as an essential overview.

If we stretch this analogy a little further, we could go on to say that you can have your fence posts where you want them: evenly spaced (ie four to the bar) or densely situated and a lot busier. It's up to you. You can also have a say in the choice of materials; there's a variety of timbers that will all do the job equally well, but they'll be different in terms of colour, texture, density, etc. Then there are totally inappropriate materials for the job of supporting our melodic beams; you wouldn't be advised to use Plasticine or balsa wood (unless the whole fence was made out of the same material, that is!) and, in much the same way, there are totally ill-advised chord forms. Of course, if you were trying for the Turner Prize, Plasticine could be an option, after all...

Naturally, there is a set of guidelines as to what is and isn't appropriate, in terms of chords supporting melody, but I thought it would serve to demonstrate the wide-openness of the subject by having a look at the subject from a slightly different angle.

In theory, you see, any chord can be used to support a melody. I've included a couple of examples on the CD of extreme cases; the harmony sounds well and truly horror-film-orientated, but you can still hear the melody over the top. This is an instance where all caution has been well and truly thrown to the wind and my choice of supporting harmony totally arbitrary, but it works. The fence stays up. You might just disagree with the colour I've painted it, that's all.

The art of choosing the appropriate chord from the possibilities available has got a lot to do with refining my arbitrary choice demonstrated above down to suit the desired arrangement. Call it chord substitution if you like, but in my book it's a matter of arrangement.

Chord Structure Versus Arrangements

Let's settle on a little definition here. When a song or piece of music is born, it has with it a basic chord structure. Remember when we talked about the 'three-chord trick'? It would probably be something along those lines. If you wanted something even more basic, you could play most melodies over a single root note or drone.

It works, in that it holds everything together – it's got to, because what's happening is that we're tying everything together by emphasising the tonal centre (the root note of the chosen key). It's as dull as anything, but it works in a very primal, rudimentary way.

But, you're far more likely to find some basic major or minor chords doing a very simple and plain job of giving the melody some harmonic support. At this stage, a song or piece of music is said to have a chord 'structure', in that basic changes are outlined – the essential superstructure.

Anything you do to the harmony from now on comes under the heading 'arrangement', even if it's a case of turning this...

‖ Cmaj / / / ‖ Cmaj / / / ‖ Fmaj / / / ‖ Fmaj / / / ‖

...into this:

‖ Cmaj7 / / / ‖ Cmaj7 / / / ‖
‖ Fmaj7 / / / ‖ Fmaj7 / / / ‖

You'll know, from what we've looked at in the section on chords, that very little has happened between these two examples. All we've done is altered slightly the hue of the chords. The major 7ths make the whole thing sound sweeter, somehow, but the original structure is still 100 per cent intact. So, in terms of arrangement, we've actually done very little – and in terms of 'chord substitution' we've done less. Now, take a look at this:

‖ Cmaj7 / / / | Amin7 / / / |
| Dmin7 / / / | Fmaj7 / / / ‖

Here, I've altered one of the C chords to an A minor and one of the F chords to a D minor – so how is this going to work?

If we go back to the basic chord formula ideas, let's take a look at what's happened, in terms of actual notes within the chords used:

Cmaj7 = C E G B
Amin7 = A C E G

Fmaj7 = F A C E
Dmin7 = D F A C

As you can see, in both instances there's only one note that's different between the C and A chords, and between the F and D chords as well. This is where substitution really begins: we've exchanged one thing for another, very similar, thing. It's a bit like having different varieties of apple – what you've got is still an apple, but it's a Granny Smith instead of a Golden Delicious.

If you play the 'substituted' arrangement shown above, you'll hear that what we've done is added variety to the sound of the arrangement – hopefully, it sounds a little more interesting now than it did when we were repeating

the same chord for two bars. But what we definitely *haven't* done is substituted our 'apples' for 'oranges'. Not yet, anyway – that's the advanced class!

Looking again at the actual content of each chord, we can see straight away why the new, substituted chords actually work. With only one note's difference between them, the C and A chords are as close as can be. In fact, remember when we looked at an Amin7 chord and found it contained exactly the same notes as a C6? Well, looking at it from another point of view, we could say that all we've done is this:

‖ Cmaj7 / / / | C6 / / / ‖

And, as we found in the 'family resemblances' section, C maj7 and C6 are so close, they're practically brothers.

Looking once more at the F and D chords, we find that another way to look at things would be this:

‖ Fmaj7 / / / | F6 / / / ‖

Once again, both chords are so close it's only natural that they could 'stand in' for each other. So why not just note down our chord arrangement like this?

‖ Cmaj7 / / / | C6 / / / | F6 / / / | Fmaj7 / / / ‖

What it all comes down to is, realistically, bass notes. Play through our little arrangement using these chords...

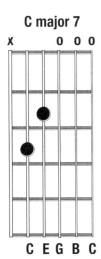

C major 7

C E G B C

A minor 7

A C G C E

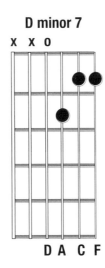

D minor 7

D A C F

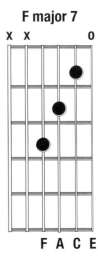

F major 7

F A C E

...and you should be able to see what I mean. If we played the first two bars with a C bass note and the next two with an F, things would still be a little dull, harmonically speaking. Certainly not as interesting as when the bass goes C–A–D–F, anyway.

You may have guessed that the root cause of chord substitution is variety; it can literally make a simple chord arrangement more interesting to listen to.

So, from the simple examples listed above, we can form a simple rule – and this is one of the most important things to remember when studying or considering chord substitution.

1   The more notes two chords share, the more likely they are to be substitutes for one another

Of course, an exact fit takes us back to the 'chord similes' idea, but I'm sure you get the idea.

A further rule would be along the same lines as the trick I taught you about never being caught short on stage if you either blank out or just don't know a chord's correct voicing:

2   Any chord can be substituted by another from the same root and family

By this, I mean that, for C major, you could substitute the following chords:

C6
Cmaj7
C6/9
Cadd9
Cmaj9
Cmaj13
C6/9 (maj7)
Csus4
Csus2

But – and it's a big 'but' – it all depends on context, once again. Quite often, a Cmaj7 or C6 chord will go almost unnoticed amongst the straightforward C majors. However, the members of the C major chord family that carry with them more distinct characteristics – Cmaj13, Csus4 and so on – would need to be slotted in at exactly the right time, otherwise, while they wouldn't exactly sound wrong, they might sound inappropriate for the moment of musical time they're supposed to fill.

So, in terms of this kind of chord substitution, it comes down to personal taste – what's your favourite shade of blue? – and context.

Obviously, the chords listed above have an awful lot in common with the chord they're replacing. If you refer to the chord-formula chart on page 89, you'll see that most have at least the basic major triad of C, E and G in common, and so it's not too difficult to see why this particular piece of musical sleight of hand works. But what about that idea of substituting an apple for an orange? When is it okay to use the colour green instead of red?

Actually, it's not really that different – neither is it some sort of arcane science, as it tends to be presented in certain music textbooks I've come across.

This particular branch of chord substitution owes quite a lot to the old 'chord similes' idea, once again. As an example, look below:

$$\| \ C9 \ / \ / \ / \ | \ C9 \ / \ / \ / \ \|$$

Two bars of C9, a member of the dominant family and the dominant chord in the key of F major. (That's what you should have been able to discern from the information in this section of the book, anyway!)

Now, look at this:

$$\| \ C9 \ / \ / \ / \ | \ Gmin7 \ / \ / \ / \ \|$$

So what's happening here? All of a sudden, we've substituted a minor 7th chord for a dominant. They're not even members of the same family, and so surely this breaks all the rules? Well, no – look at the notes in these two apparent strangers:

$$C9 = C \quad E \quad G \quad B\flat \quad D$$
$$Gmin7 = G \quad B\flat \quad D \quad F$$

Maybe they do share something in common after all: to be precise, they share three notes in common and, according to the first rule of chord substitution, this makes them plausible substitutes for each other.

Putting the chord arrangements above into some sort of context, imagine that you've been asked to play about eight bars of C9, like this:

$$\| \ C9 \ / \ / \ / \ | \ C9 \ / \ / \ / \ | \ C9 \ / \ / \ / \ | \ C9 \ / \ / \ / \ |$$
$$| \ C9 \ / \ / \ / \ | \ C9 \ / \ / \ / \ | \ C9 \ / \ / \ / \ | \ C9 \ / \ / \ / \ \|$$

Now, I don't know about you, but to me that sounds quite boring. It's not moving at all – and by 'moving' I mean harmonic movement. In other words, the chord stays still, exactly where it is, and doesn't really go anywhere. But, if we want to change things at all and make the part more interesting to play – and, hopefully, to listen to – we've got to remember that, basically, C9 is what the songwriter or composer wanted you to play at this point – or, at least, something very similar. So, in other words, you'd probably get away with something like this...

$$\| \ C9 \ / \ / \ / \ | \ Gmin7 \ / \ / \ / \ | \ C9 \ / \ / \ | \ Gmin7 \ / \ / \ / \ |$$
$$| \ C9 \ / \ / \ / \ | \ Gmin7 \ / \ / \ / \ | \ C9 \ / \ / \ / \ | \ Gmin7 \ / \ / \ / \ \|$$

...without upsetting anyone. In fact, you'd be doing the audience a favour, as our slightly modified example is much easier to listen to. Then, of course, having established that we've got two slightly different but fundamentally the same chords going on in the background, you're quite at liberty to exercise the first kind of chord substitution and invite the separate families around.

$$\| \; C_7 \; / \; C_9 \; / \; | \; Gmin7 \; / \; Gmin6 \; / \; |$$
$$| \; C13 \; / \; / \; / \; | \; Gmin \; / \; Gmin7 \; / \; | \; C_7 \; / \; / \; / \; \|$$

And so on. I'm not guaranteeing that the above substituted arrangement would actually work in every context, but hopefully you're beginning to get the idea of what's possible. But remember that the theme here is one of offering variety for the listener: literally making the harmony 'move' a little and take on a more interesting demeanour. It's not science; we're not applying secret formulae that have a magical effect on the chord arrangement. We've proved how all the notes within the chords we've used orbit around the same essential centre of gravity. All we're doing is providing the occasional dash of a different colour.

Believe it or not, that's about all there is to chord substitution in the popular sense. There are other little practices that crop up, mainly in jazz, but as far as the musical mainstream is concerned, that's about it. But perhaps you'll come across one other term which really sounds terrifying but is actually quite easily explained. We call it 'tritone substitution'.

Tritone Substitution

A tutor I used when I was a mere lad had a paragraph on tritone substitution that held up my development as a musical human being for about five months. I just couldn't get my overheated brain to understand it. Then, one day, it clicked and I've not looked back. What's more, I discovered that it wasn't so important after all and quite easily understood.

Tritone substitution is all to do with the Devil's Interval – remember that? The demonic flat 5th that was banned from Church music by our unenlightened forefathers who were still scared of their own shadows? Well, I won't bore you with more explanations, merely invite you to revise the section on the more unsociable aspects of this particular interval (see page 61).

The basis of tritone substitution (also known as 'flat 5th substitution') is this: any dominant 7th chord can be substituted for another dominant chord exactly a flat 5th away from it. Take my word, there's no easier way of summing it up. But, to explain, this means that, for C7, we can substitute F♯7. Ouch.

On paper, this looks like bad news. Whereas before we were merely mixing up family members, or introducing chord similes or, at least, chords with a few of the same notes in, this time, we've got two entirely separate dominant

chords that can't possibly be related in any shape or form. Or can they? Take a look:

$$C_7 = C \quad E \quad G \quad B♭$$
$$F♯7 = F♯ \quad A♯ \quad C♯ \quad E$$

Now, given that A♯ occasionally answers to the name B♭, we've got something of a match: both chords contain E and B♭ – a 50 per cent match. If we apply the rule that, the more notes in common between two chords, the more likely they are to be substitutes for each other, we can't deny that half of each chord being the same as the other has got to make both contenders in the substitution game. In this case, the two notes in common are the vital element of all dominant 7th chords: the flat 5th.

$$B♭ - E = ♭5th$$
$$E - B♭ = ♭5th$$

The root notes are different, but the flat-5 interval still resolves into a major root – its function. Watch:

$$| \; G_7 \; / \; / \; / \; | \; Cmaj \; \|$$

Could become:

$$| \; G_7 \; / \; D♭7 \; / \; | \; Cmaj \; \|$$

Okay, so D♭7 can move a semitone down into C major and still sound okay. Big deal. Here's another example:

$$| \; D_7 \; / \; / \; / \; | \; Gmaj \; \|$$

Becomes…

$$| \; D_7 \; / \; A♭7♭5 \; | \; Gmaj \; \|$$

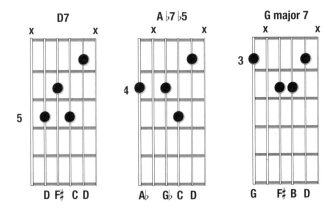

What's happened here is that the A♭ chord – being a flat 5th away from D – provides a slightly smoother transition between the D and G chords. Again, it wouldn't work in some contexts; it all depends on how you want to hear things.

Taking Things To Extremes

If you take this concept still further, you could substitute just about every chord in any given arrangement and come up with something really harmonically complex but still relevant to the basic task of harmonising a melody in a sympathetic and supportive way.

My guess is that, unless you're set on a course which is bound to take you headlong into the world of jazz, we've gone far enough in our look at how several chords can do each other's jobs with varying degrees of success. If I was to add that an awful lot of the ground we've covered remains totally subjective and that something that sounds like choirs of angels to one will sound like the screaming grind of malfunctioning machinery to another, this should strengthen the impression that we are indeed painting from a large paint box.

The most important thing to hold onto here is why this game of chordal musical chairs works and not to allow yourself to become in any way intimidated by it. Just think of it as yet another way in which a melody can be 'lit' by choosing from the many colourful variations harmony can offer. Some like their musical lighting calm, subdued and moody, while others like the brightest glare available. I really can't overstate how subjective an area it is that we've been dealing with!

Chord Construction Summary
Major Chords

Major = 1 3 5
Major 6 = 1 3 5 6
Major 7 = 1 3 5 7
Major 9 = 1 3 5 7 9
Add 9 = 1 3 5 9
Major 11 = 1 (3) 5 7 9 11
Major 13 = 1 3 5 7 9 (11) 13
Major 6/9 = 1 3 5 6 9
Major 6/9 (maj 7) = 1 3 5 6 7 9
Sus 4 = 1 4 5
Sus 2 = 1 2 5

Major 7♭5 = 1 3 ♭5 7
Major 7♯5 = 1 3 ♯5 7
Major 9♭5 = 1 3 ♭5 7 9

Dominant Chords

Dom 7 = 1 3 5 7
Dom 9 = 1 3 5 7 9
Dom 11 = 1 (3) 5 7 9 11
Dom 13 = 1 3 5 7 9 (11) 13
7♭5 = 1 3 ♭5 7
7♯5 = 1 3 ♯5 7
7♭9 = 1 3 5 7 ♭9
7♯9 = 1 3 5 7 ♯9
7♭5♭9 = 1 3 ♭5 7 ♭9
7♭5♯9 = 1 3 ♭5 8 ♯9
7♯5♭9 = 1 3 ♯5 7 ♭9
7♯5♯9 = 1 3 ♯5 7 ♯9
9♭5 = 1 3 ♭5 7 9
9♯11 = 1 3 5 7 9 ♯11
9♯5 = 1 3 ♯5 7 9
11♭9 = 1 (3) 5 7 ♭9 11
13♯11 = 1 3 5 7 9 ♯11 13
13♭9 = 1 3 5 7 ♭9 13
13♯9 = 1 3 5 7 ♯9 13
13♭9♯11 = 1 3 5 7 ♭9 ♯11 13
13♯5♯9 = 1 3 ♯5 7 ♯9 13

Minor Chords

Minor = 1 3 5
Minor 6 = 1 3 5 6
Minor 7 = 1 3 5 7
Minor 9 = 1 3 5 7 9
Minor 11 = 1 3 5 7 9 11
Minor 6/9 = 1 3 5 6 9
Minor 7♭5 = 1 3 ♭5 7
Min (nat 7) = 1 3 5 nat7

Diminished = 1 ♭3 ♭5
Diminished 7 = 1 ♭3 ♭5 6 (aka ♭7)

Augmented = 1 3 ♯5
Augmented 7th = 1 3 ♯5 ♭7

8 THE ORIGIN OF THE SPECIES

'To see the world in a grain of sand...' So wrote the poet William Blake. Well, believe it or not, it's possible to see music in a single note and give ourselves a fairly good idea of where it all came from.

Without getting scientific about things, each note is made up from a series of harmonics – a little like a colour is rarely pure but made up from a mixture of other colours. So, when you sound a string on the guitar, it's not just the note you are hearing, but a mixture of many different notes all blending together.

Harmonics

This is partly why a middle C on a piano sounds different from the same note on a guitar or flute; in each case, a different blend of harmonics – or 'partials'– is at work. As guitarists, we know that we can find harmonics along a string by pressing lightly on the 12th, seventh or fifth frets and plucking the string. At the 12th and fifth, the note produced is the same as the open string, but an octave or two octaves higher. At the seventh fret, the note produced is an octave and a 5th higher than the open string. So, on the bass E string, the harmonic on the seventh fret produces a B – an octave above its fretted value.

There are other, less pronounced, harmonics available along the string – in fact, technically speaking, they're everywhere, but you might like to try finding the harmonic on the fourth fret. There's even an excruciatingly high one available at the second fret on the top E string, allegedly the highest note you can play on the guitar, but it takes some looking for.

If you want to hear someone who must have found about every harmonic possible, listen to the bass player Jaco Pastorius's solo album (called *Jaco Pastorius*) and the track 'Portrait Of Tracy'. Another player who can wring a harmonic out of a guitar in the most unexpected places is Jeff Beck – listen to the album *Guitar Shop*, particularly 'Where Were You'. The man's a genius.

In any case, we all know that there are harmonics available to us along a string and are probably more than happy to remain blissfully ignorant as to why. I'm not going to get too scientific here – I can't, I'm no physicist; I'm a musician! – but the rules say that, when a string vibrates, it does so not only from one end to another but also along fractions of its length.

I'll leave you to reread that last sentence at your leisure. What it means is that instead of one wobbly line like this:

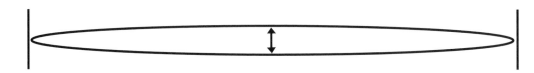

A string doesn't just vibrate along its length...

What we end up with looks more like this:

...it vibrates along fractions of its length

Now, if I can indulge your patience a little while longer (this all gets startlingly relevant later on, I promise), if you can imagine all those wavy lines having a centre, like this...

At these points, the string is technically 'still'

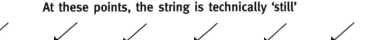

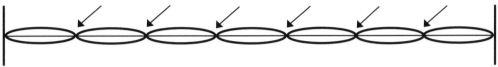

...then it means that the string is, in fact, still at various points along it. These points are called 'nodes' (as opposed to 'modes' – music can be tiresomely confusing at times) and these are the points at which we find our harmonics.

All the harmonics are present in the original note, so when you pluck your open E string, what you're really hearing is a rainbow of different pitches with a single, dominant fundamental – in this case, the note E. So, the E on your bass string is far from being a pure musical note, by any means. If you want to hear what a pure E sounds like, you'll have to ask someone who owns a synthesiser to play you an E using a sine wave. Careful how you phrase the question, though: funny people, keyboard players.

A sine wave is an electronic signal that contains no harmonics whatsoever, and if you get a chance to hear one, you might agree that it sounds like the 'unobtainable' tone from a UK telephone – and about as musically interesting. Lacking harmonics has the effect of reducing the note down to its barest essentials and stripping it of any characteristics that playing it on a harmonically rich instrument would give it.

The Overtone Series

Having said all that – and I know you're sitting there wondering what all this science has to do with the art of making music – this means that harmonics are as much a part of music as anything else and that they must have some sort of story to tell. Well, indeed they do, and the story concerned is known as the 'overtone series'.

The overtone series defines the order in which these harmonics ring out; it's fixed and the same on every instrument. The difference is how pronounced the harmonics are, and this varies dramatically from instrument to instrument.

If you sound a low C on a piano, the first harmonic you'll hear within the note is another C an octave higher, then a G (5th), another C, then an E (major 3rd), another G (5th), a pitch that's very close to B♭ (harmonics can actually be slightly out of tune with the fundamental), then another C, D, E, F♯ (another slightly out-of-tune note), G, A (out of tune) and then a series of ever-diminishing intervals (semitones, microtones and so on). So, as you can see, there's more to the note C than just...well, C!

C C G C E G B♭ C D E F♯ G A etc...

Play a low C on a piano and you'll hear a mixture of all these notes, represented by harmonics

It is widely thought by musicologists that the overtone series traces the development of music harmony, in that it establishes the order in which certain intervals were embraced within polyphonic music.

In other words (and plainer English), in early music, intervals like the octave, 4th and 5th – all low down in the overtone-series pecking order – were the first to be used in plainsong (just think of monks singing) and early Church music. After a while, thirds became involved, most notably in such a way as to give us the core of music harmony: the triad. Gradually, the chromatic scale as we know it today evolved from the swamps and has remained in place as the master scale from which all Western music is drawn.

9 SCALES

There is an awful lot of muddled thinking on the subject of scales. In many ways, scales themselves are irrelevant to much of what you need to learn in order to be a creative musician. They are the contents of your musical toolbox, nothing more, and should never be mistaken for some sort of wonder drug to cure all musical ills. Even an encyclopaedic knowledge of chords and scales is no substitute for an attuned creative sensibility – and neither is it a guarantee of enhanced improvising skills.

To put it another way, a house is more than simply a pile of bricks; a book is more than a collection of words; a car is more than an assemblage of parts. And scales should never be looked at as anything other than building blocks from which great things can be built or achieved.

So, before we even start our look at the world of melody and its relationship with some rather peculiarly named reference areas, let's get one thing absolutely clear: scales are not music. To be more realistic, possibly the most useful aspect concerned with the practising of scales is the way in which they can develop physical skills on the guitar. Other than that, scales are just different permutations and subdivisions of the musical motherlode: the chromatic scale.

We've already considered how nature's overtone series maps out our tonal understanding and how it provides a rather fascinating insight into the very birth of music itself. But now it's time to get down to the business of looking at scales in terms of common usage.

As with chords, I believe that the most practical way to study scales is to start with the most common and work our way gradually and methodically towards the more exotic realms of melodic expression. Here, as we found with the more rarefied chord forms available to us, there exist scales which probably only ever see the light of day on very special occasions. But, to begin, let's start with the everyday varieties.

The Major Scale

Without a shadow of a doubt, the most common scale in use today is the major scale. You'll hear it 1,000 times a day on the radio or the television. And there's a good chance that most of your record collection will call upon this particular scale most of the time.

The major scale, as with all of the other subdivisions of the chromatic scale, is basically a template that sees certain notes in a specific order, as precise as a mathematical series, and which results in a specific sound.

In the case of C major, we find that the notes which add up to make the sound of this particular scale are these:

$$C \quad D \quad E \quad F \quad G \quad A \quad B \quad C$$
$$1 \quad 2 \quad 3 \quad 4 \quad 5 \quad 6 \quad 7 \quad 1$$

Here it is in the form of tab and a fretboard diagram:

Exercise 1

C major scale

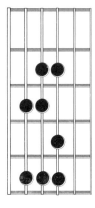

Track 10

So, given that this is purely a mathematical sequence, the major scale can be formed from every note of the chromatic scale, as long as we use the same 'template' to do so every time.

There's an awful lot of confusion surrounding the subject of keys and even more surrounding key signatures, and so it's probably wise to explain it to you so that it's absolutely clear. This sort of thing is a lot easier to understand than a lot of people think.

Key Signatures

As I have already said, the C major scale is formed using the notes shown above. On the piano keyboard, these would be the white notes. Played sequentially from the note C, you end up with this happy-sounding major scale every time. But what happens if we want to form another major scale starting on any other note from within the parent chromatic scale?

The answer is that, as long as you apply the 'template' or 'key', in as much as there is always exactly the same distance in scale steps between each of the notes in the scale, you'll get a major scale from any point you care to start on.

As far as guitarists – who don't enjoy the benefit of having any 'white notes' to base their essential scale-hunting facilities upon – are concerned, it's probably easier to look at things like this. Here's a one-octave scale shape for the C major scale:

C major

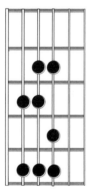

And here's another major scale, this time starting on C♯:

C♯ major

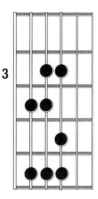

And another starting on D:

D major

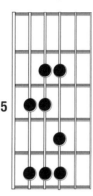

You don't need me to tell you that they are all the same shape, but starting at different points along the fretboard. Why is this? It's a convenience that we don't share with many other instruments (the different scales are all different fingerings on wind and keyboard instruments, for example), but why does it work?

The answer lies with the note order – what we call the 'tone/semitone order' within the major scale. This order is shown below:

C (t) D (t) E (st) F (t) G (t) A (t) B (st) C

(t = tone; st = semitone)

On the guitar, a semitone is the distance between two frets next door to each other, like this:

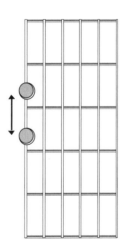

These two notes are a semitone apart – to us guitarists that means they are next-door neighbours

A tone, meanwhile, is next door but one, like this:

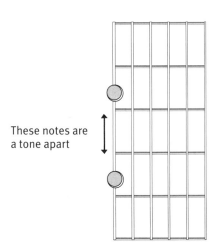

These notes are a tone apart

So, you'll be able to appreciate how the tone/semitone order of the major scale works by considering a major scale along a single string, as shown opposite. In this instance, we have this:

E (tone) F♯ (tone) G♯ (semitone) A (tone)
B (tone) C♯ (tone) D♯ (semitone) E

The following tab diagram shows it again in a more familiar way – and please forgive me for being really heavy-handed with this explanation, but it's an important point to get across:

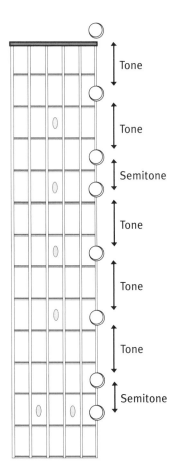

The E major scale played along the top E string showing the tone/semitone order

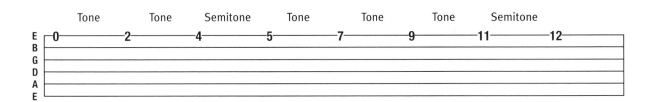

This, essentially, is the key – or the code, if you like – to making a major scale from any given point along the chromatic scale. At the top of the next page are three examples of how you might visualise this happening.

As far as key signatures are concerned, those mysterious-looking hieroglyphics at the start of a piece of music...

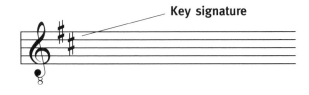

Key signature

...are, once again, a form of shorthand that tells a

musician what flats or sharps are necessary in order to make the scale at hand toe the line and 'imitate' the sound of C major.

If you look at the E major scale above, you'll notice that we need four 'sharp' notes in order to make the scale template fit perfectly. For the key of B♭, we need two 'flat' notes in order to achieve the right tone/semitone order. And so the 'key signature' for E major is four sharps:

The 'key' of C major

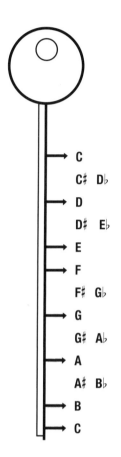

→	C
	C♯ D♭
→	D
	D♯ E♭
→	E
→	F
	F♯ G♭
→	G
	G♯ A♭
→	A
	A♯ B♭
→	B
→	C

The 'key' of E major

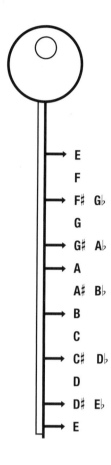

→	E
	F
→	F♯ G♭
→	G
→	G♯ A♭
→	A
	A♯ B♭
→	B
	C
→	C♯ D♭
	D
→	D♯ E♭
→	E

The 'key' of B♭ major

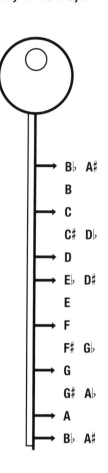

→	B♭ A♯
	B
→	C
	C♯ D♭
→	D
→	E♭ D♯
	E
→	F
	F♯ G♭
→	G
	G♯ A♭
→	A
→	B♭ A♯

And the key signature for B♭ is two flats:

If you want some sort of table showing all the key signatures, look no further:

0 x ♯ = C major
♯ = G major
♯♯ = D major
♯♯♯ = A major
♯♯♯♯ = E major
♯♯♯♯♯ = B major
♯♯♯♯♯♯ = F♯ major

♭ = F major
♭♭ = B♭ major
♭♭♭ = E♭ major

♭♭♭♭ = A♭ major
♭♭♭♭♭ = D♭ major
♭♭♭♭♭♭ = G♭ major

As you can see here, there is a minor scale (the Aeolian) contained within the individual notes of every major scale, so in fact all key signatures indicate both a major and a minor key.

0 x ♯ = A minor
♯ = E minor
♯♯ = B minor
♯♯♯ = F♯ minor
♯♯♯♯ = C♯ minor
♯♯♯♯♯ = G♯ minor
♯♯♯♯♯♯ = D♯ minor

♭ = D minor
♭♭ = G minor
♭♭♭ = C minor
♭♭♭♭ = F minor
♭♭♭♭♭ = B♭ minor
♭♭♭♭♭♭ = E♭ minor

If you want a system for remembering the order, you're on your own, because I've never found one that works. I went for ages trying to remember it like this:

```
C   F   B♭  E♭  A♭  D♭  G♭  B   E   A   D   G
0   1   2   3   4   5   6   5   4   3   2   1
```

Flats..................................I Sharps...........

I'd tell myself that it spelled 'BEAD-G BEAD-G', where the first series was flats and the second sharps. It didn't really work and so I asked as many people as I could find, including some of my own pupils who were learning music at school, and the best anyone could come up with was the equally fallible mnemonic 'Father Charles Goes Downstairs And Eats Breakfast', which, as you've probably already noticed, is backwards.

In the end, I became used to which key signature is which merely by being confronted with them continuously. I now automatically think 'four sharps' if someone mentions the key of E major.

But, if your memory isn't good at processing this kind of information, then don't be disheartened, because, from a fretboard point of view, all scale shapes of the same type are similar to each other in terms of shape, regardless of key.

Back To The Major Scale

So why this particular order and not some other? Well, the short answer is that the major scale was all part of music's 'evolution' and was probably decided upon by many years of trial and error. But the major scale represents just another day's work at the scale foundry because this is how every scale comes about. Essentially all scales are templates that switch from one root to another in exactly the same way.

Now, I'm emphasising this point because I believe that

it's the only practical way of looking at this business of where scales spring from. By seeing them as variations on a central resource – the chromatic scale – it's easier to see where the various scale shapes on the guitar fretboard come from.

So, as far as our scale of C major is concerned, we have one shape on the fretboard fully up and running. But if you look at it, you'll see that we're using only a fraction of the playing area available to us. And so, before we leap in and find some other ways of playing this one scale, a bit more orienteering is perhaps necessary.

We've already seen how the guitar's musical range is slightly less than four octaves, given that the most common scale length is around 22 frets. If you have a guitar with a 24-fret span, you've got yourself four whole octaves to play with.

We've also seen that the hand covers just over two octaves – over half the guitar's full range – when it covers any four-fret span. So, weighing these two facts up against each other, it's tempting to say that one contradicts the other. Rather than looking at the fretboard as a mysterious length of wood with lots of notes on it, it's much better to get this set of references well in mind:

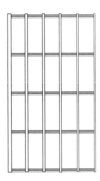

This area of the fretboard contains a little over two octaves – over half the full range of the guitar

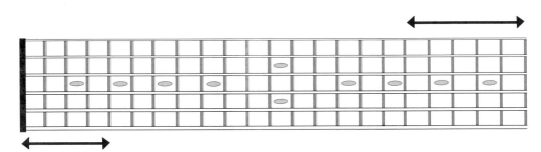

The only notes on the fretboard that aren't repeated elsewhere on the neck are the first five on the bass string and the top five on the top E

From this, it's possible to see that many of the notes on the fretboard are shared in common between the six strings. In fact, it's only really the first five notes on the bass string and the top five on the top E that are unique. This might explain the apparent conundrum of how you can hold half the guitar's range in your hand at any one time.

So, when we consider the other scale shapes that are possible, in order to make sure that we've got the entire fretboard covered with playing positions for any given scale, it's more healthy to look at them as mere variations of each other and not as something entirely new.

One of the things that unfortunately holds many guitarists back is their reluctance to venture much further than knowing just a couple of scale shapes. This means that they are robbing themselves not simply of actual notes, but of many useful alternatives, too.

C Major Scale Positions

Here are the five basic positions for the C major scale, spanning the entire fretboard:

Exercise 15

Track 10

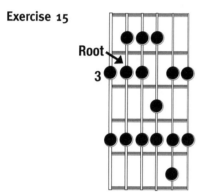

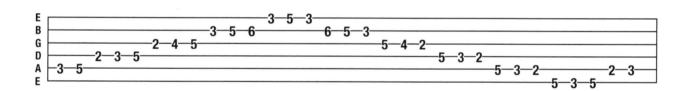

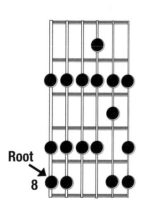

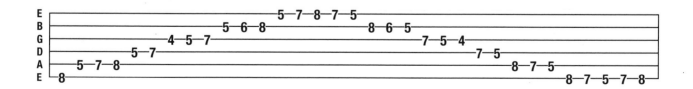

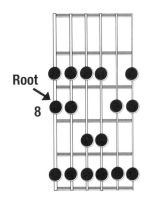

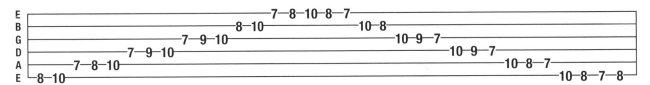

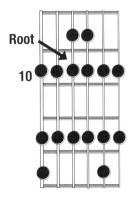

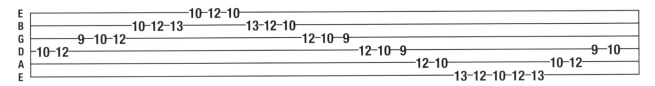

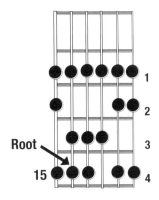

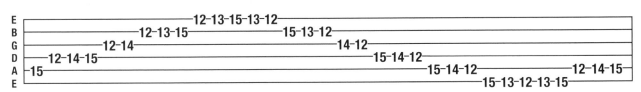

Please check the section on recommended fingerings and so on before initiating a practice routine based on the information presented here.

By the side of the diagrams above, you'll notice I've shown you where the roots for each scale are located. You'll notice, too, that the tab requires you to play each scale from root to root, which sometimes involves you repeating a few notes at the top or bottom.

Despite the fact that this might seem a weird way of going about things, it's very important that you should play every scale in this way.

Remember that what we're really doing here is exploring the various possibilities that lurk within the chromatic scale, and this kind of information can only be expected to make its way into your brain if you're hearing the scale played with these essential reference points – the roots – in place. Otherwise, it's possible to confuse yourself into mistaking some of the vital aural clues that should accompany scale practice.

The other thing that knowing the position of the various roots will do for you is you'll know how and where to line things up to swap scales into different keys. As an example, have a look at how the major-scale shapes appear if we choose to write them out in E major:

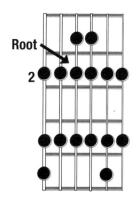

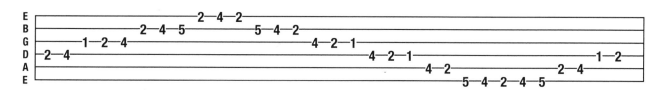

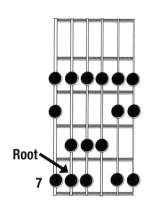

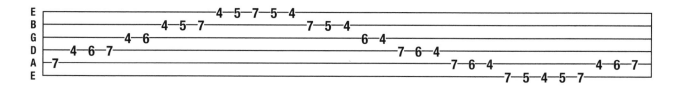

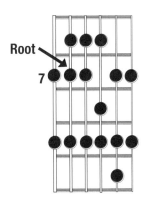

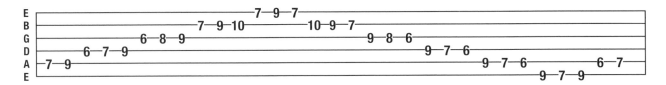

```
E ─────────────────────────────────────7─9─7──────────────────────────────────
B ──────────────────────────7─9─10──────────────10─9─7─────────────────────────
G ──────────────6─8─9────────────────────────────────────9─8─6─────────────────
D ──────6─7─9──────────────────────────────────────────────────9─7─6────────────
A ──7─9──────────────────────────────────────────────────────────────9─7─6──────6─7──
E ─────────────────────────────────────────────────────────────────────9─7─9────────
```

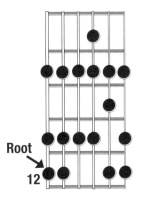

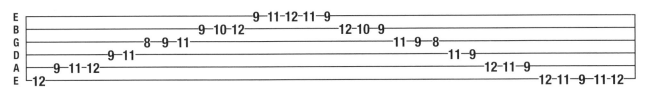

```
E ──────────────────────────────────9─11─12─11─9──────────────────────────────────
B ──────────────────────9─10─12──────────────────12─10─9──────────────────────────
G ──────────────8─9─11─────────────────────────────────────11─9─8─────────────────
D ──────────9─11──────────────────────────────────────────────────11─9────────────
A ──9─11─12──────────────────────────────────────────────────────────────12─11─9────
E ─12──────────────────────────────────────────────────────────────────────────12─11─9─11─12─
```

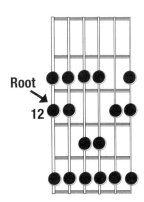

```
E ──────────────────────────────────11─12─14─12─11──────────────────────────────────
B ──────────────────────12─14──────────────────────14─12──────────────────────────
G ──────────────11─13─14───────────────────────────────────14─13─11─────────────────
D ──────────11─13─14──────────────────────────────────────────────14─13─11──────────
A ──11─12─14──────────────────────────────────────────────────────────────14─12─11────
E ─12─14────────────────────────────────────────────────────────────────────────14─12─11─12─
```

All the shapes remain exactly the same, but all the positions have changed and all the roots are now lined up with the note E, as opposed to C.

At first, this kind of thing can appear bewildering, but, with practice, it will become easier and easier – especially when it's linked up with the CAGED idea.

The major scale is, without any doubt, the most important scale in music: everybody's used it, from Beethoven to Nirvana, from Bach to The Beatles, so having a thorough knowledge of it on the guitar fretboard is vitally important.

Pentatonic Scales

Another scale you'll find in popular use in pop and rock music is the minor pentatonic scale. This scale is a favourite amongst guitarists, to the extent that many put off learning anything else. It's very primal, and every music culture in the world seems to have one. There are Chinese and Japanese pentatonic scales, Indian pentatonics – even a Scottish one! It's a very adaptable scale, and it's able to break quite a few of music's rules.

The basic minor pentatonic shape on the guitar fretboard looks like this:

Exercise 17　　**C minor pentatonic**

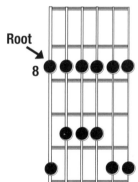

I wouldn't be at all surprised if you've come across this particular shape before, even if you didn't what it actually was. It's one that tends to be handed down from one generation of guitar players to the next.

One of the most obvious differences between the pentatonic scale and the major we've just looked at is that this scale is only five-notes long…

C min pentatonic = C　E♭　F　G　B♭　C
　　　　　　　　　　1　2　3　4　5　1

…although its makeup is generally looked at in terms of intervals, which merely becomes another means to identify its essential template. And so, if we look at what's going on inside the scale, we come up with this:

C min pentatonic = C　E♭　F　G　B♭　C
　　　　　　　　　　1　♭3　4　5　♭7　1

So, it contains a root, a minor 3rd, a 4th, a 5th and a dominant, or 'flat' 7th. It's always interesting to look at pentatonic scales as if they were chords – check out the note content and imagine you were looking at a chord formula. In the case of the minor pentatonic, it would most resemble a minor 11th chord (see page 72), and this gives us something of a clue to its character and, indeed, what set of chords it's most likely to feel at home with from a melodic point of view.

Just as with the major scale, there are five pentatonic fretboard locations to learn in every key. Here's a more complete picture, with the root notes in place and tab that tells you how to play each of the shapes:

Exercise 18

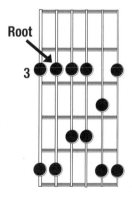

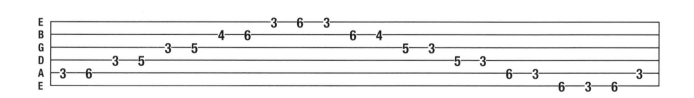

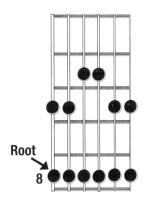

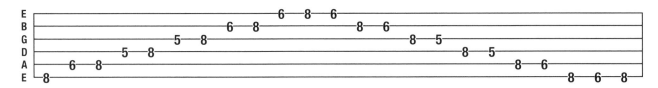

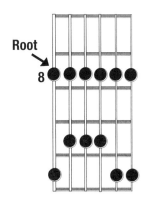

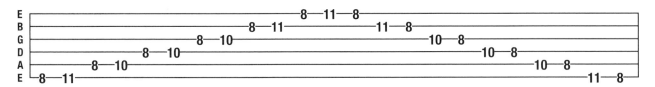

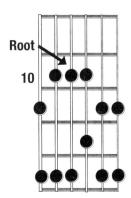

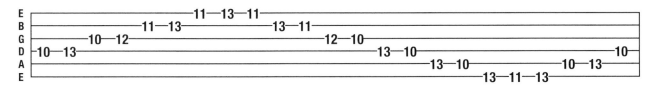

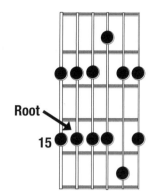

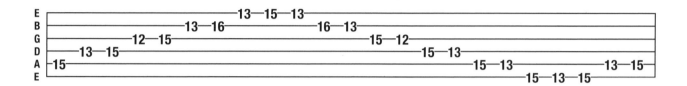

Remember that the most important thing here is to focus on the actual sound of this scale. Compare it to the sound of the major scale by playing them both one after the other; in fact, a good practice plan is to play the major scale and the minor pentatonic scale from the same root, like this:

Exercise 19

Track 11

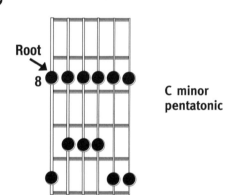

C minor pentatonic

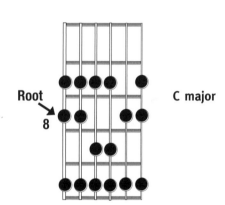

C major

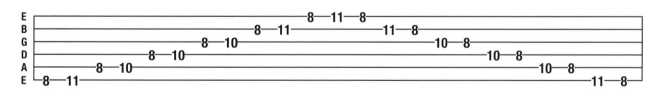

C minor pentatonic

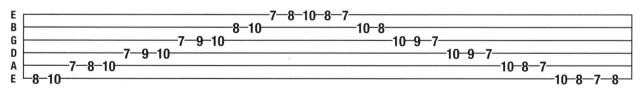

C major

This way, you're hearing the contrast between the two more clearly and you should be able to assign some sort of character to both in much the same way as we did when we looked at chords. In this way, the major scale may sound bold, or happy, whereas the minor pentatonic may sound sombre, or even a bit rocky. I'll leave the definitions to you, though; it's better that you come up with your own set of criteria for how the scales sound.

The Natural Minor

When we took a look at minor chords, you'll remember that I said that there was quite a lot of confusion about which minor scale it is which is responsible for the formation of the minor chords. The same sort of illogic applies here, I'm afraid. But, if we apply the law of 'common usage' and look at the minor scale that crops up in guitar music more than any other, we land on the natural minor. We will be looking at the harmonic and melodic varieties

later on, but it's this critter that sits atop the minor-scale pile as far as we're concerned.

C natural minor = C D E♭ F G A♭ B♭ C
                    1 2 3 4 5 6 7 1

Here's what C natural minor looks like on the fretboard:

Exercise 20

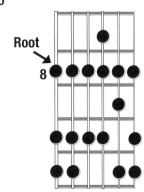

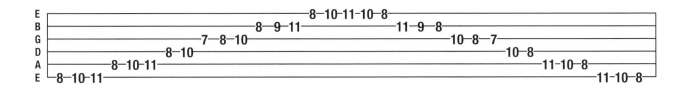

We're back to seven-note scales now, but it will make an interesting exercise if we compare the natural minor to the minor pentatonic and then to the major. As before, keep

all scales based on a single root to give your ears the best chance of forming an opinion:

Exercise 21

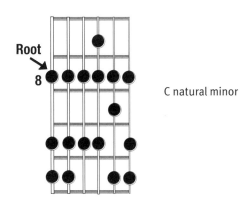

C natural minor

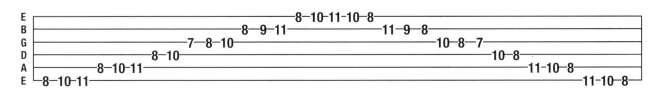

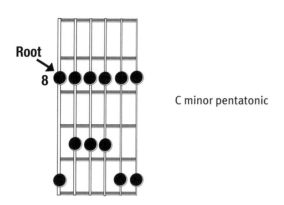

C minor pentatonic

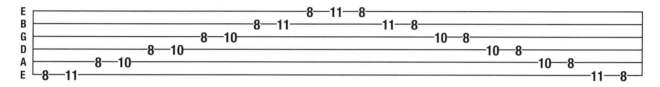

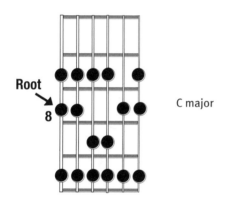

C major

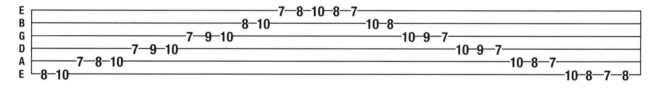

In exactly the same way as before, there are five positions for the natural minor, if we intend to cover the entire fretboard.

If you take a look at the fretboard diagrams here, though, you'll probably notice something a bit odd.

First, though, here are the rest of the diagrams:

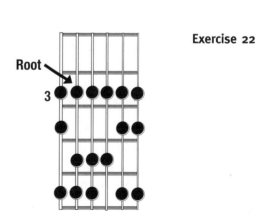

▲ Track 12

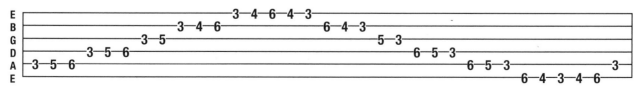

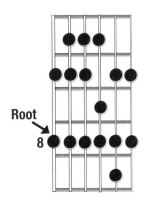

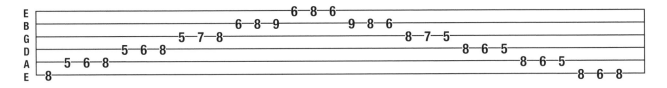

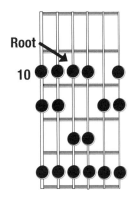

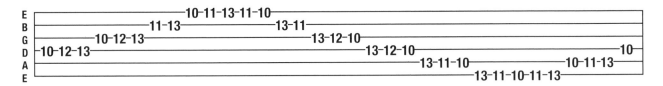

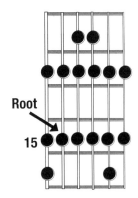

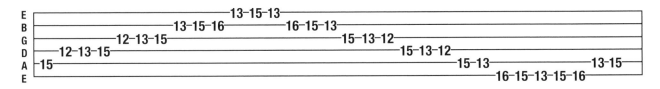

Notice anything? As far as the fretboard diagrams are concerned, these natural minor shapes correspond to the shapes we looked at for the major scale earlier on… Surely some mistake? Well, no, actually; the explanation is really quite straightforward – as far as music is concerned, anyway – and needs only a little careful thought to understand.

Take another look at the tone/semitone order of the major scale:

C (t) D (t) E (st) F (t) G (t) A (t) B (st) C

(t = tone; st = semitone)

Now look at it for the natural minor:

C (t) D (st) E♭ (t) F (t) G (st) A♭ (t) B♭ (t) C

Now, look at this:

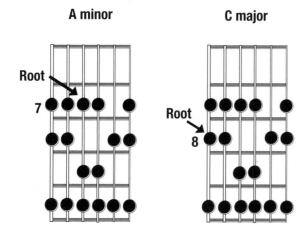

A minor   **C major**

Root

7

Root

8

Apart from the different position for the root, these two scale shapes are identical

It looks exactly the same on the face of it, wouldn't you agree? However, if you pause for a moment and carefully consider the actual tone/semitone order of these two scales, you might begin see just why this is the case.

C major
C (t) D (t) E (st) F (t) G (t) A (t) B (st) C

A natural minor
A (t) B (st) C (t) D (t) E (st) F (t) G (t) A

The two scales contain exactly the same notes, but they begin on different roots. If you look at the tone/semitone order once again, you'll get exactly the same answer: it's the same, but it starts at a different place.

When you think about it, this is fantastically useful and cuts down the number of shapes you have to learn significantly. And, quite naturally, this is a trick that works for other scales, too…

The Major Pentatonic
Just as the major and minor scales involve similar shapes for different scales, the major pentatonic bears an uncanny resemblance to the minor. Take a look:

Exercise 23

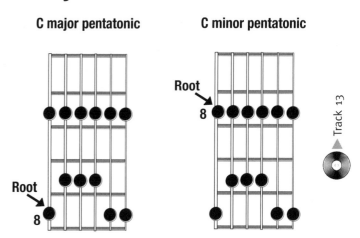

C major pentatonic   **C minor pentatonic**

Root

8

Root

8

▲ Track 13

Once again, you'll notice that the only difference is that the scales start at different points on the neck. Let's look a little more closely at the inner workings of the major pentatonic.

C major pentatonic = C   D   E   G   A   C

And, again, the numbering system below is traditionally representative of the notes' positions in the major scale.

C major = C   D   E   F   G   A   B   C
             1   2   3   4   5   6   7   1

C major pentatonic = C   D   E   G   A   C
                     1   2   3   5   6   1

If the note content of the major pentatonic was a chord, we'd say it was reminiscent of a major 6/9 (see page 50), and the scale has much the same sweet character – so much so, in fact, that it's often unwisely disregarded by the rock-guitar fraternity in favour of the grittier, bluesier minor pentatonic. But the major pentatonic is also used in blues, as we'll discover a little later on.

Here are the remaining shapes for the C major pentatonic scale, with the usual tab. Don't forget to play the scales from root to root all the time; it's the only way you'll be able to hear their contrasting effect.

Exercise 24

Track 13

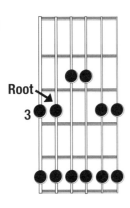

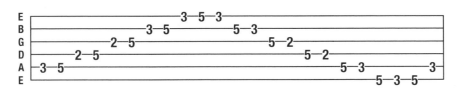

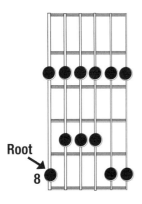

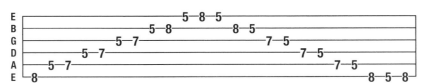

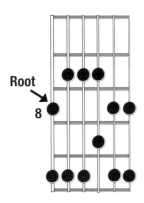

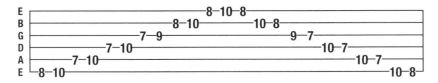

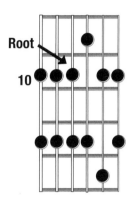

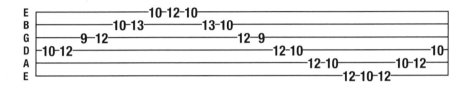

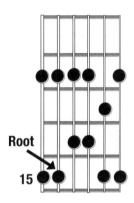

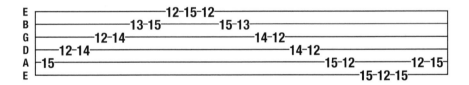

The Blues Scale

There's an awful lot of controversy about this particular scale. I've said before that I don't believe it's ever written down accurately, but we must remember that scales come after the fact. The great blues pioneers like Robert Johnson, Charlie Patton, Son House and Mississippi John Hurt didn't write their music from a text book – or from any academic point of view at all. Blues was a 'folk' music in the most traditional sense of the word. It was handed down by ear from generation to generation, each adding its own unique nuances as the music evolved.

Many learned musicologists have tried to trace the origins of the blues back as far as they can. There are books that compare the music of the West African tribes to the blues of the Mississippi Delta, finding some sort of family resemblance along the way. But most are decided that the blues is an American music, born and bred in the cotton fields of the Mississippi Delta.

But the fact is that, whatever its origins, you cannot tie something as free-form as the blues down to a single reservoir of notes. Every time someone tries, they come up with an answer which is rapidly contradicted somewhere else.

And so, having thought long and hard about the subject, I've come up with something that I believe is closest to the facts. But I'm going to show you the traditional route as well as my theoretical standpoint, so that we've got as many bases covered as possible!

As far as guitar lore is concerned, the blues scale is based upon the minor pentatonic. However, it's almost certainly the other way around: the minor pentatonic scale we use on the guitar today is more likely to be under the influence of the blues. So, to begin with, here's the minor pentatonic scale:

Exercise 25

▲ Track 14

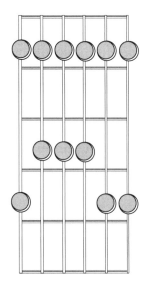

One of the main characteristics of the blues, which was doubtless derived from how the music was vocalised, is that it contains certain imprecise pitches. The 3rd and 5th notes of the blues scale are usually not 'spot on', in terms of pitch. The pitch of the 3rd lies somewhere between the minor and major variations. In other words, it's not exactly this...

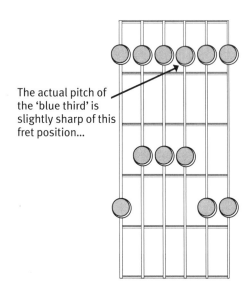

The actual pitch of the 'blue third' is slightly sharp of this fret position...

...or this...

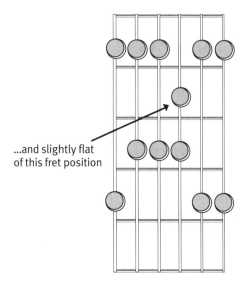

...and slightly flat of this fret position

...but somewhere in between. When we're playing it on the guitar, of course, we get around this anomaly by bending the string slightly here, to make the necessary alteration:

Exercise 28

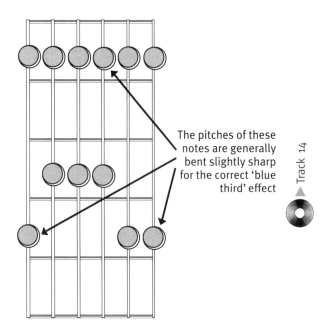

The pitches of these notes are generally bent slightly sharp for the correct 'blue third' effect

▲ Track 14

What you end up with by doing this is one of those microtones we found present in the overtone series earlier in the book.

Microtones are common in Oriental and Eastern music, but not so common in the West – except in the blues and the music derived from it (and I would certainly include jazz here, too).

The other 'indeterminate pitch' is the 5th. Sometimes you'll hear the 5th played pretty much 'as is'; at other times it will be flattened, just like the flat 5th we find in some altered dominant chords (see page 61).

Therefore, instead of having another 'blurred note', if you like, in the scale, the flat 5th is inserted in its own right. Play through the following example, taking care to bend the 3rd but also playing both versions of the 5th, and you should be able to hear something seriously bluesy beginning to happen, although it might take a bit of work to get it spot on.

Track 14

Exercise 29

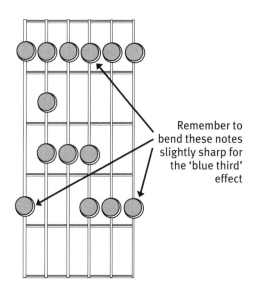

The flat 5th – the dissonant driving force behind the blues

So now we are in a position to make an attempt at writing down the contents of the blues scale:

C blues scale = C Eb/E F Gb/G Bb C
               1 b3/3 4 b5/5 b7 1

And a fretboard diagram would look like this:

Remember to bend these notes slightly sharp for the 'blue third' effect

But I don't believe this explanation goes far enough in summing up the melodic content of the blues, although this is where a lot of people stop adding notes. Remember when I said that the major pentatonic crops up now and again in blues and is – unwisely – ignored by many players for simply being too 'soft and sweet' for playing good old, rugged blues? Well, let's see what happens if we add the major pentatonic to the minor and come up with the C maj/min pentatonic:

C maj pentatonic = C D E G A C
                 1 2 3 5 6 1

C min pentatonic = C Eb F G Bb C
                1 b3 4 5 b7 1

Add them together:

C maj/min pentatonic = C D Eb/E F G A Bb C
                    1 2 b3/3 4 5 6 b7 1

And now, if we add the flat 5th interval:

C blues = C D Eb/E F Gb/G A Bb C
          1 2 b3/3 4 b5/5 6 b7 1

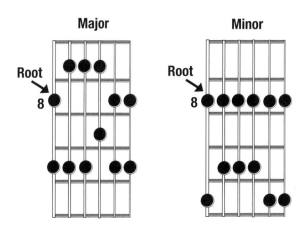

Major   **Minor**

Root   Root

8   8

Superimpose the two scales above and you end up with this:

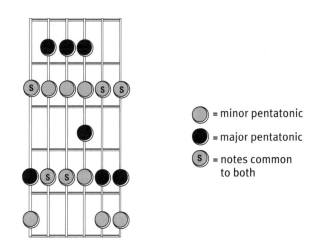

⬤ = minor pentatonic

⬤ = major pentatonic

Ⓢ = notes common to both

This is, to my ears at least, far more likely to be an accurate reading of the blues scale.

If you write it down as a diagram, though, I'll be among the first to admit that the minor pentatonic with the bent 3rd and the flat 5th sounds more 'instant blues'.

But, if the case against the blues scale as I've written it here is that it doesn't sound enough like the blues, I'd counter that by saying that the major scale doesn't sound like the pieces by Beethoven, Bach, The Beatles, Abba, Led Zeppelin and so on that have been based on it, either! However, I'd be the first to admit that it's not particularly helpful when training the ear to recognise the essential building blocks of the blues – despite being, to all intents and purposes, accurate enough.

Full blues scale   **Minor pentatonic with added ♭5ths**

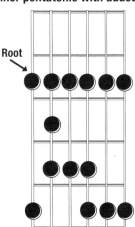

Although the diagram on the left is more technically representative of the actual note content prevalent in the blues, the diagram on the right is a more manageable and better-sounding starting point

The enhanced minor pentatonic version of the scale is unquestionably more manageable from a fretboard point of view, and it's to this end that blues is still taught as being a collision between minor and major pentatonic scales. As a thumbnail guide, it is probably sufficient, and so, if our purpose here is to look at scales in their proper context – ie as mere builders' yards from which melodies are constructed – I believe that the enhanced minor pentatonic (with added flat 5th) is a better introduction, melodically, to the blues for both hand and ear. So here, for completeness's sake, is a fretboard full of what may be dubbed 'the blues pentatonic':

Exercise 32

Track 14

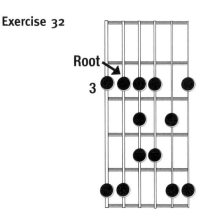

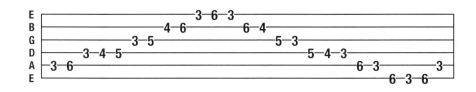

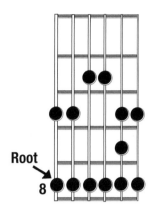

Root
8

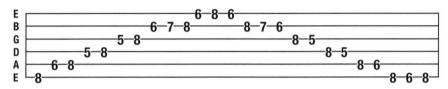

```
E ───────────────────6─8─6───────────────────────
B ─────────────6─7─8───────8─7─6─────────────────
G ───────5─8─────────────────────8─5─────────────
D ───5─8─────────────────────────────8─5─────────
A ─6─8───────────────────────────────────8─6─────
E ─8───────────────────────────────────────8─6─8─
```

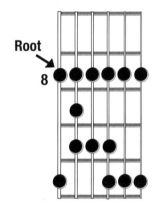

Root
8

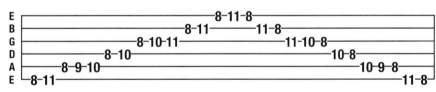

```
E ──────────────────────8─11─8───────────────────────
B ──────────────8─11──────────11─8────────────────────
G ──────8─10─11────────────────────11─10─8────────────
D ──8─10──────────────────────────────────10─8────────
A ─8─9─10──────────────────────────────────────10─9─8─
E ─8─11──────────────────────────────────────────11─8─
```

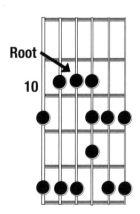

Root
10

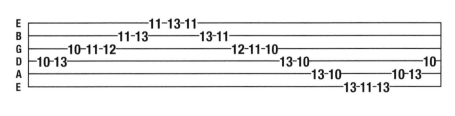

```
E ─────────────────11─13─11────────────────────────
B ──────────────11─13──────────13─11───────────────
G ──────10─11─12──────────────────────12─11─10──────
D ─10─13──────────────────────────────────────13─10──────────10─
A ───────────────────────────────────────────────────13─10──────10─13─
E ───────────────────────────────────────────────────13─11─13─
```

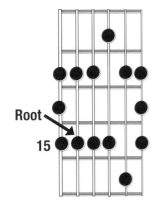

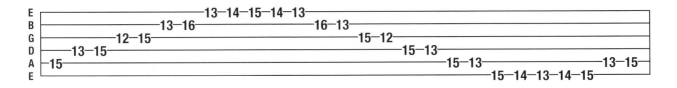

* Note: although technically there are more flat 5ths available on the fretboard, the ones I've included here are the most practical in terms of fingering

▲ Track 15

How To Find A Scale From A Melody

Now that we're a fair way down the line in our look at scales – and, so far, we've looked at what are arguably the most common in use – it's worth looking at how you can make up your own scales from any given melody.

I would urge you to read this section, even if you think that you're unlikely ever to be in the position where you need to play the role of being a music architect. This information has got me out of trouble a number of times!

Let's consider the facts: all scales are representative of 'backwards engineering', as music didn't start off with a scale book and instructions for use. There is a definition I really like: 'Science is the means by which we try to understand nature.' The same applies to music: scales are part of the essential machinery of music, and a means by which we try to understand the creative force that underlies it. Apart from that, they're as relevant to music as Boyle's Law is to making a cup of tea.

Deconstruction For Beginners

First, we need to take a melody, so here's the well-known UK National Anthem written out in tab:

Exercise 33

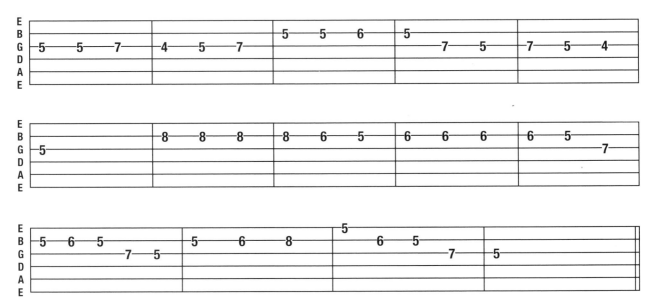

And here's what you do: take a blank fretboard diagram, like this...

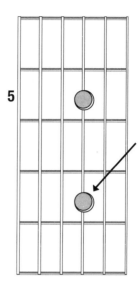

...and write down each note of the melody on it. At first, you'll need to do this with a guitar in your hands, and there will be plenty of going backwards and forwards between fretboard, pen, paper, book, and so on. Our first melody note is C, and so this would appear here:

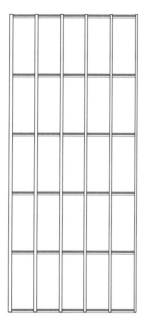

The second melody note to deal with is D, and so this would fit here:

Eventually, after having written down all the melody notes, you should come up with something that looks like this:

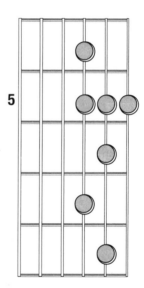

Look familiar? If not, look again:

*R = root

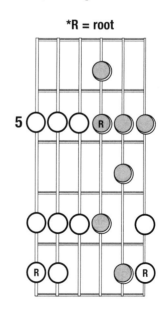

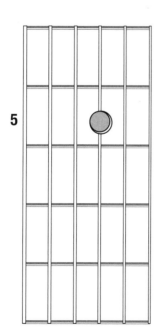

It makes a scale of C major, and this tells us two things: that the melody is drawn exclusively from the scale of C, and that any guitar solos or counter-melodies we might feel inclined to play over the chord arrangement would be expected to follow suit.

This also illustrates the relationship between actual melody and scales even more. There's no way that the C major scale in its basic form could possibly be mistaken for 'God Save The Queen' and yet the melody is in fact there all along.

So you can see how futile it would be to substitute the scale itself randomly for the melody. The results wouldn't be at all musical, although you might get lucky a couple of times and play something that fits well enough. Also, 'God Save The Queen' is a simple melody and, musically, very straightforward, but other melodies may raise questions that this process has the power to answer. I have found my way melodically into Egyptian and Indian music by doing this little sum and so, as a creative device, it's pretty much priceless.

Assessing What We've Got

So far, we have looked at five different scales: the major, natural minor, minor pentatonic, major pentatonic and blues. Now, believe it or not, we've covered an immense amount of ground with just these five. A thorough knowledge of these scales in all keys will provide you with enough melodic information to carry you through as much as 90 per cent of your musical needs.

Did you notice those three words I slipped in there, 'in all keys'? With the guitar being so 'shape-orientated', in terms of chords and scales, there's no excuse for not being able to transpose (change the key) of everything we've looked at so far. The section on CAGED is going to help you out here, but I'll add a few words of caution: don't allow yourself to become stuck in the rut of being fluent in only one or two keys. I've seen this sort of thing happen too many times. It's a simple trap to fall into, with rock music, blues and so on having their favourite keys (A, E, G, D, C and so on), but being adept in all keys is a fantastic resource to have at your disposal.

Despite the guitar fretboard being so easily partitioned into scale and chord shapes that merely move around between keys, you would think that it's an easy thing to do just to move everything one fret up or down to suit a different key, but it's not.

Once, I had the enviable task of keeping the jazz-guitar legend Tal Farlow company for two or three hours before a gig. I sat with him while he wrote out his set list and I noted that he was writing out keys alongside the various titles. Many of them were 'flat keys' – A♭, B♭, E♭, D♭ and so

on – and I mentioned the difficulty I had in playing in D♭. Part of the problem, I mused, was probably due to that particular key's proximity to C major (they're next-door neighbours), and it confused me to look at the fretboard and see myself so close to a key I was more familiar with.

Tal told me that it was the other way around for him: he was so used to playing in bands with horn players – who like playing in flat keys – that it was C major that was the problem, whereas D♭ felt and looked right!

So don't let yourself off here and think that you might never need some of the keys and hence avoid practising them. Practise them all; you'll be building yourself a far broader base if you do.

Scale Similarity

The next important thing for us to focus on is the similarity between the four scale types that we've looked at so far. (I'm actually missing out the blues scale here but I can assure you that I have my reasons, so please be patient!)

Look at the similarity between the C major and C major pentatonic scales:

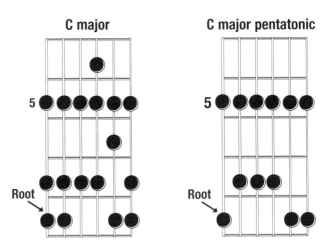

Now look at the two minor-scale variations:

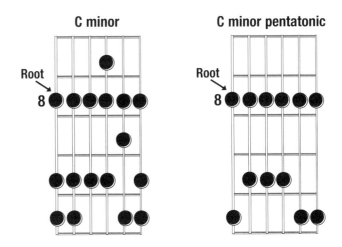

If we take all four, try to see the basic similarity between them.

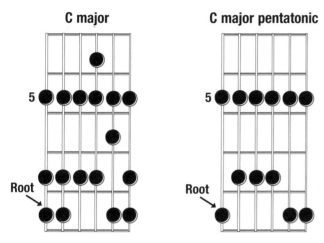

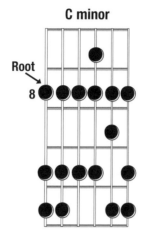

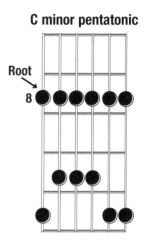

If you agree that there are, in fact, more similarities than real differences, you're well on your way towards being able to take the fullest advantage of applying the CAGED idea later on.

Practice Schedule

Before we go any further in our look at scale variations, it's best that I offer up some sort of advice with regards to practising the ones that we've looked at so far. At the risk of repeating myself, I'll say again that these four scales, along with the hard-to-define blues scale, are by far the most common in use where guitar music is concerned. A thorough knowledge of what we've looked at so far will cover you for most of the music you come across. The other permutations are far more rarefied and, in many cases, too exotic for mainstream usage.

Don't allow yourself to believe that becoming a walking scale repository will help you too much at all. Most of your musical achievements that lie in the future will be drawn from basic major and minor scales – in either five- or seven-note form – and these are the ones that really require the most conscientious committal to memory. Worry about the rest later on and you'll enjoy the advantage of being able to see what lies ahead as mere variations on what you've already learned.

So, my suggested practice routine for the four scales we've looked at (leave the blues scale a while longer) is this:

- Make a fretboard chart, showing the notes on the strings (I know I've asked you to do this before, but repeating good advice never hurts, in my opinion). Remember not to clutter things up overmuch; just the 'whole' notes – like A, B, C, D and so on – will do as reference points. Including all the sharps and flats makes things look impenetrable and hard to read

- Every time you sit down to practise, pick a key at random from your chart and play the major, natural minor, pentatonic major and minor from that one root in a single position

- If you have access to one, use a metronome to keep your playing in time. Just synchronise each note with a click from the metronome at around 80–100 beats per minute. Don't try to speed things up too much – we're not entering you for the Olympics; part of the exercise is to give your ears time to hear each note of each scale and the contrast between them

- Spend no longer than five minutes in total on the scales before moving on to whatever you want to do next. This way, scale practice should never become a chore. (Take it from someone who used to spend three hours a day practising scales!)

- Repeat daily

If you follow these simple guidelines, I can guarantee that you will gradually build up the necessary information in both your ears and hands that will form the basis for your melody playing in the future. Remember that solid foundations yield the strongest constructions.

The Blues Scale Revisited

The reason why I wanted to keep this particular scale separate from the rest is because I think it's important that you try to practise it in context and not by simple unaccompanied repetition. In fact, you will eventually begin to practise all scales over the backing tracks that I've recorded on the accompanying CD.

The blues scale is singular in that it requires some degree

of technique even to play it 'cold'. With the other scales, as long as you can pick each note cleanly and with reasonable fluency, everything will be pretty much fine and you will be drawing benefit from mere repetition.

The blues scale, on the other hand, has those indeterminate pitches we discovered earlier, and so your-string bending technique has to be quite advanced to make these musical aberrations work in their proper context.

In other words, if you can't bend a string in tune – or at

least bend the 3rd out of tune to the correct extent – everything is going to start sounding very nasty indeed.

So here, it's best to put on the blues backing track from the CD and play along – but play along strategically! We haven't reached the point where you're practising your blues playing as such; here we want to be sure that your blues technique is up to scratch. Getting it right now will save frustration later on, so here are a few strategies which should sharpen up your blues technique.

◢ Track 20

Exercise 42

◢ Track 16

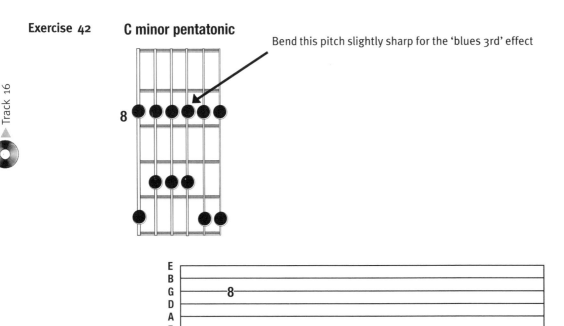

Here, you are bending the minor 3rd of the minor pentatonic scale slightly sharp to give it that 'bluesy' edge. Listen to the example on the CD for reference; in fact, if it's still

unclear how much you should bend the string, play along with my example until you get a perfect fit.

Exercise 43

◢ Track 16

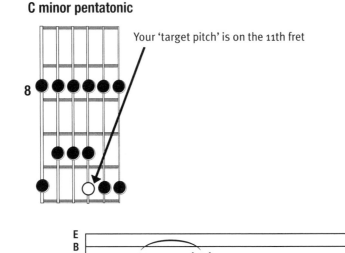

Now it's time to bend the 4th up to that demonic flat 5th for another bluesy nuance. Again, watch how far you push the string; this sort of thing may not be an exact science, but there is clearly a right and a wrong type of bend, and your ears should enable you to hit the spot every time. It's all down to practice in the end.

Exercise 44   **C minor pentatonic**

Track 16

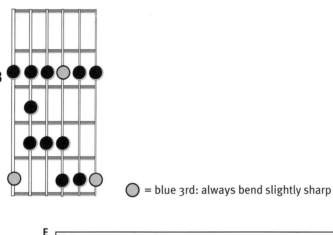

◯ = blue 3rd: always bend slightly sharp

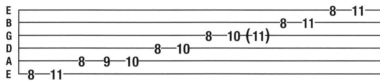

Here's the minor pentatonic over two octaves with both the 3rd and flat 5th anomalies in place. When you can perform this correctly every time, you're ready to use the scale in your practice routine – but definitely not before!

The Modes Of The Major Scale

This is another area that has attracted somewhat more attention than it probably deserves. Once, the modes were given almost semi-religious standing in the music community, mainly due to jazz-trumpet-playing legend Miles Davis. In 1959, Miles recorded an album called *Kind Of Blue*, on which the musicians involved were invited to improvise on the prevailing modes rather than a given melody (you'll understand all this in a minute, I promise you). This idea was pretty controversial in its day, because for years jazz musicians had been training themselves to play around a melody or chord progression, and now all Miles was telling them was what scale to use over a static chord. It was a bit like saying that you've got four bars of C major, six bars of F major and then back to C.

In any case, the album went on to change not only the face of jazz but also the way in which musicians thought about improvising in general. 'Modal jazz' was the way to go and the place to be, from a musician's point of view.

Fast-forward to around 25 years later, when rock guitarists such as Joe Satriani and Steve Vai started using modes in their own music. Suddenly, practice and rehearsal rooms across the world rang out to the sound of guitarists massaging modes into their fretboards, hoping it would unlock The Secret Of Being A Really Cool Guitarist.

What they didn't know, of course, was that, in the musical universe, the modes come around about as regularly as Halley's Comet. They started life long ago and enjoy periodic resurgence – albeit mainly in classical music.

So, what exactly are the modes? The good news is that you already know them – from a fretboard point of view, at least. Let me explain this a little more clearly. Have another look at the by now very familiar C major scale:

Exercise 45

Track 17

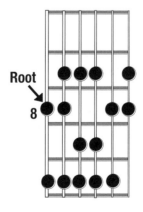

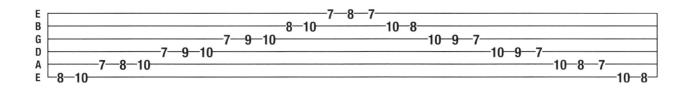

Played in this way, from C through to C, the scale sounds exactly the way it always does – as you would expect.

But what happens if we choose to play it in a slightly different way?

Exercise 46

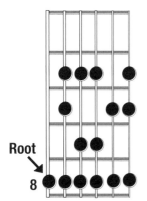

The C major scale played from D to D – sounds different, doesn't it?

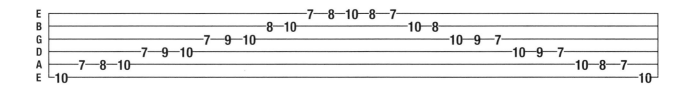

Here, it's still the notes of C major that we're playing, but this time we're playing it from D to D. It changes the sound of the scale almost completely, and here's why:

$$\begin{array}{ccccccccc} \text{C major} = \text{C} & \text{D} & \text{E} & \text{F} & \text{G} & \text{A} & \text{B} & \text{C} \\ 1 & 2 & 3 & 4 & 5 & 6 & 7 & 1 \end{array}$$

$$\begin{array}{ccccccccc} \text{D to D} = \text{D} & \text{E} & \text{F} & \text{G} & \text{A} & \text{B} & \text{C} & \text{D} \\ 1 & 2 & 3 & 4 & 5 & 6 & 7 & 1 \end{array}$$

If we compare the two scales, we'll find that the D-to-D variation is a minor scale with a flat 7th, making it a sort of 'minor 7' scale, if we were going to try to sum up its sound like we did when we were looking at chords. You'll have a chance to hear how different it is to its parent major scale in a moment, but for now we'll consider looking at the major scale from the point of view of all its individual working parts.

The D-to-D version of the scale has a name, of course, and, this being music, you can bet that it's not a particularly easy one to commit to memory. It's called the Dorian mode.

For that matter, the C major scale has another name under the modal system: the Ionian mode. There is absolutely no difference between the major scale and the Ionian mode; it's just like one thing having two names – 'car' and 'automobile', for instance.

The next mode we encounter as we traverse the major scale is the one that starts and finishes on E – known to its mates as the Phrygian (pronounced 'Fridge-Ian') mode.

$$\begin{array}{cccccccc} \text{Phrygian mode} = \text{E} & \text{F} & \text{G} & \text{A} & \text{B} & \text{C} & \text{D} & \text{E} \\ 1 & 2 & 3 & 4 & 5 & 6 & 7 & 1 \end{array}$$

This is another minor scale with a flat 7th, but before we dub it as such, another element contained within it – and one that makes all the difference to how it sounds – is a flat 2nd (or flat 9th, if we're thinking along similar lines to chord formulae).

So, a sort of easy, shorthand description of the Phrygian would be that of a minor7♭9 scale. In use, it has Spanish overtones and is great for the odd flamenco interlude.

Next in line we find the F-to-F variation, which is named the Lydian (pronounced 'Lid-Ian') and looks like this:

Lydian mode = F G A B C D E F
1 2 3 4 5 6 7 1

A quick analysis reveals that the Lydian is a major scale with a sharpened 4th (note that we can't use the term 'flat 5th' here because there is a perfectly normal 5th present in the scale, but the 4th is sharp).

To me, this particular mode sounds like a sort of sweet-and-sour scale: all the sweetness we would normally associate with the major scale, with the bitter twist of the sharpened 4th degree.

In chordal terms, we have here a bit of an anomaly – seeing that the root, 3rd and 5th of the scale gives us a perfectly normal major triad, the chord doesn't really spell out the sound of the scale. We could call it a major7#11, if we wanted to, though. Interestingly enough, Steve Vai once told me that he was so fond of the sound of this scale in rock improvisation that he almost gave himself a 'Lydian hernia'...

If we look at the C major scale from G to G, we get quite a straightforward scale with a heck of an non-straightforward name: the Mixolydian.

Mixolydian mode = G A B C D E F G
1 2 3 4 5 6 7 1

The definition here is that of a major scale with a flat 7th – in other words, it's a dominant 7th scale and a perfect fit for the chord of the same name. This is a scale that turns up quite often in jazz, fusion and funk guitar, and it can be thought of as another starting point for playing the blues, too. It's got that same sort of 'unresolved' sound that the dominant chord has and therefore suits anything remotely blues-based.

Considering the C scale from the point of view of A to A reveals another old friend under the pseudonym the Aeolian mode.

Aeolian mode = A B C D E F G A
1 2 3 4 5 6 7 1

Not only does a quick look reveal that we're dealing once again with a minor scale plus flat 6th and 7th degrees, but also that we've got an absolute thumbprint-exact match for the natural minor scale.

If you remember when we looked at why the major and minor scale shapes were very similar to each other, you'll recall how they're the same scale taken from different starting points – the very basis of modal scale construction itself. So

here is a scale that you're already very familiar with, in terms of both fingering and sound – or, at least, you should be, if you've been following my practice-plan recommendations!

The last modal variation we've got left in the box is possibly the weirdest; it runs from B to B across the compass of the C major scale and calls itself the Locrian mode.

The Locrian mode = B C D E F G A B
1 2 3 4 5 6 7 1

This scale is the living proof that there's always someone in an otherwise perfectly well-behaved crowd who is going to give you a hard time. Played in its basic naked form, it sounds absolutely unusable, and a quick look at its moving parts will give us a clue as to why.

It clocks in as a minor scale with a flat 7th, a flat 5th and a flat 2nd (or 9th). So, what we have here is a Bmin7♭5♭9, and a quick flick back to the section on chords will tell you that a chord with so many alterations present is going to be extremely 'highly flavoured' and greatly restricted in its usefulness in everyday terms.

The Modes In Context

On the CD, I've recorded a series of seven backing tracks for you to play the modes over, because these particular scales only really take on their true characteristics when heard in context. If you practise them unaccompanied, one after another, it will end up sounding like C major all the time. Hearing them set against suitable backdrops enables you to hear the animals in their natural surroundings, so to speak!

But, before you rush off to your CD player, a word or two more on playing through the modes. For a start, you're going to need some diagrams and fingerings. Because all these scales are so patently related to C, we don't want to detract from that with another set of shapes to learn. As you already know the fingering for the major scale itself, I recommend that you play them like this:

Exercise 47

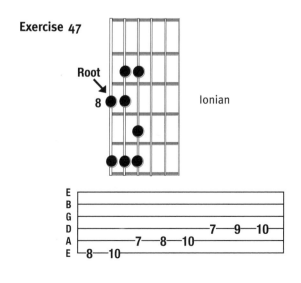

121

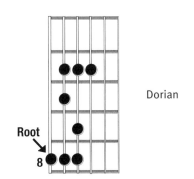

Dorian

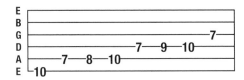

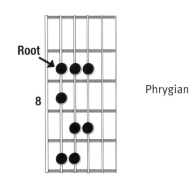

Phrygian

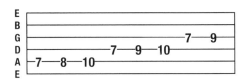

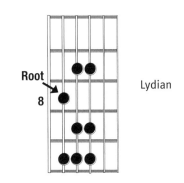

Lydian

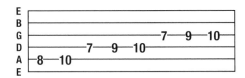

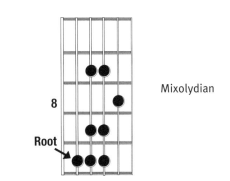

Mixolydian

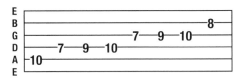

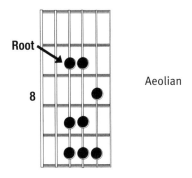

Aeolian

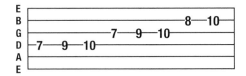

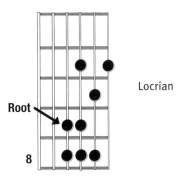

Locrian

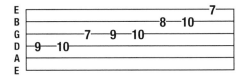

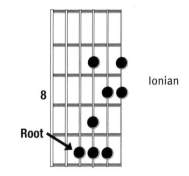

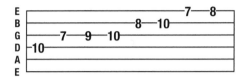

Use this fingering plan when you play them against the backing tracks. This way, you're not inputting any new information into the hands – they already know this area pretty well. What's happening is that you're introducing your ears to the different parameters available to you from a single fingering. Economic learning, eh?

The most important lesson to be learned here is that of becoming aware of the different sounds or musical textures available to you through the modes – or any new scale you're reviewing. So practising these 'new' scales against the backing tracks provided on the CD is vital in order for you to be able to make a proper evaluation as to whether the sounds they produce are ever likely to be useful to you in your music.

This has got to become your commanding factor, asking the question, 'What does the sound of this chord or scale suggest to me?'

I went through this process years ago and, out of interest, my own summing up of the individual modes went something like this:

- Ionian: ordinary major
- Dorian: sweet-sounding minor
- Phrygian: Spanish
- Lydian: slightly sour major
- Mixolydian: jazz/funk
- Aeolian: natural minor/slight Spanish sound
- Locrian: almost unusable!

This way, I gave myself a series of approximate reference points which allowed me to head off in a particular direction, or examine new musical terrain with some sort of guideline already in place. For instance, if you wanted to play something that sounded a little jazzy, knowing that the Mixolydian mode was there ready and waiting for you,

like a sure foothold on a tricky cliff face, then you'd be off with a headstart.

As a further example to their use, I was once doing a jazz fusion gig somewhere in the wilds of Suffolk. The bandleader had a habit of setting up tunes that none of us really knew too well and he came over to me and asked me if I could play something with a Spanish vibe to it (I think he had a sort of Miles Davis 'Sketches Of Spain' hang-up at that time). On the spur of the moment, I couldn't actually think of anything that would fit the sort of laid-back groove the band was putting down behind me – and I wasn't too sure I knew what he meant, anyway! But the one thing I did know was that the Phrygian mode could provide me with instant access to a sort of Spanish sound, and so I applied it. The key we were playing in was D minor, and so I set about playing in the Phrygian mode based on D and was rewarded by a smile and a 'That's it!' from the bandleader. It really didn't do my reputation as a guitar polymath any harm at all...

The story I've just told you is one of the rare occasions when musical theory has helped me out on-stage. Usually, I'm not thinking in actual musical terms at all; I'm using instincts gained from years of practice and experience. But the point is that, having worked with the Phrygian in the practice room, I knew it could get me out of trouble and gain me a few brownie points with my employer at the same time. Once I established that I was in the right musical area, I forgot all about what I was playing from an academic point of view, and my musicianship took over and led the way.

Even if you don't think you're ready to use the modes in your guitar solos, or you want to apply the sort of musical mental arithmetic necessary to perform tricks like the one above, it's still advisable to go through the process of letting yourself hear and evaluate them.

Modal Fingerings

It still might appear that we've got another five scale fingerings to learn (seeing as you already know the Ionian and Aeolian modes), but it's best not to allow yourself to think that way at all. As you can see, all the new information we're considering here springs from a central resource with which we're already very familiar – the major scale. So what should be happening is that we're merely reprocessing information, not learning it from scratch.

So a practice routine that includes modal scale study would necessarily involve using backing tracks, so that the flavour of each mode has the optimum chance to get through, and fingerings that are slight variations on those you know already.

As an example, here are the fingerings for C Dorian (ie the Dorian mode starting on C):

Exercise 48

Track 17

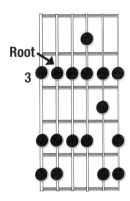

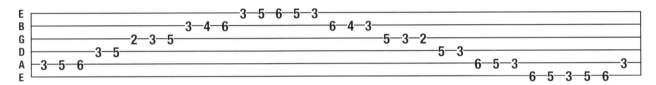

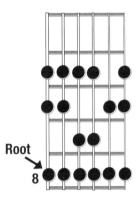

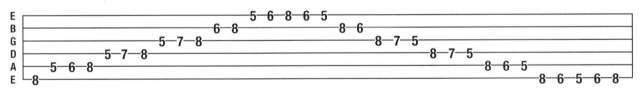

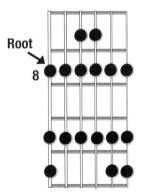

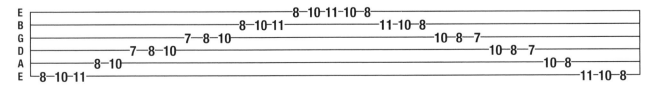

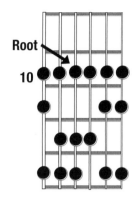

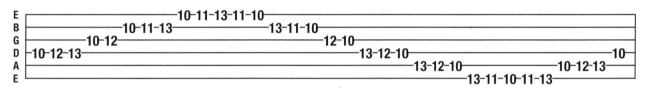

```
E ┌──────────────────10-11-13-11-10──────────────────────────────┐
B │───────────10-11-13───────────────13-11-10────────────────────│
G │──────10-12──────────────────────────────12-10────────────────│
D │─10-12-13──────────────────────────────────────13-12-10───10──│
A │──────────────────────────────────────13-12-10────10-12-13────│
E └───────────────────────────────13-11-10-11-13─────────────────┘
```

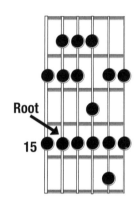

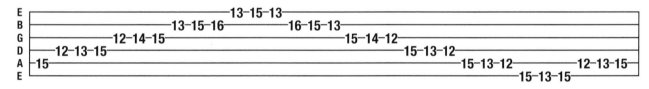

```
E ┌──────────────────13-15-13─────────────────────────────────────┐
B │───────────13-15-16───────────16-15-13─────────────────────────│
G │──────12-14-15────────────────────────15-14-12─────────────────│
D │─12-13-15──────────────────────────────────15-13-12────────────│
A │─15──────────────────────────────────────────15-13-12──12-13-15─│
E └─────────────────────────────────────15-13-15──────────────────┘
```

You'll agree that they look very familiar! What's more, they'll feel familiar, too – as long as you're following my guidelines for a scale practice routine, that is.

To continue, here's the C Phrygian mode:

Exercise 49

Track 17

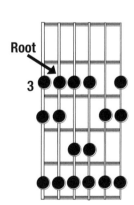

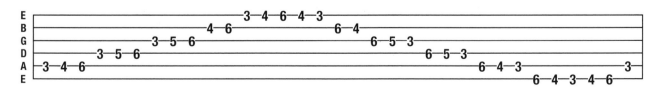

```
E ┌──────────────3─4─6─4─3────────────────────────────┐
B │──────────4─6──────────6─4─────────────────────────│
G │────────3─5─6────────────────6─5─3─────────────────│
D │──────3─5─6────────────────────────6─5─3───────────│
A │─3─4─6──────────────────────────────────6─4─3────3─│
E └───────────────────────────────────6─4─3─4─6──────┘
```

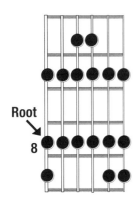

Root

8

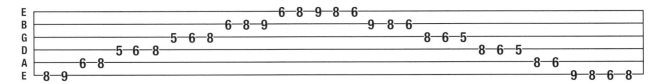

```
E |------------------6-8-9-8-6----------------------------|
B |------------6-8-9----------9-8-6-----------------------|
G |--------5-6-8--------------------8-6-5-----------------|
D |----5-6-8--------------------------------8-6-5---------|
A |--6-8------------------------------------------8-6-----|
E |-8-9-------------------------------------------9-8-6-8-|
```

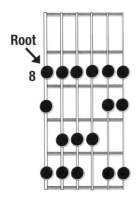

Root

8

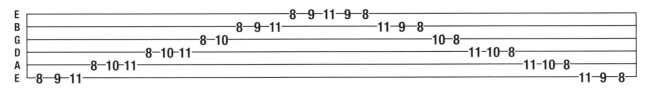

```
E |---------------------8-9-11-9-8------------------------------|
B |----------------8-9-11----------11-9-8----------------------|
G |----------8-10--------------------------10-8----------------|
D |-----8-10-11--------------------------------11-10-8---------|
A |---8-10-11--------------------------------------11-10-8-----|
E |-8-9-11-------------------------------------------------11-9-8-|
```

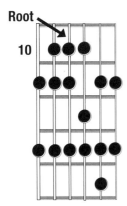

Root

10

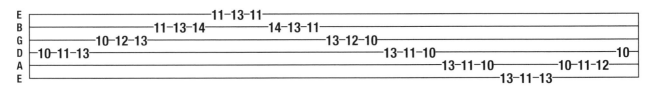

```
E |-----------------11-13-11-----------------------------------------|
B |-----------11-13-14----------14-13-11-----------------------------|
G |------10-12-13------------------------13-12-10--------------------|
D |-10-11-13----------------------------------13-11-10-------------10-|
A |--------------------------------------------------13-11-10--10-11-12-|
E |-----------------------------------------------------13-11-13-------|
```

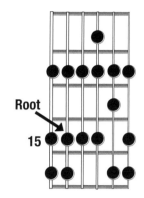

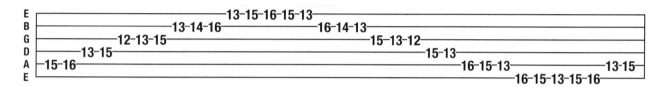

The C Lydian:

Exercise 50

Track 17

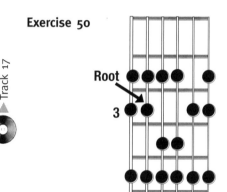

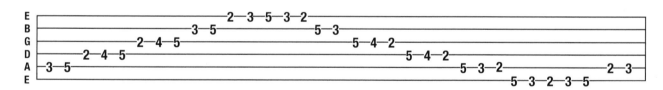

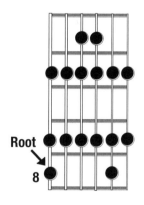

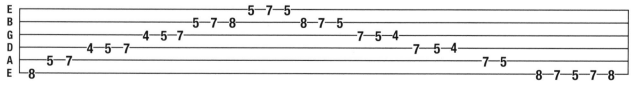

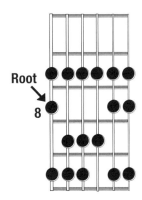

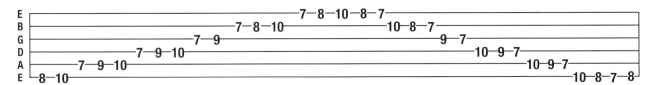

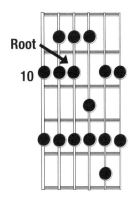

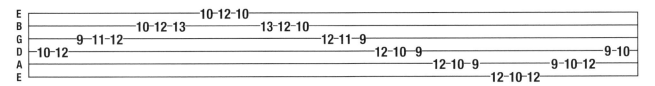

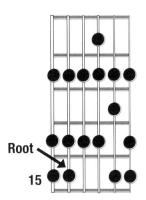

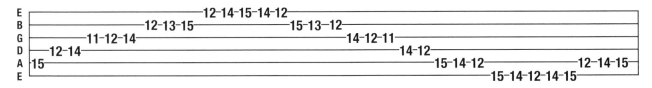

The C Mixolydian:

Exercise 51

Track 17

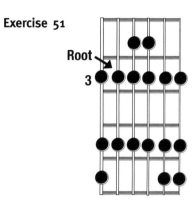

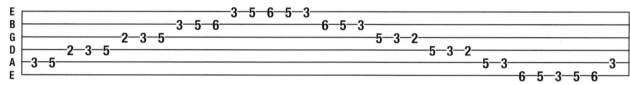

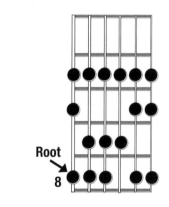

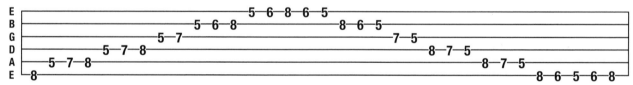

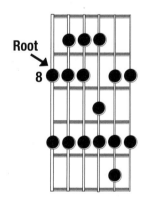

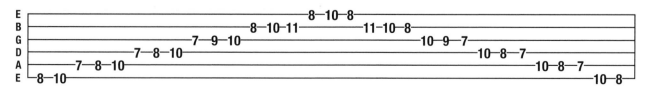

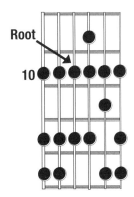

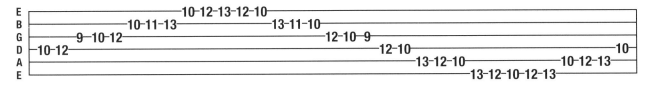

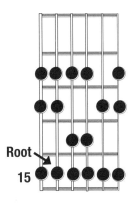

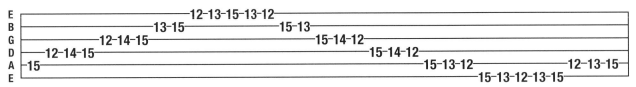

The C Locrian:

Exercise 52

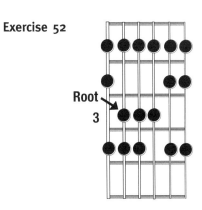

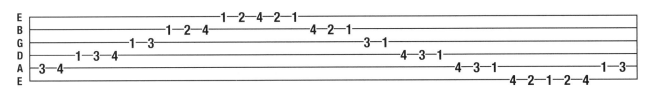

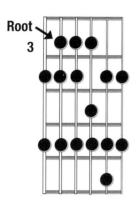

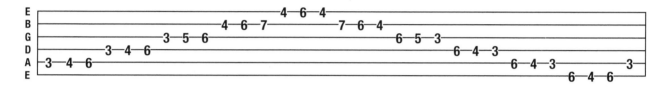

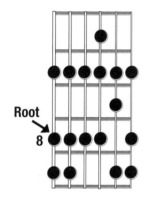

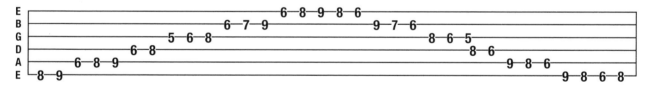

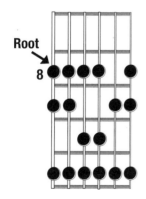

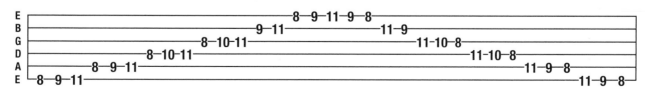

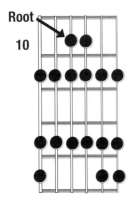

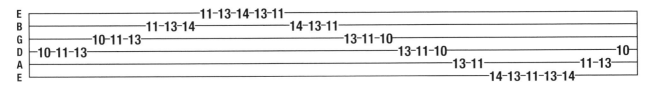

Play all of the scales as shown, starting on C. This way, you're giving your ear the optimum chance to make comparisons and build up something of a catalogue of things you may or may not find useful in the future.

Melodic And Harmonic Minor Scales

If you cast your mind back to the section on chords where we were discussing minor scales (page 69), you'll remember that there are no less than three to consider. I've always found this something of a confusing inconvenience, from the point of view of being a teacher trying to introduce students to the concept of minor melody and harmony, but the truth is that we rarely run across the two minor scales we've not looked at so far. In any case, they're far less popular in rock, blues or whatever than they would be in traditional classical music, anyway.

The reason for this is that we're primarily concerned with music that has been derived from 'pop' or 'folk' culture – as I've said before, blues or jazz didn't start out with the same rule book that classical music did; blues, jazz and the various styles that evolved from them came from fairly humble folk origins. So, whereas you're quite likely to find the melodic and harmonic minor scales throughout classical music, they are both assigned only the privileges of 'occasional guest' in the rock and pop arenas.

This is why we've been able to get this far in our scale safari before even mentioning them. You are really more likely to find one of the modal minor scales cropping up (and in there, of course, we have the natural minor in any case) than you are one of these beasties.

As back-up information here, I should mention a musicologist by the name of Cecil Sharp, who studied folk music intensely and came to the conclusion that, nearly 100 per cent of the time, the tunes we would determine as being minor are, in fact, modally derived. In other words, they are based on either the Dorian, Aeolian or very occasionally Phrygian modes rather than the harmonic or melodic forms.

But, seeing as both the harmonic and melodic forms of minor scale are variations on ones we already know, it's worth taking a look at how and where these differences occur and listening to how they sound.

Let's have a look at the natural minor once again:

C natural minor = C D E♭ F G A♭ B♭ C
                  1 2 3   4 5 6   7   1

So, it's the 3rd, 6th and 7th notes of the scale that make the natural minor scale different from the major. There's the minor 3rd, which needs to be there to tell us that the scale belongs to the minor family – in fact, one of the numerous theory books I've read said that the minor 3rd is the only constant factor in the minor-scale family tree, and the author was right, as we will see. I always thought that this was a little vague, but we're stuck with it.

The harmonic minor scale looks similar to the natural minor:

C harmonic minor = C D E♭ F G A♭ B C
                   1 2 3   4 5 6   7 1

We've only 'unflattened' the 7th, but it makes the scale sound almost completely different. It's shown here, so play through it for yourself:

Exercise 53

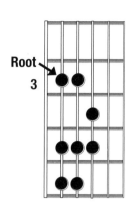

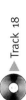

```
E
B
G ----------------4--5--4----------------------
D ----------3--5--6----------6--5--3-----------
A --3--5--6----------------------------6--5--3-
E
```

The main area of difference – in terms of sound, at least – is in those last two notes. The relationship between the B and C gives this scale a sort of Middle Eastern flavour. It's this piece of exotica that makes the harmonic minor beloved of the neo-classical guitar movement. As I have said, this scale is at home in classical music and so it's an almost instant passport to the sound of the Baroque era – just like the Phrygian gains you access to pseudo-flamenco.

I'm not telling you that learning to play the harmonic minor scale will make you sound like Yngwie Malmsteen – it might not even get you into the ball park. You'll be outside queuing for tickets until your musicianship develops to the extent where your taste and choice of notes, degree of expression and so on develops to a high degree. In much the same way, teaching you the alphabet wouldn't be teaching you to write.

The Melodic Minor

If I told you that there is a scale in music which is different depending on whether you're playing it in ascending or descending order, you'd be forgiven for thinking I was, shall we say, taking liberties. But it exists, and we're about to meet it.

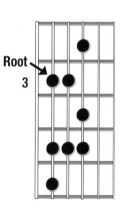

Ascending

```
E
B
G ----------------------2--4--5-
D ----------3--5----------------
A --3--5--6--------------------
E
```

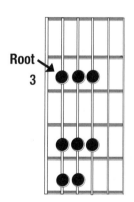

Descending

```
E
B
G --5--3----------------------
D --------6--5--3-------------
A -----------------6--5--3----
E
```

C melodic minor (ascending) = C D E♭ F G A B C
                                 1 2 3 4 5 6 7 1

C melodic minor (descending) = C D E♭ F G A♭ B♭ C
                                 1 2 3 4 5 6 7 1

Before we discuss the melodic minor, it's best to hear it; play both the ascending and descending forms to hear the full effect. Here's C melodic minor:

You may have noticed that the descending version of the melodic minor sounded somewhat familiar. If so, reward yourself with something nice because you're spot on. It is, in fact, our old friend the natural minor or Aeolian mode assuming a third identity. Except, of course, in rock circles, the natural minor contains the same notes in both directions.

I expect you'll want something of an explanation as to why this little minor-scale anomaly should exist. I certainly did when I first encountered it, and my teacher wouldn't – or couldn't – tell me.

The reason is all to do with the so-called 'melodic' quality of the scale. It was considered that the melodic minor in its ascending form was fine when used in melodies, but didn't sound right when descending. So it was decided (and I've often wondered if there was an actual meeting about this) that the scale should be altered in its descending form in the interests of having everything running smoothly in both directions.

Now, I'm not sure that knowing the explanation makes things any clearer or easier to understand, but before you slam the book shut in frustration at the sheer arbitrariness of music's Highway Code, it's wise to remember what I said about the natural minor being more common in rock and popular music.

Don't give yourself a haemorrhage worrying that you'll never be a complete musician if you can't rattle off every scale in the book. We're primarily concerned with common usage here and not some of the madder inclinations of classical music theory.

Your watchwords should be that you're aware of the anomalies concerning minor scales and you know what they sound like, but you're equally aware that you're familiar with the variations you're likely to meet.

Minor Modes

A lot of people ask, usually with a fair amount of fear in their eyes, if there are such things as minor scale modes, in the same way that we find some really useful modes from the major scale.

Well, technically speaking, this is true, there are, but the fact that there isn't one definitive minor scale makes the question of minor modes very tentative, to say the least. For a start, you'd need to choose a minor scale to extract a system of modes from, and that's where the trouble usually begins.

Deriving modes from the natural minor scale would only give us the major modes once again, but this time in a different order, because we would be dealing with exactly the same notebase as we had when we were working with the major scale:

Aeolian

Locrian

Ionian

Dorian

Phrygian

Lydian

Mixolydian

So that's no good – or, at least, it doesn't really get us anywhere we haven't already been. Let's see, then, what happens if we look for modes in the melodic minor:

$$\text{C melodic minor} = \begin{array}{cccccccc} C & D & E\flat & F & G & A & B & C \\ 1 & 2 & 3 & 4 & 5 & 6 & 7 & 1 \end{array}$$

When discerning the content of the minor modes, I like to think of them in much the same way as we did when looking at chords. In this way, the melodic minor could be looked at as being a minor scale with a natural 6th and 7th (conversely, you could say that it's merely a major scale with a minor 3rd, but it really is better to look at things from a minor-scale perspective, in order to keep everything in the correct family grouping).

There isn't a standard naming convention with the minor modes in the same way as there is with the major. Different books/teachers tend to call them different things – which I realise isn't particularly helpful, either. This is all to do with conventions: the modes of the minor scales are less 'in-built' than those of the majors, and arguably much rarer in use.

Add to this the fact that the true melodic minor scale doesn't crop up in 'popular' forms of music as often as it does in classical music and you can be forgiven for thinking that looking at these particular modes could be something of a futile mission. But the individual scales that result from the application of modal theory can be quite interesting, and they certainly serve to demonstrate where some of the more obscure and exotic-sounding scales have come from.

One final point before we dive in: a lot of these scales have been adopted by jazz fusionists as a means for getting unexpected (but theoretically stable, and hence justified in the name of music lore) dissonance in their solos. Like I said, I tend to prefer to look at them in a similar way to looking at chords: finding some common denominators so that the scale concerned can be attributed a kind of 'shorthand' sonic identity. Saying, 'It's a dominant scale with a flat sixth' tells us more than making up a name for it could – although I believe that comparing these modes to those from the major scale is quite justified.

In this case, the scale I just mentioned might assume a name like 'Mixolydian ♭6'. It really is a case of whatever works for you. The most important thing is to take a look at all of these variations and listen to what they sound like. Only then will you be able to make choices and decisions.

And so, starting on the second note of the melodic minor will give us this:

2nd melodic minor mode = D E♭ F G A B C D
                          1   2   3 4 5 6 7 1

This would be a minor 7th scale with a flat 2nd. So, if we were looking for a chord-like formula, we could say that this is a min13♭9 scale. Play through it to hear what it sounds like.

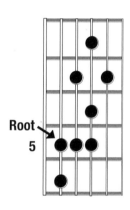

Some people refer to this particular scale as the Phrygian natural 6th, because it differs from the Phrygian in this one respect.

D Phrygian = D E♭ F G A B♭ C D
              1   2   3 4 5   6   7 1

D Phrygian nat 6th = D E♭ F G A B C D
                      1   2   3 4 5 6 7 1

Play them side by side for comparison:

D Phrygian Nat 6   **D Phrygian**

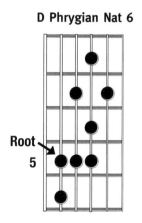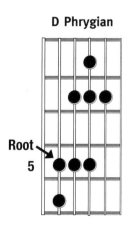

D Phrygian Nat 6

D Phrygian

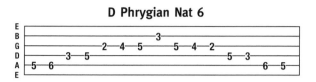

The third mode of the melodic minor would involve beginning and ending on the E♭:

3rd melodic minor mode = E♭ F G A B C D E♭
                           1   2 3 4 5 6 7   1

A definition here would result in a sort of E♭maj♭5♯5 configuration. But both the flat and sharp 5ths present in the same scale makes things sound very exotic indeed – take a listen:

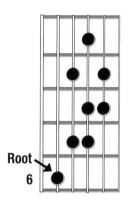

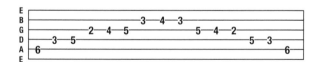

The other name for this particular scale is the Lydian augmented scale. The Lydian mode is basically a major scale with a sharp 4th degree. This minor-mode variation sharpens the 5th – hence, Lydian augmented.

Next in line, we've the melodic minor mode that starts on the fourth degree of the scale; in this case, F.

4th melodic minor mode = F G A B C D E♭ F
                          1   2 3 4 5 6   7   1

A quick look at this scale reveals it to be one of the more straightforward melodic minor modes because, apart from the sharpened 4th, it's a dominant 7th scale. So, this scale could be referred to as a 7#4 (or 7#11) scale – a sort of Lydian dominant, if you prefer. Take a listen:

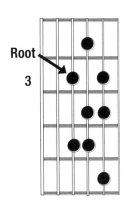

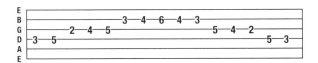

Onwards to the fifth mode:

5th melodic minor mode = G A B C D E♭ F G

                           1 2 3 4 5 6 7 1

Another fairly straightforward scale to analyse. Most of it, once again, is a perfectly intact dominant 7th scale; it's just that E♭ that causes a grinding of gears...

We know from our chord analysis that the 5th and flat 6th aren't particularly good neighbours; that old 'garlic sandwich' situation where one of the important members of the scale (in this case, the 5th) has a semitone 'leaning in' on it.

Of course, with a scale, where the notes aren't meant to be sounded simultaneously, the effect is smoothed out a little.

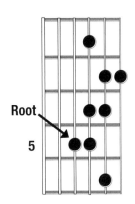

I mentioned earlier that this scale is also referred to as the Mixolydian flat 6 scale, but whatever naming convention you want to adopt to enable your own categorisation (heck, make some names up – no one's going to notice!) it's more important that you hear these scales and come back to them occasionally to review them. As you develop as a musician, you might find that you have use for some of these lesser-walked areas of guitar melody.

The sixth mode of the melodic minor scale looks like this:

6th melodic minor mode = A B C D E♭ F G A

                           1 2 3 4 5 6 7 1

At first glance, it looks like we're dealing with something fairly regular. The triad (1st, 3rd and 5th) is diminished, but then everything continues as it would if this were a natural minor scale. The 6th and 7th degrees are both flat – and so it's only really that flat 5th that causes problems.

Because of its similarity to the almost unusable Locrian mode, this scale is sometimes referred to as a Locrian ♮2 (or 'nat 2nd'), but I think it's easier to come to terms with if you think of it as a natural minor with a flat 5th. Whatever you decide (after all, this sort of thing is hardly likely to come up in conversation with anyone outside a music academy), it sounds like this:

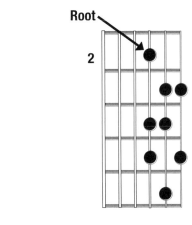

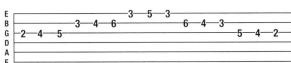

I don't know what it is – although, if you've got the time, I'll gladly come up with some sort of theory – but it always seems to be the 7th mode that turns out to be the weird one. Remember the Locrian? This one's worse...

7th melodic minor mode = B C D E♭ F G A B

                           1 2 3 4 5 6 7 1

Almost nothing works here, practically. The case for the prosecution opens with the fact that we've got a flat 2nd, flat 3rd, flat 4th (I'll explain in a minute), flat 5th, flat 6th *and* a flat 7th.

If you were thinking, 'Hang on; surely a flat 4th is the same as a major 3rd?' you'd be absolutely right, and if I was handing out gold stars, you'd be wearing one right now. This is just an example of a musical naming convention that causes migraines amongst the noviciate. The answer is that the 'flat 4th' can't be thought of as being a 3rd, because it's the 4th note in the scale, and so it's got to be looked at as being some kind of 4th. Simple explanation, eh?

Anyway, back to this dissonant monster we have before us. Before I wax poetic about it, take a listen.

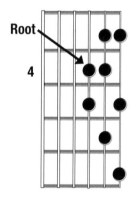

The fingering for this scale is a bit of a horror, but it keeps in line with the rest of the melodic minor examples

Bit of a stinker, eh? Especially if you hear it with a steady bass note under it. But, strangely enough – paradoxically, even – it's the very weirdness inherent in this scale that makes it useable. Of course, we're talking 'useable in its proper context', and that context happens to be jazz and fusion once again. You're not likely to hear it on a Kylie Minogue record.

If we are going to dream up some sort of name for the beast, we'd end up with something along the lines of a 7♭9♭5♯9♯5. In other words, none of the component parts are necessarily what you might like to call 'stable'. (In jazz fusion, it's the type of scale you'd use if you wanted only the tiniest relevance to the ongoing key.) Obviously, '7♭9♭5♯9♯5' is not exactly a shorthand term, and so this

scale has earned itself several identities, including Superlocrian. (Anything 'super' in music doesn't necessarily mean 'smashing' or 'great'; it just means 'more than'. In this case, the scale has more altered notes in it than the Locrian, and so Superlocrian it is.)

Others names include the 'altered scale' (because just about everything in it has been 'altered' if you look at it from the point of view of a simple dominant 7th scale) or 'diminished whole-tone' scale – this one, I think, describes it vaguest of all.

And there you have it: the melodic minor dissected into modes. Listen to them, but don't dismiss them. Remember some of the things you didn't like when you were young – spinach, beer, garlic, pepperoni, wine and so on? It's a bit like that with music: when you're first confronted with quite large amounts of dissonance, as there is present in these modes, you tend to disregard it, but later on, when you've developed more of a discerning ear and feel confident enough to be a little bit more adventurous, you might feel like using some of them, even thinking that they don't sound as bad as you thought they did!

If I seem to be somewhat dismissive of these particular scales, don't think I don't use them in my music, because I do. I play more jazz than is probably healthy, but, as we'll see later on, I don't necessarily think along the lines of what scale I'm using at the time. I just throw the occasional hint of garlic into an otherwise sweet-sounding melody, and that 'garlic' would definitely involve flattening or sharpening 5ths and 9ths quite liberally. It all adds up to differing points of view.

The Harmonic Minor Modes

Forgive me if you're experiencing *déjà vu* here. If you're thinking that surely breaking the harmonic minor down into separate modes is going to result in more dissonant-sounding bewilderment, then you're partly right, but it's unwise to bar yourself from experiencing this sort of thing. The secret to becoming a fully rounded musician is, at least in part, the ability to keep an open mind. You'll be glad I told you that one day.

And so, here's a quick review of the harmonic minor scale:

C harmonic minor = C D E♭ F G A♭ B C
                 1 2 3 4 5 6 7 1

You might require an aural prompt, too, so the chord box and tab are shown at the top of the next page. You might have categorised this particular representative of the minor scale family as being 'the one with the Eastern twist at the

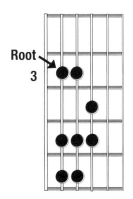

Root
3

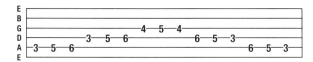

```
E
B
G           4  5  4
D       3  5  6          6  5  3
A  3  5  6                        6  5  3
E
```

end'. Whatever, it's certainly distinctive with that sudden leap of a tone and a half between its 6th and 7th:

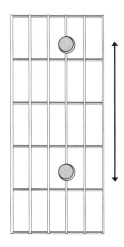

The gap between the 6th and 7th in the harmonic minor scale looks like this – a tone and a half, or a minor third, if you prefer. This sort of interval is more common in pentatonic scales

And that turn at the top end of the scale:

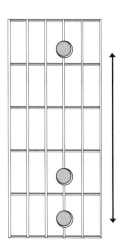

The configuration of notes at the top of the harmonic minor scale gives it a distinct Eastern flavour

So, before we start splitting things up into different modes, you know these anomalies are going to have an effect wherever they crop up in the general batting order.

Our second mode, then, looks like this:

2nd mode of the harmonic minor =

D	E♭	F	G	A♭	B	C	D
1	2	3	4	5	6	7	1

Basically, this is a minor 7♭5 scale with a twist, because it contains a flat 9th, too. Compared to what we were looking at a moment ago with the melodic minor modes, this scale seems almost totally normal.

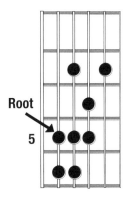

Root

5

```
E
B                    3
G            4  5        5  4
D        3  5  6              6  5  3
A  5  6                             6  5
E
```

Once again, there's no official naming convention with these modes, but you might find this particular one compared to the Locrian mode from the major family. The difference is that this version contains a natural 6th, as opposed to the Locrian's flat 6th degree.

Moving on, we reach the mode based on the third note of the harmonic minor, and it looks like this:

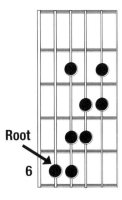

Root

6

```
E
B              3  4  3
G          4  5        5  4
D      3  5  6              6  5  3
A  6                              6
E
```

3rd mode of the harmonic minor =

E♭ F G A♭ B C D E♭
1 2 3 4 5 6 7 1

Remarkably, this turns out to be quite a respectable citizen in the world of scales, too. The only dissonance it contains is a sharp 5th – otherwise, it's a major scale from top to toe. The sharp 5th has the effect of adding a certain 'piquancy' to the proceedings, none the less.

Now for the fourth mode of the harmonic minor:

4th mode of the harmonic minor =

F G A♭ B C D E♭ F
1 2 3 4 5 6 7 1

Another surprisingly normal variation, in that this scale turns out to be a minor 7 with a sharp 4th (or 11th):

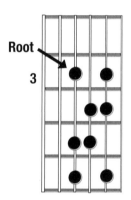

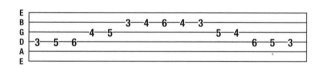

Some teachers compare this scale to the Dorian mode – the Dorian being basically a minor 7th – whereas this mode has a sharp 4th, but what it's called isn't as important as its sound. Later, I'll submit my Sensible Way To Look At Scale Construction, but for now we've reached the fifth mode of the harmonic minor scale:

5th mode of the harmonic minor =

G A♭ B C D E♭ F G
1 2 3 4 5 6 7 1

This is another scale with a bit of a Spanish accent; it's that minor-second (semitone) gap between notes 1 and 2. Loosely speaking, any scale that contains this particular interval in this position is going to take on a slightly gypsy or Spanish air. It's one of the characteristics of that sort of music style. Handy to know, if you're in the position I

was when the bandleader wanted me to play 'something Spanish-sounding'.

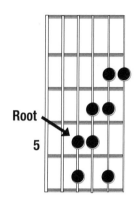

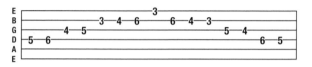

Naturally, this scale has been compared to the Spanish-sounding Phrygian mode and is sometimes referred to as the 'Phrygian major'.

Time to bring out the sixth mode.

6th mode of the harmonic minor =

A♭ B C D E♭ F G A♭
1 2 3 4 5 6 7 1

This time, we have another major scale with a sharp 4th, very similar to the major scale's Lydian mode, only here that 'gap' of a tone and a half that sits within the harmonic minor crops up between the root and second note, meaning that the scale's second degree checks out as a sharp 2nd (or 9th).

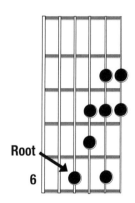

The beginning of this scale compares to the minor pentatonic in that both begin with a minor 3rd, and it's already got that sharp 4th (corresponding to a flat 5th), so you might even try using this mode in a blues, just to see what happens.

The seventh and final harmonic minor mode ends our look at modes. Now, remember when I said that it always seems to be the seventh mode that's the crazy one? Well, guess what...

7th mode of the harmonic minor =

B	C	D	E♭	F	G	A♭	B
1	2	3	4	5	6	7	1

By now, you'd have thought that we would be pretty used to 'weird' wouldn't you? But this mode, like its cousins in the melodic minor and major modes, could out-weird at Olympic level.

The roll-call reveals there to be a flat 2nd, flat 3rd, flat 4th, flat 5th, flat 6th – and that's not all. The 'big gap' in the harmonic minor has worked up to being between the 7th and root, meaning that, technically speaking (and we're well inside music naming conventions now), it's a double-flat 7th (that's ♭♭7th).

I expect you want to hear it...

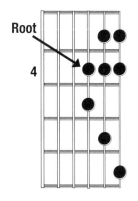

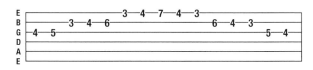

Once again, apologies for the somewhat torturous fingering, but we have to keep things in line with some sort of symmetry

Strangely enough, the harmonic minor 7th mode is quite similar in construction to the diminished scale. But we're not quite there yet.

The Sensible Way To Look At Scale Construction

I realise that our whistle-stop tour around the scale safari park has probably left you with your head in a bit of a spin, but I believe that there is a way in which we can categorise everything we've looked at so far and make it work somehow. It might sound unbelievable, but you'll soon see why this is true.

Back in the section on chords, I said that the most important distinction to learn in music is that of whether a chord is major or minor, because this is the most fundamental musical difference we have to deal with. I said that it was as important as gender differences are in people, and definitely an area in which early homework should be done.

Then we went on to establish three essential families – major, minor and dominant – and categorised everything that we found accordingly. Well, I want to establish the same kind of system here. It's far easier to think of the independent scales as belonging to one of the three families – even the modal scales would be used as independent, stand-alone entities, and so they can escape their scale 'parentage' and become fully mature offspring in their own right.

For example, we now know that the Dorian mode 'belongs' to the major scale, but as long as we continue to think of it in that way, it will never be able to leave home and assume an identity strictly of its own – that of being a minor scale. Can you see the distinction?

This way, all major scales become variations of *the* major scale, and the same can be said for all minors and dominants, too.

This kind of thinking and methodology helps you on the fretboard, as well: if you establish the basic shapes in your mind and fingers, everything can be seen as a simple variation.

As an example, let's do a little bit of a comparison. Here's the major scale:

C	D	E	F	G	A	B	C
1	2	3	4	5	6	7	1

And here's the dominant scale:

C	D	E	F	G	A	B♭	C
1	2	3	4	5	6	7	1

Only one note's different, and yet the two scales are so different in context. If we take a look at the same thing on the fretboard, this simple adjustment is arguably even more pronounced:

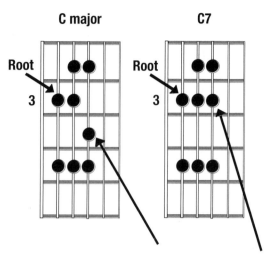

C major   C7

Keep your eye on the ball, boys and girls: the only difference between these two scales is the position of a single note. This sort of thinking aids memorisation enormously...

Once again, it's just a question of using a different finger for the dominant 7th.

We can extend this idea further to include all of the scales we've looked at so far. Classify each of them as belonging to one of the three families, understand how their individual formulae differ from the norm and then apply them.

This is by far the quickest way to begin organising scales on your fretboard, as you cease thinking that there are 25 scales to learn in 12 keys and start considering them as variations on something you already know very well (at least, you should know the basic major and minor scales very well if you've been following the book closely so far!).

As a further example, let's take a dominant 7th scale – or the Mixolydian, if you want to call it that.

C	D	E	F	G	A	B♭	C
1	2	3	4	5	6	7	1

Now then, say we wanted a scale to include any number of variations, or 'altered tones'. If we wanted to turn that particular scale into a 7♭5, it's really no big deal...

C	D	E	F	G♭	A	B♭	C
1	2	3	4	5	6	7	1

In other words, what's happened is this:

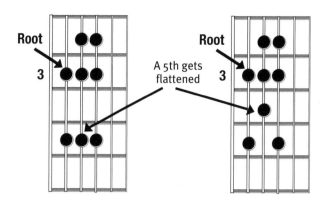

A 5th gets flattened

Again, it's a case of moving only one finger out of place from a scale that we know well.

Now, if we want to add a flat 9th to the scale, we get this formula:

C	D♭	E	F	G♭	A	B♭	C
1	2	3	4	5	6	7	1

And this fretboard diagram:

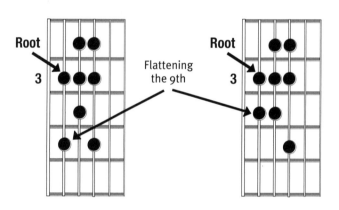

Flattening the 9th

It's important to keep this shape in your mind, though:

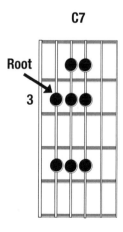

C7

The basic template from which all 'altered' 7th scale sounds come. Keep this shape in mind and learn how to alter various voices within

Always remember where things come from and how they've changed. This simple act of visualisation will save you a lot of time and trouble later on and, given time, will develop into a valuable instinct that will allow your fingers to make all the necessary changes without your brain being engaged at all!

We can apply the same logic to the major scale. If we want a major scale with a sharpened 4th, we think like this:

Major Scale:

C	D	E	F	G	A	B	C
1	2	3	4	5	6	7	1

Major ♯4th

C	D	E	F♯	G	A	B	C
1	2	3	4	5	6	7	1

And on the fretboard:

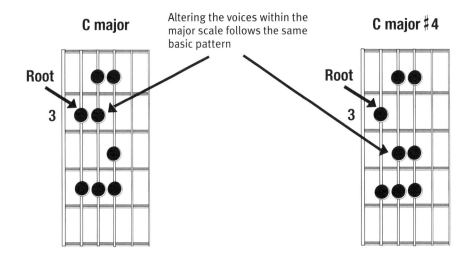

Altering the voices within the major scale follows the same basic pattern

A question arises with the minor scale: which one do you use as your basic template? I believe it's more useful to think of the natural minor scale as being the 'parent' scale, because it's used more than the harmonic or melodic variations in rock music. This would mean that you'd think of a C minor scale as being this:

C	D	E♭	F	G	A♭	B♭	C
1	2	3	4	5	6	7	1

The difference between this basic model and the other two involves the 6th and 7th degrees of the scale – in C's case, this would be the A♭ and B♭. To produce the melodic minor,

take both of them away, leaving the E♭ as the sole minor-scale representative:

C	D	E♭	F	G	A	B	C
1	2	3	4	5	6	7	1

To get the harmonic minor, all you have to do is lose the B♭:

C	D	E♭	F	G	A♭	B	C
1	2	3	4	5	6	7	1

On the fretboard, the equation looks like this:

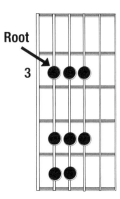

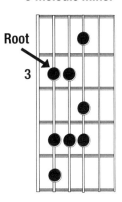

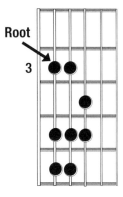

An example of how the natural minor can provide a template from which the melodic and harmonic variations can be drawn. This kind of thinking really can save you hours of toil learning 'shapes' for the various scales...

You can see that the differences are not so radical – and far easier to think about than to consider three separate scales, each with a different fingering to learn. Think of the parent scale and learn to vary it.

We'll be expanding on this kind of thinking when we apply the CAGED idea. Eventually, virtually everything you do you will look at as being a variation on a basic form, whether it's a chord or a scale. I believe this is healthy because, after all, every melody is basically a variation on a scale and every harmony is a variation on a chord.

Music Maths

I'm no mathematician, and that's probably why I can't get into the music maths that some teaching systems recommend. I can't think, 'If you want the C Lydian scale, think of it as being the G major scale played from the 4th'. To me, the Lydian mode is a couple of words that describe a sound and my head knows how to find that sound without doing any sums beforehand.

It's the same sort of doctrine that teaches us that 'when we're playing over X, play the major scale a Xth above the root'. I just can't think like that! Of course, a certain amount of formulaic thinking is necessary to begin with: 'A 7♯9th chord is a member of the dominant family and is basically a 7th with the second note of the scale pushed up a fret.' All right, that's okay in the initial stages, but it's by no means a system for life.

My method has always been to expose people to sounds they can use, starting with the most common (major scales, major and minor chords, and so on) and then, when their ears have absorbed the basic information, leading them on to learn how to vary what they already know.

Musicians – great musicians – don't apply a set of mathematic formulae to what they're doing. That's done afterwards by guys like me! We need some sort of Highway Code to enable students to start their individual journeys in the right direction. But, at the end of the day, it's your ears that will lead you on to making a set of decisions based on what they know, where they've been before and what they've heard. Your fingers, if properly schooled and developed by playing chords and scales, will develop physically to the extent that they can act instantly on what you hear in your head and playing music will become as natural to you as speaking.

To sum up, what I'm selling you here is meant to minimise having to think while you're playing. Every great player I've ever spoken to tells me that, if you're 'thinking' while you play, you're going down the wrong route, the same way as we have considered previously that it would be impossible to drive a car if you had to think about every mechanical operation you perform. You rely on instinct which has been founded on experience and is tempered continually by further experience.

Scale Classification

So, if we were going to classify every scale we've looked at so far as being members of one or other of the three family groups, we'd have something like this:

Major Scales

Basic major (or Ionian mode):

C D E F G A B C

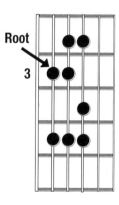

Lydian mode:

C D E F♯ G A B C

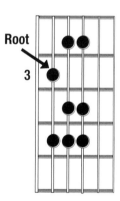

Lydian augmented scale:

C D E F♯ G♯ A B C

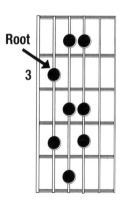

Harmonic minor – mode 3:

    C D E F G♯ A B C

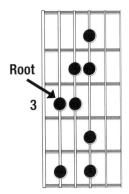

Minor Scales

Natural minor (or Aeolian mode):

    C D E♭ F G A♭ B♭ C

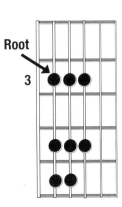

Harmonic minor – mode 6:

    C D♯ E F♯ G A B C

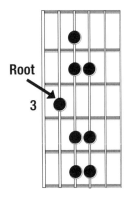

Harmonic minor:

    C D E♭ F G A♭ B C

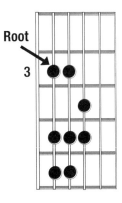

Major pentatonic:

    C D E G A C

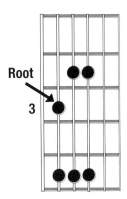

Harmonic minor – mode 2:

    C D♭ E♭ F G♭ A B♭ C

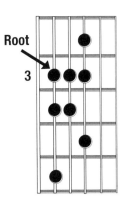

Dorian mode:

C D E♭ F G A B♭ C

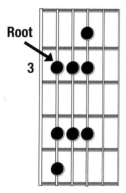

Melodic minor:

C D E♭ F G A B C

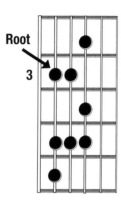

Phrygian mode:

C D♭ E♭ F G A♭ B♭ C

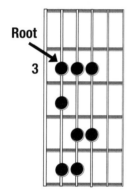

Melodic minor – mode 2:

C D♭ E♭ F G A B♭ C

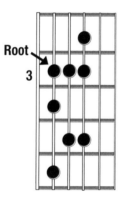

Locrian mode:

C D♭ E♭ F G♭ A♭ B♭ C

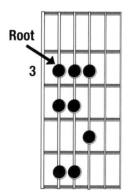

Could be seen as being an altered dominant scale, too.

Melodic minor – mode 6:

C D E♭ F G♭ A♭ B♭ C

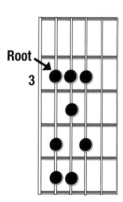

Minor pentatonic:

C E♭ F G B♭ C

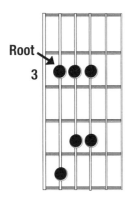

Melodic minor – mode 5:

C D E F G A♭ B♭ C

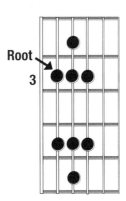

Dominant Scales

Basic dominant (or Mixolydian mode):

C D E F G A B♭ C

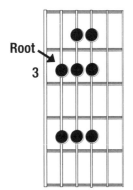

Melodic minor – mode 7:

C D♭ E♭ F♭ G♭ A♭ B♭ C

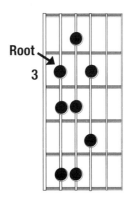

I include this scale in the dominant series rather than the minor because it's usually looked at as being an 'altered dominant' scale.

Melodic minor – mode 4:

C D E F♯ G A B♭ C

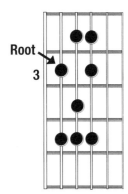

Harmonic minor – mode 5:

C D♭ E F G A♭ B♭ C

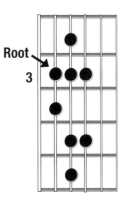

Harmonic minor – mode 7:

C D♭ E♭ F♭ G♭ A♭ B♭♭ C

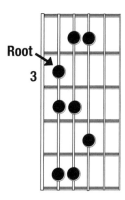

Like mode 5, this scale is more or less considered to be an altered dominant with seriously diminished tendencies!

Blues scale:

C D E♭/E F G♭/G A B♭ C

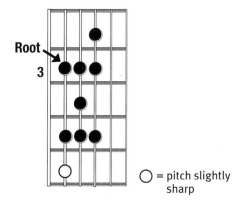

◯ = pitch slightly sharp

Looney Tunes

So far, we have looked at scales that are in common use – and we've covered a vast musical area. You've probably experienced more different scale types than you could possibly apply in a whole career in music. So, from here on in, we're into a highly eclectic area; everything now becomes extremely specific and very limited in terms of its suitability for general use.

Of course, at this stage we also have to confront the question 'How many scales are there?' once again. The answer is really the number of variations there are on the chromatic scale if it's split into five-, six-, seven- or eight-note segments.

Obviously (and I've told you already that I'm no mathematician) there are thousands, if we look at each

from the point of view of looking at each in every key. I know for a fact that there are books available as thick as the New York phone book that list most of the feasible permutations, but, at the end of the day, is it really worth the effort? Apart from the academic profundity of the situation, what's the point of finding a combination of notes that hasn't seen the light of day in 100 years or more, giving it a name, learning it and filing it away when the chances of it actually being useful to you are practically nil? It may seem that we're taking a headlong dive into the eclectic here, but I thought it might be worthwhile looking at just a few of the more common variations that are in use at least somewhere in the world. Just look at it as an exercise to bring a sort of international flavour to the proceedings and an introduction to some of music's more rarefied forms.

Diminished And Augmented Scales

You might be wondering exactly why I'm including diminished and augmented scales under the banners 'rare' and 'exotic'. The reason for this lies in the simple fact that both of these particular scales have been invented, if you like: they represent symmetrical divisions of the chromatic scale which happen to coincide with the chords of the same name.

I know of very, very few melodies that have ever sprung from either (that said, there's a tune by the jazz guitarist Jim Hall called 'Careful' which is based on the diminished scale).

As melodic tools, the usefulness of diminished scales probably gets pegged somewhere around the lower end, along with some of the weirder modal moments we've just been looking at.

Of course, when you get down to it, the real reason why they aren't in common use is that neither diminished nor augmented melodies sound particularly good!

Let's start with a look at the diminished scale. Here, the chromatic scale has been divided up into consecutive tone/semitone units, like this:

C diminished: C D E♭ F G♭ A♭ A B C
               1 2 3   4   5   6   7 8 1

The reason why we refer to this scale as being 'diminished' is because all the important chord tones have been dropped a semitone. The third, fifth and seventh have all come down one scalar notch and become 'diminished' by one degree. Obviously, a scale which has suffered alteration to this degree has a somewhat special set of rules and a certain name to match.

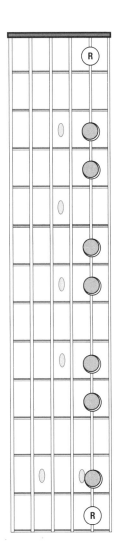

C diminished

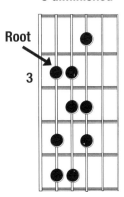

The C diminished scale laid out along a single string to give you a better idea of the symmetry involved. In my experience, though, if it looks perfectly neat and symmetrical on the fretboard, it usually sounds absolutely dreadful!

The next synthetic scale out of the pen is the whole-tone scale – often wrongly accused of being the 'augmented scale'.

C whole tone: C D E F♯ G♯ A♯ C
                1 2 3 4   5   6   1

Everything starts off as if it was an ordinary major scale – until we reach the fourth degree, where all intervals become sharpened, or 'augmented'. Again, here's the scale shown along a single string to make its symmetry stand out better:

See what's happening? What's more, have you counted how many notes there have to be in this scale to make the sum work properly? The diminished scale boasts eight notes instead of the more humble seven – but this still makes the chords derived from it work:

C dim: C E♭ G♭
       1 3   5

C dim7: C E♭ G♭ A
        1 3   5   7

As I've said, the whole scale bends the rules a little bit, and if you take a listen, you'll hear just how limited it is in terms of use:

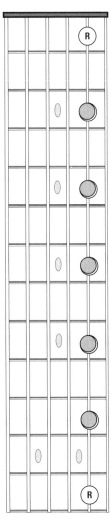

The C whole tone scale along a single string. Again, it looks organised – but musically speaking, it's not too pretty...

Once again, you'll notice that the whole-tone scale isn't the more conventional seven notes long; it clocks in at only six. This means that the augmented triad can quite happily thrive within its ranks:

C augmented: C   E   G♯
            1   3   5

But, despite the fact that there's a B♭ present in the scale (under the pseudonym of A♯), it logs in as being the 6th and not the 7th. So, for once, the old chord-formula routine doesn't quite pan out:

Caug7: C   E   G♯   A♯(B♭)
        1   3   5   6

I think that this makes a stronger case for considering the augmented 7th chord as being a member of the dominant family – a 7♯5th.

The whole-tone scale sounds like a major scale that goes horribly wrong after the 3rd:

C whole tone

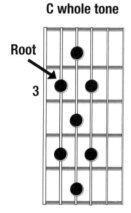

Even when viewed this way, the whole-tone scale takes on quite a pleasing shape!

It's distinctive, but not particularly melodic. However, it used to be a favourite improvisational tool of Frank Zappa, who would include it, seemingly at random, in his guitar solos. But hardly anyone else has employed it quite as much – in rock circles, anyway.

So now to the augmented scale, which differs a little from the whole tone, though it's still a six-note scale:

C augmented: C D♯ E G G♯ B C
            1   2   3 4   5 6 1

To my eyes, this looks very unlike a scale in the truest sense of the word; its formula is symmetrical, being a minor 3rd followed by a semitone all the way through.

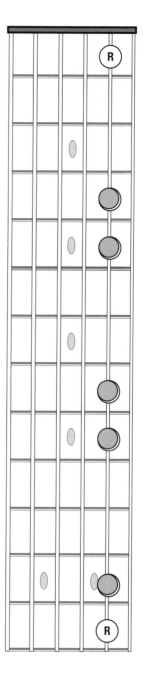

The augmented scale, with its alternating minor 3rd/semitone configuration, tumbles up the fretboard

The augmented triad lies inside it, but not the augmented 7th chord (that makes even more of a case for thinking of the 7♯5th as being a strictly dominant anomaly).

C aug: C E G♯
      1   3   5

But don't you think we're stretching things here a little? This is really where actual music and scales take entirely separate and divergent routes, in my opinion. These scales have got more to do with maths than melody. Take a listen:

C augmented

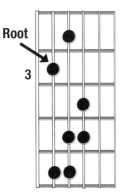

The large gaps in this scale make practically any fingering you can come up with feel awkward

More Pentatonic Variations

Students often laugh when I tell them that there is actually a Scottish pentatonic scale, but there is...

C Scottish pentatonic: C   D   F   G   A   C
                1   2   3   4   5   1

Having looked at the modes from the major and minor scales, you'd be forgiven for thinking that the pentatonic scales don't follow suit – but, of course, they do. So this is, if you like, one of the 'modes' of the major pentatonic scale (in fact, as we've seen, the minor pentatonic is, strictly speaking, a mode of the major pentatonic, too).

C 'Scottish' pentatonic

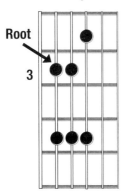

As is typical of all scales, this isn't an 'instant fix' by any means, but if you play through the scale and listen hard, you can definitely hear how a lot of Scottish folk music might be derived from these five notes. Interestingly, the Scottish pentatonic contains the same notes as one of the so-called 'Japanese' pentatonic variations. Incredibly, you can hear the sounds of both these diverse cultures present in this single scale (as long as you keep an open mind, of course).

Taking the Japanese pentatonic theme a frame or two further forward – and this time we do manage to leave the rolling hills of the Scottish Highlands far behind – there are basically three more to consider: the Iwato, Hirajoshi and Kumoi.

C Iwato: C   D♭   F   G♭   B♭   C
         1   2   3   4   5   1

C 'Iwato' pentatonic

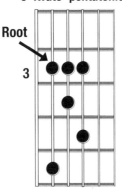

C Hirajoshi: C   D   E♭   G   A♭   C
             1   2   3   4   5   1

C 'Hirajoshi' pentatonic

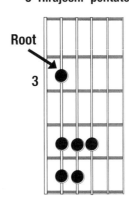

C Kumoi: C   D   E♭   G   A   C
          1   2   3   4   5   1

C 'Kumoi' pentatonic

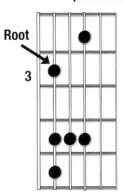

Another pentatonic scale with Japanese overtones is a variation on the minor pentatonic. Remember that these scales only really come into their own when heard against a backing track...

C 'Japan' pentatonic: C D♭ F G B♭ C
                       1   2   3 4   5   1

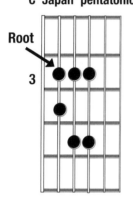

C 'Japan' pentatonic

Root

3

In fact, remember when I said that there is a pentatonic scale in just about every folk culture in the world? Well, let's look at what happens when you change another of the notes from the minor pentatonic. This scale has notable Indian qualities:

C 'Indian' pentatonic: C E F G B♭ C
                        1 2 3 4   5   1

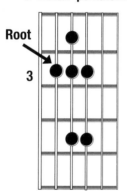

C 'Indian' pentatonic

Root

3

Other pentatonic scales prevail, of course, but even this brief example shows how just five notes can provide a free pass into another musical culture.

More Seven-Note Variations

One particular scale enjoyed a brief day in the sun back in the '80s when Joe Satriani based one of his pieces on the Enigmatic scale. (On the album *Not Of This Earth*; the track was called 'The Enigmatic'.)

C Enigmatic: C D♭ E F♯ G♯ A♯ B C
              1   2   3 4   5   6   7 1

And it sounds like this:

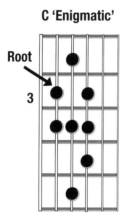

C 'Enigmatic'

Root

3

Joe's piece is a great example of how a musical exercise – that is, melodic variations on a given scale – can assume a life of its own.

To be honest, we could spend a lot longer looking at all of the rare examples of scales that have seen action at varying times during music's long life, but I think that the selection presented here serves as a thorough introduction to the idea of where the theory of scales begins and just where it can lead. The mathematical potential is practically limitless, but, as I've said before, exactly how many of the variations would be musically useful is doubtful.

Exploration, it has to be said, comes after a thorough appraisal of the basics. Pursuing your interest in scales any further before assimilating the information held with the fundamental major and minor scales would be worth little in the long run. Once you have established the sound of these most important scales in your head, only then will all the rest be seen in their true light – that is, as variations on a given norm.

Before moving on to look at the CAGED idea in much greater detail in the next chapter, it's a good plan to review the basic layout of chords – shown on the next page – as they proceed up the neck. Get yourself familiar with the pattern and pay particular attention to your barre technique, as any problems you encounter in this department should be ironed out as soon as possible.

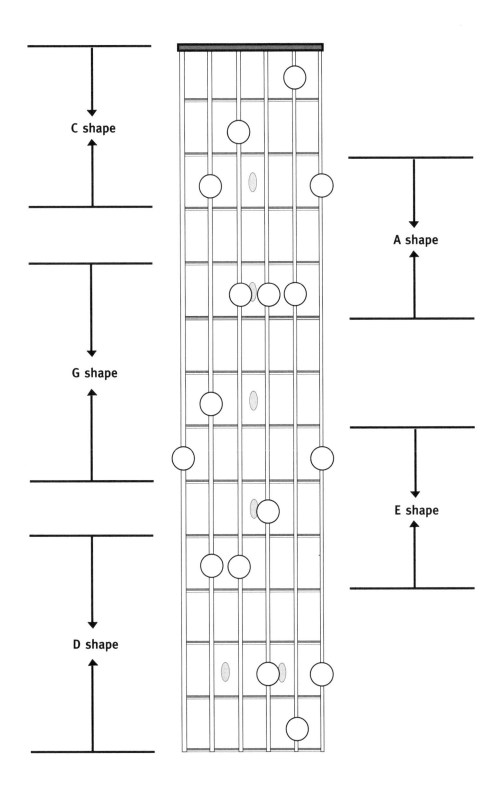

C shape

A shape

G shape

E shape

D shape

10 THE CAGED IDEA

We looked at the basics of the CAGED idea, where the five chord shapes C, A, G, E and D follow each other up the guitar neck in order in any given key (see page 18). Now we're going to tie scale and chord shapes together to form one single, cohesive system.

This is really more a lesson in visualisation. The great jazz guitarist Tal Farlow once told me that you've got to use your eyes and learn to 'see' the scale shapes spread over the neck. It's a question of orienteering – and you're not going to need it all your playing life. As I've said before, this kind of thing becomes instinctive: you stop thinking in terms of shapes and positions; you hear melodies in your head and your fingers know where to find them. Or, at least, that's the idea...

The C Shape

Let's look once again at the C major chord. Here's the fretboard diagram:

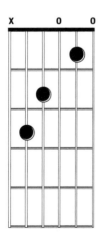

Root-position chord shape

This is a shape that you're no doubt very familiar with, and when we promote it to a barre chord, it still retains its major characteristics, as shown on the next page:

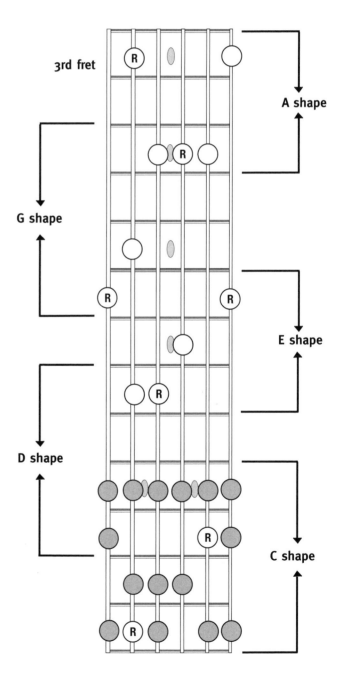

7th fret

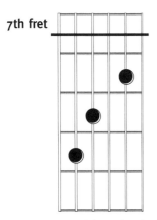

Barre-position chord shape

All well and good. Let's see what happens if we fill in the scale over the chord shape:

'C-shape' scale

With any luck, you'll be pretty familiar with both the scale shape and barre chord here. But you might not have considered them superimposed in quite this way before.

Taking things a step further, let's name all the intervals of the scale.

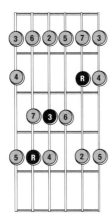

'C-shape' scale showing the positions of chord tones

Now, what you have before you is a lot of incredibly useful information. Remember that this shape can be found in every key – not just C – and so this will give you access to all the various chords and scales we've looked at in this book, in every key. Mindblowing, isn't it?

For instance, if you want to find an F6 chord shape, match the root of the scale with a C and think about the formula:

$$\text{Major 6th} = 1 \quad 3 \quad 5 \quad 6$$

And here's the chord shape:

F maj 6

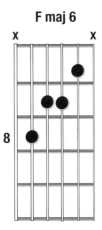

It's vital that you don't see the major chord and the major 6th as two separate entities, but rather as variations. The major becomes the 6th by the simple addition of a single note. In much the same way, we can turn this shape into a dominant chord by another single addition. First, locate the flat 7th – there's one on the third string – and put it into the regular major chord shape:

F7

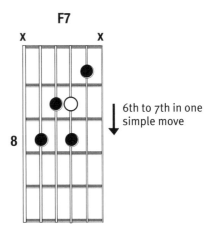

6th to 7th in one simple move

You know that a dominant chord starts life as a major triad – once again, it's a variation on what you already know.

Now, if you want to add a 9th, an 11th or whatever, it's all right in front of you.

This kind of thinking works with scales, too. If you want a major scale with a sharp 4th (aka the Lydian mode), think of the shape for the 'C-shape' major scale, locate the 4th and sharpen it by a single fret:

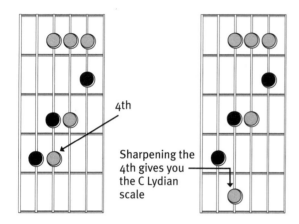

4th

Sharpening the 4th gives you the C Lydian scale

Turning the major scale into a dominant is an easy task to perform, too. Just as we did with the chord a moment ago, locate the flat 7th and insert it into the scale instead of the major 7th:

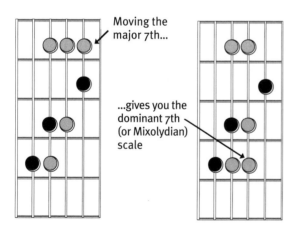

Moving the major 7th...

...gives you the dominant 7th (or Mixolydian) scale

Now, the idea of playing a 7♭5 scale doesn't need to be scary – and you don't have to remember a separate scale shape, because the flat-5th part of the equation is really just a variation on a known quantity.

Again, it may sound like we're trying to apply dry scientific principles to a subject that should remain rooted in something more arty, but we're not. This doesn't remain in the 'conscious' zone for long, but as a system for organising scales and chords on the neck in the formative stages, it reigns supreme.

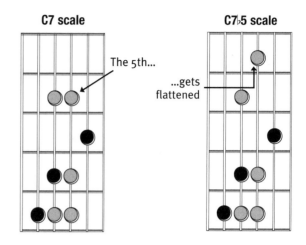

C7 scale

The 5th...

C7♭5 scale

...gets flattened

The CAGED idea makes the concept of chord 'editing' much easier to contemplate as well. Given that this is the barre shape for a C-type chord...

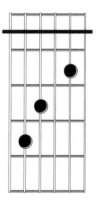

...we know that any smaller part of that shape will in some way still represent the chord (after all, it contains only the root, 3rd and 5th), so it's easy to see that this would also be a major chord:

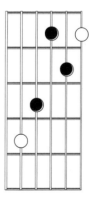

This is a perfectly workable major chord 'fragment' as it contains a root, 3rd and 5th. The most important thing to be able to 'see' is that it belongs to the larger 'C shape' (the white circles are there to help with visualisation)

That last shape is a fragment of a bigger chord, but it's still a viable shape in its own right. This is what I mean by the process of visualisation – the ability to classify chord shapes as belonging to one of the five master shapes. Here are some chord shapes that belong to the C-shape area:

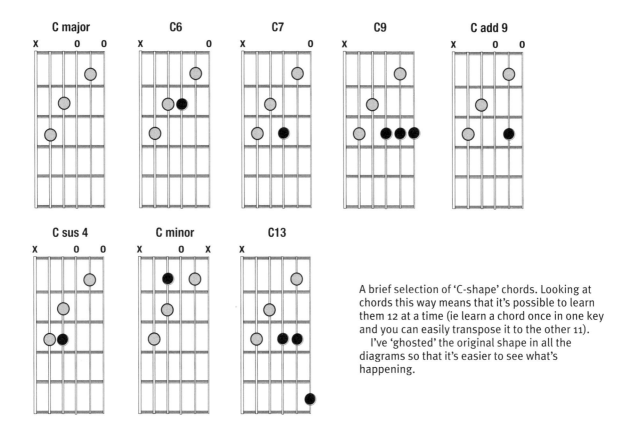

A brief selection of 'C-shape' chords. Looking at chords this way means that it's possible to learn them 12 at a time (ie learn a chord once in one key and you can easily transpose it to the other 11).

I've 'ghosted' the original shape in all the diagrams so that it's easier to see what's happening.

The Maths

In order to try to sell you the CAGED idea still further, let's look at a few facts and figures before moving on to the other four shapes in the series.

If you learned one complete set of 'C-shape' derivatives – say, 10 chords – then, by applying the CAGED idea, you can transpose everything you've learned into all 12 other keys. This means your original 10 becomes 120 with no further learning necessary.

It's the same for scales. By learning what a 7♭5 scale looks like in this single position – and by seeing it as a variation on the major scale shape – you now know it in 12 keys.

This is the kind of fretboard logic applied by the pros. It may seem like another ungainly system that has to be learned, but eventually you'll be applying it without thinking. The bottom line is that the ability to 'evolve' fingerings for scales and chords from a single template opens up the entire fretboard, which means that an unbelievable amount of music now lies within your grasp. It makes learning easier, too. If, for instance, you come across a chord shape you like the sound of in a book or a piece of music, by relating it to one of the five CAGED master chords, you won't forget it.

I've been showing pupils this system for years and even the ones who thought they'd never grasp it have surprised themselves in the end.

Let's consider another of the CAGED series chords – the A shape. Once again, think about the basic 'root-position' chord first and foremost:

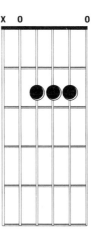

Root-position chord shape

Then we have the barre-chord version, which gets it away from the nut:

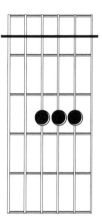

Barre-position chord shape

Then look at the chord and scale superimposed, taking note of where the chord tones are positioned in the scale (it's just the chord shape, so nothing too much to remember). Don't forget, these are your 'target notes' when improvising, so their positions are important.

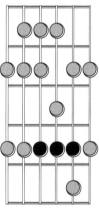

'A-shape' scale

Finally, have a look at where all the scale tones appear by name:

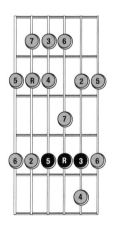

'A-shape' scale showing the positions of chord tones

How the CAGED idea looks on the fretboard from the point of view of the 'A-shape' chord. Notice that the corresponding scale tones have been added around the basic shape to give an idea of how harmony and melody cross over at this point

C shape

A shape

G shape

E shape

D shape

This means that, once again, if we wanted to form a major 6th shape, just checking the chart above reveals that a handy 6th lies on the top E string, and so a suitable chord shape would look like this:

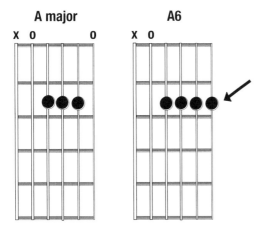

Adding the 6th on the top string turns the basic A shape into an A6

Remember that it's not only important to be able to see how the sixth superimposes itself over the basic chord shape, it's also important to be able to predict what sort of change it will have on the sound of the chord itself. The more work you do in this area now, the more it will be of benefit to you later on.

Forming a major 7th would involve inserting the 7th, like this:

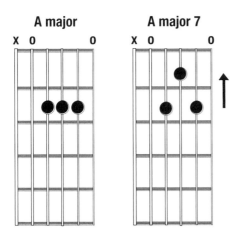

Shift the root back one fret and you've got an instant major 7th chord

Whereas the dominant 7th is close behind:

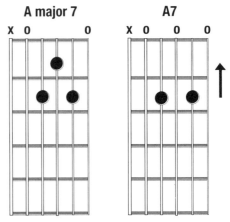

The dominant 7 is just behind the major 7

If this still sounds a bit like some kind of advanced biology to you, maybe there's just cause in turning back to the section on chord formulae and reviewing it in light of what you have learned since. Every new concept starts life in the brain as something unfathomable, but patience and persistence pay dividends in the end, so don't get put off!

Turning the major chord shape into a minor would go something like this:

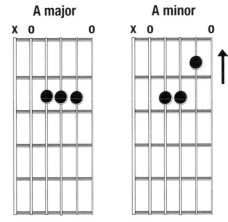

Switch the major 3rd to the minor 3rd and there's an instant minor chord

And a minor 7th would look like this:

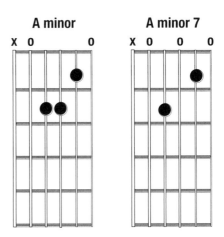

The 'A-shape' barre chord is definitely one of the two most commonly used barre shapes on the guitar (the other being the very familiar 'E shape'), and so having a number of alternative chord voicings under your fingers here will give you a distinct advantage on the bandstand.

In many instances, a guitarist either stands or falls on his ability to generate new or fresh-sounding ideas in everyday situations. So, having a broad palette of chordal hues is a definite advantage!

Here are a few other shapes derived from the 'A' area:

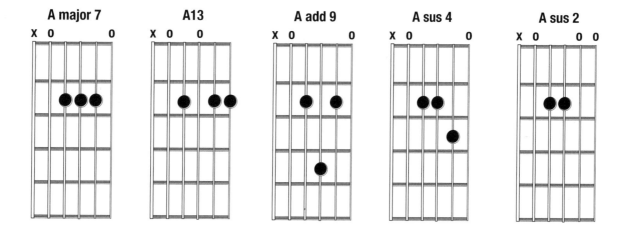

When it comes to looking at the A-shape scale, once again variations are no big deal. Turning the major shape to the dom 7th shape involves a change of only one note:

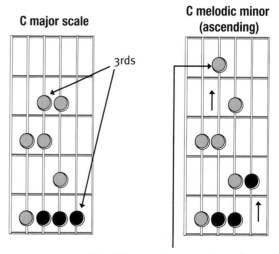

The difference between the major and melodic minor is the position of the 3rd; in the major scale the 3rd is major, in the minor, it's minor. Simple, eh?

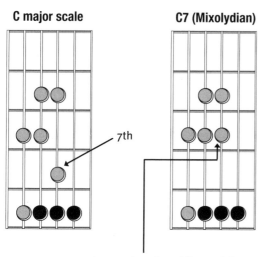

Locate the 7th and flatten it by one fret to transform the major scale into the Mixolydian mode

Compare the sound of the two scales above and try to 'see' the change you're making as well as hear it. This way, your fingers and ears will be effectively singing from the same songbook and you'll find 'perfect harmony' easier to achieve!

Changing the major to the melodic minor involves only one note's difference, too:

I must emphasise that this kind of thinking – call it 'research' if you want to – is all well and good in the practice room, but that's effectively where it should be left if you go out on a gig. By all means experiment on stage, but don't do anything that's too risky, like trying out a totally new harmonic concept while the rest of the band is playing a Carpenters song. The art of successful science calls upon a certain amount of predictability in the outcome of any equation...

When you become experienced at visualising the different scales as being variations on one another, cooking up a Lydian mode from the major won't pose too much of a problem.

C major scale   **C Lydian**

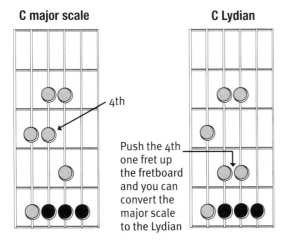

4th

Push the 4th one fret up the fretboard and you can convert the major scale to the Lydian

Neither would converting a Mixolydian to a 7♭5...

C7 (Mixolydian)   **C7♭5**

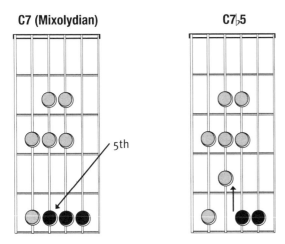

5th

Remember that your soloing mainstays are going to be the straightforward major, minor, dominant 7th and pentatonic scales for the most part and so you won't find yourself having to delve into the more exotic variations too often. But it's knowing that you can – knowing that they're available to you without the need to rummage through a scale book.

What's more, using the maths once again, when you've worked either a scale or chord shape out in a single key, it's instantly transposable to 11 others. I know that sounds a mammoth task, but it becomes easier and easier as you go along – trust me!

The G Shape

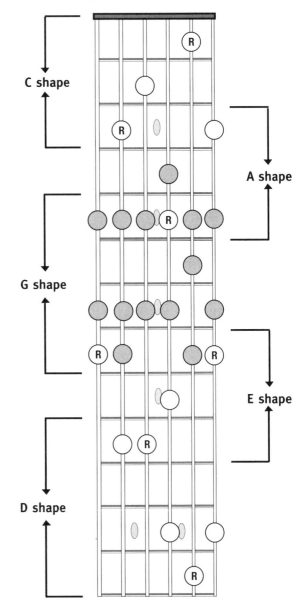

C shape

A shape

G shape

E shape

D shape

This is how the guitar fretboard looks from the point of view of the 'G-shape' chord and scale position

The procedure here is exactly as before. First, the root position chord:

0 0 0

Root-position chord shape

Then the barre version:

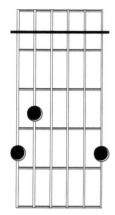

Barre-position chord shape

If you recall, the G-shape barre is something that has more theoretical value than practical. It's a tough shape to get your fingers around until practice has rendered them more flexible. Just don't hurt yourself on my account!

Now, the chord shape and scale superimposed:

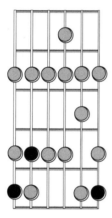

'G-shape' scale

Finally, the names of the scale tones with the chord still showing inside:

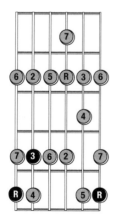

'G-shape' scale showing the positions of chord tones

From this information, it is possible to see that, whereas the barre G is practically unmanageable, chord fragments are readily available that can all be called upon to represent major shapes.

Fragments are incredibly useful if you're playing in a situation where 'big' six-string chords would be inappropriate and can add significantly to your chord vocabulary. All it takes is the ability to see smaller shapes within the parent chord.

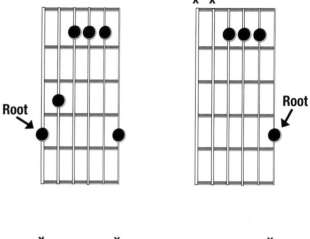

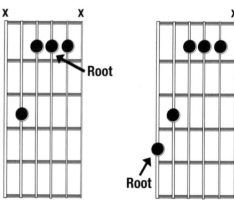

G major – unmanageable as a barre, but the basic shape breaks down to some very useable shapes

Another way of thinking about the different variations is to think about chords you know down at the nut and, despite the fact they might not be possible as barre chords, apply them to this template shape anyway. Listed over the page are examples of a memorable and useful version of a dominant 7th chord, a workman-like major 7th and a surprisingly straightforward 6th:

G7

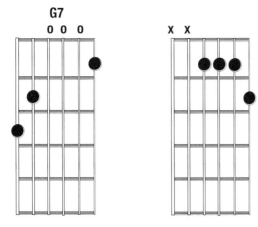

G major 7

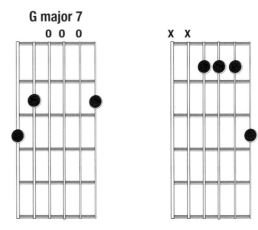

This 'nut-position' 7th chord becomes a very useful, moveable 'G-shape' chord

Similarly, this major 7th chord shape turns into a very useful 'G-shape' chord

G6

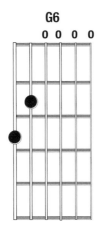

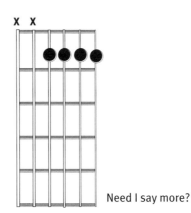

Need I say more?

The scale that is derived from the G shape is very common and equally useful – and we'll see in a minute how the pentatonic shapes tally with the CAGED idea, too.

Inserting the dominant 7th into the scale makes for a good Mixolydian scale, and that brings about a whole series of dominant chords:

A melodic minor shape falls within reach with the absolute minimum effort:

G shape major scale   **Mixolydian scale**

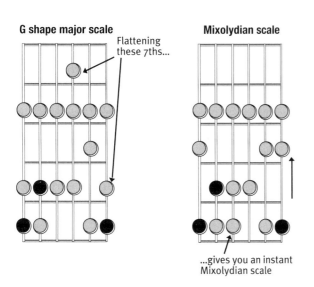

Flattening these 7ths...

...gives you an instant Mixolydian scale

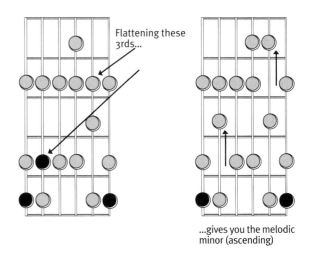

Flattening these 3rds...

...gives you the melodic minor (ascending)

And the Lydian mode is just a step away:

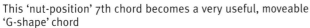

162

'G Shape' Scale

4ths

To convert the 'G shape' into the Lydian mode, first locate the 4ths...

Lydian mode

...and then sharpen them

The E Shape

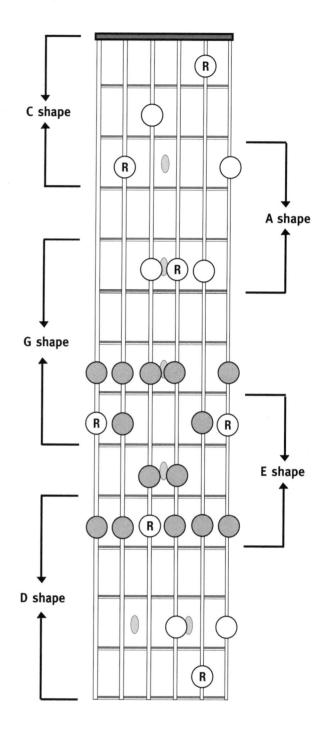

C shape

A shape

G shape

E shape

D shape

The 'E shape' takes its place on the fretboard amidst the other CAGED idea chord forms

The G-shape area of the fretboard is often overlooked, having the reputation of being too hard to handle as a barre chord. This means that it represents a rich area in which to experiment with both chord voicings and scale shapes.

The lesson here is not to dismiss something out of hand immediately just because it appears tricky at first. Just try to remember how difficult you found it to play things like barre chords – or even playing your first 'F' chord down at the nut – compared to how easy you find them now.

Arguably, this chord shape is one of the easiest to remember, as we tend to come across it as a barre version fairly early on when learning chords. But, just for the sake of following the same sort of logic as before, we'll start with the nut position:

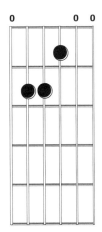

Root-position chord shape

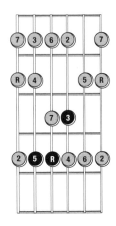

'E-shape' scale showing the
positions of chord tones

Then the barre version:

Barre-position chord shape

Along with the 'A shape', this barre chord has to be the
most well known.

Now look at the scale and chord shapes superimposed:

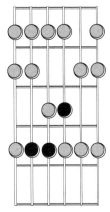

'E-shape' scale

And finally, the identities of the individual constituent parts:

The diagram above contains some absolutely vital musical
information that can really add scope to your musicianship.
All it takes is patient practice in becoming familiar with the
shape's inner workings.

When it comes to considering exactly what type of useful
information we can derive from the 'E shape', we find
immediately that the basic chord shape yields some
instantly recognisable variations. Here we have dom7th,
minor and minor 7th shapes – three chord shapes that
represent most players' first foray into barre chords:

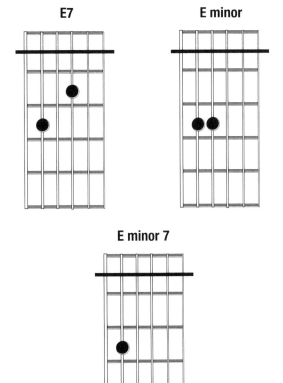

Theme and variation in action – some members of the 'E-shape'
chord family

You should now be able to see how this system of theme and variation works and how all chords bear some family resemblance to one of the basic five master templates. It should be beginning to become clear how the scale can be varied quite simply to reveal its relatives, too.

The D Shape

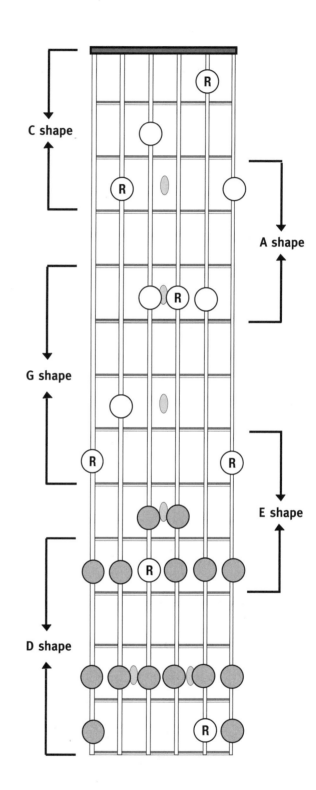

E shape scale

Mixolydian mode

Flatten the 7ths for the Mixolydian mode

Lydian mode

Dorian mode

Sharpen the 4ths for the Lydian

Flatten the 3rds and 7ths for the Dorian

This is the last shape in the series and cannot really be considered as being a barre shape as such. It incorporates the top four strings and seeps into the top of the C shape. But it's a heck of a handy 'moveable' chord shape to have in your chordal arsenal, yielding some distinctive chord voicings...

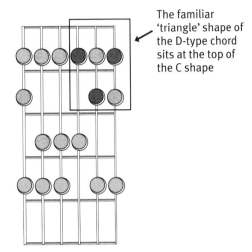

The familiar 'triangle' shape of the D-type chord sits at the top of the C shape

Once again, look at the root position...

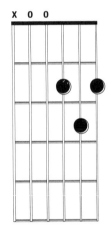

X 0 0

Root-position chord shape

...and then the moveable shape:

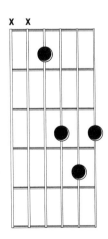

X X

Moveable chord shape

Then, by superimposing chord and scale shapes...

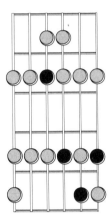

'D-shape' scale

And naming the individual scale tones...

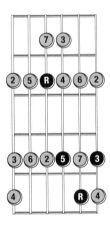

'D-shape' scale showing the positions of chord tones

...we build up a complete picture of the D shape and how it looks on the fretboard. Like the G shape, the D shape is often overlooked, yet some serious study will reveal just how useful it can be when committed to memory. The chord forms that it contains have their own unique sounds and are especially useful whenever you find yourself playing with a keyboard player.

Incidentally, this particular little chord shape is often ignored by many players in the rock guitar fraternity because its comparatively high voicing – ie residing on the top four strings – is thought to add up to a general lack of power. This is definitely not so, however! Try a few shapes through a reasonable amount of gain on an amp and you've got yourself quite an imposing little monster.

Initially, it reveals the major and dominant 7th chords:

Major 7
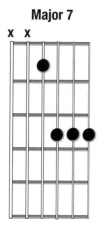

Dominant 7
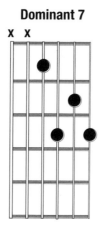

And major 6th and sus2 chords:

6th
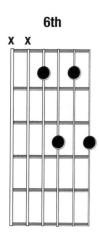

Sus 2

All these chords are effective additions to your rapidly growing stockpile, mainly because chords formed on the top four strings tend to have a slightly different timbre or tonality than the fuller six-string variations.

Considering the scale formed around the D shape, we find that, once again, it's a fairly easy job to permutate all the variations needed. Here are a few examples:

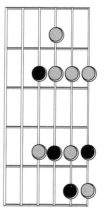

The basic D-shape major scale...

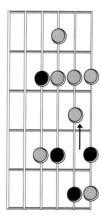

...becomes the Mixolydian mode...

If you cast your mind back to the section on chord inversions, it's worth noting that the version of the major seventh chord here is in the order root, fifth, major seventh and third. If you compare this to some of the other variations available and take a side-by-side listen, you'll be able to detect why there isn't a simple answer to the question 'What shape is a major-seventh chord?' If you exploit the slight differences in timbre via these different shapes, you'll be taking the fullest advantage of the new material you're learning.

This is the most common minor 7th shape from the D:

Minor 7
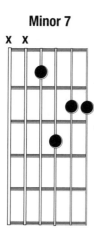

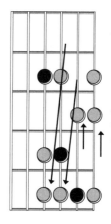

Even though converting the D shape major into the Aeolian mode represents a major construction job, it's possible to see how visualisation eases the path and offers up some essential landmarks that make learning scales easier

...or the Aeolian mode by flattening the 3rd, 6th and 7th

In order to simplify things a little, this represents the D-shape scale in abbreviated form. However, when you practise this particular version of the scale, be sure to take advantage of the whole scale. There are some useful intervals in there!

F – The Unofficial Sixth Shape?

If you remember when we were looking at fretboard orienteering (page 24), we saw that chord roots were placed on the sixth, fifth and fourth strings, with the G and E shapes on the sixth string, the C and A shapes on the fifth and the D and an unofficial member of the CAGED team on the fourth.

This particular squad member turns out to be the top of the E shape and so isn't really counted as a shape in its own right. However, I've come across many of guitar students who cannot link the F and E shapes together – and so I thought I'd spend a few moments clearing this matter up.

This really is a case in point, in terms of fretboard visualisation. First of all, here's the E shape as a barre chord once again:

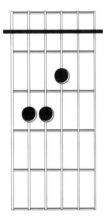

And here's the F:

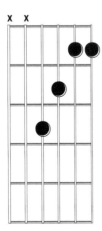

It should be immediately obvious that the two are, in fact, one.

Don't worry if all this sleight of hand still feels a little bewildering at the moment, because, given time, it won't. It took me ages before I was capable of taking those all-important steps back and seeing this sort of thing with any real clarity! If you need another visual clue to the dual identity of the 'F shape', here's one:

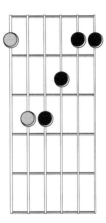

And so all the chord shapes derived from the F shape actually belong to the E.

The F is useful to us from the point of view that it falls into 'root position' note order from the word go.

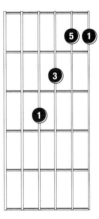

The 'F' shape conveniently falls into 'root, 3rd, 5th, root' order – a perfect textbook example of a root-position chord!

It is, therefore, very good for experimenting with different voicings.

Pentatonic CAGED

So, does the CAGED idea work for pentatonic scales as well? You bet it does. In fact, I think it's time to draw a comparison between the major scales and the pentatonic scales.

When you think about it, a pentatonic scale is really only an abbreviated form of a major or minor scale.

C natural minor: C D E♭ F G A♭ B♭ C
                 1 2   3 4 5   6   7 1

C minor pentatonic: C E♭ F G B♭ C
                    1   2 3 4   5 1

C major: C D E F G A B C
         1 2 3 4 5 6 7 1

C major pentatonic: C D E G A C
                    1 2 3 4 5 1

So it's a dead cert that the CAGED idea is going to work here. Here's a chart that compares the major CAGED shapes to their relevant major pentatonic versions:

'G Shape' Scale

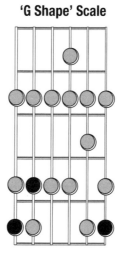

'G Shape' Major Pentatonic Scale

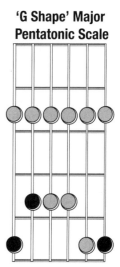

'C Shape' Scale

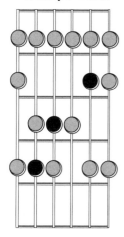

'C Shape' Major Pentatonic Scale

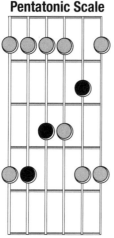

'E Shape' Scale

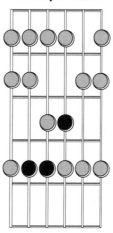

'E Shape' Major Pentatonic Scale

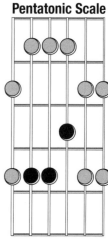

'A Shape' Scale

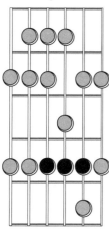

'A Shape' Major Pentatonic Scale

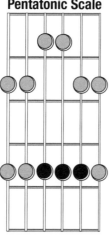

'D Shape' Scale

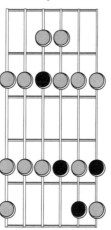

'D Shape' Major Pentatonic Scale

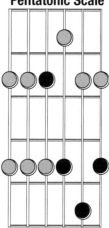

Does it work for minor pentatonics, too? Well, yes, it does. All you have to do is convert the five major shapes to their minor counterparts and all is revealed:

'C Minor Shape' Scale

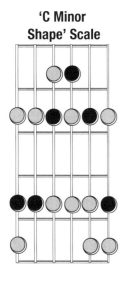

'C Shape' Minor Pentatonic Scale

'A Minor Shape' Scale

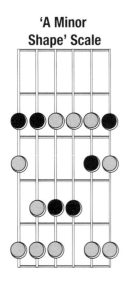

'A Shape' Minor Pentatonic Scale

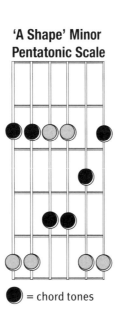

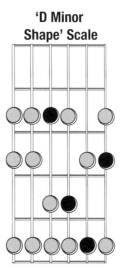 = chord tones

'G Minor Shape' Scale

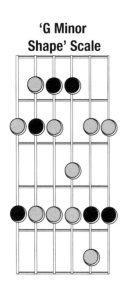

'G Shape' Minor Pentatonic Scale

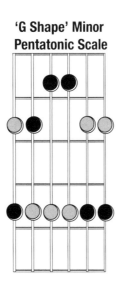

'E Minor Shape' Scale

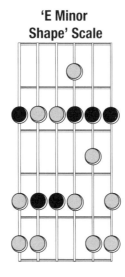

'E Shape' Minor Pentatonic Scale

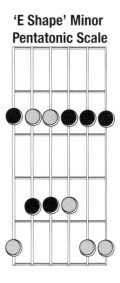

'D Minor Shape' Scale

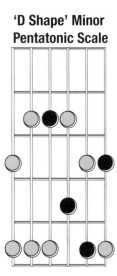

'D Shape' Minor Pentatonic Scale

Bit of a mind-boggler, isn't it? But it proves that the system still holds even when converted to minor shapes.

So hopefully you can see how the CAGED idea works in pulling together everything we've looked at. Scale and chord shapes collide to form an indelible system for learning and remembering reams of vital musical data that, once formulated, can form the backbone of everything you play on the instrument.

Practice Routine

Having read back that last paragraph, which even I think sounds like something from an early episode of *Star Trek*, you're probably thinking that it's a long job, taking all this information in and working with it to the extent that it becomes useable in the 'drop-of-a-hat' sense. But it's no good being aware of a system like CAGED without structuring it somehow into a daily practice routine so that you get a chance to explore its depths.

I've already suggested that you pick a different key every day and work out the major, minor and pentatonic scales from the appropriate roots, using the neck chart you wrote out (you did do one, didn't you?) as a guide.

To take the CAGED idea a few steps forward, you need to set yourself some tasks that involve cross-referencing all the information in this book. In order to give some starting points, try these:

1 Find a major, minor, dominant 7th and minor 7th chord shape in each of the CAGED locations.

    This gives you access to five different versions of the most useful guitar chords in every key – you'll be learning 60 chords at a time!

2 Turn each of the CAGED major scales into dominant 7ths (Mixolydian mode) by flattening the 7th in each case

3 Pick a type of chord – anything you like – and try to find a version in each of the CAGED positions.

    For instance, you might decide to find add 9 chords in every position, or major 6ths, major 9ths, sus chords, whatever. By doing so, you'll find that gradually you'll be able to find things you need quicker and easier.

4 Do some reverse engineering. Look up some chord shapes in a chord book and try to work out which shape is the 'parent' in each case.

This is particularly useful if you stumble on a chord voicing you like and need a way to remember it. By relating it to its parent shape, you've got it locked into a system – and made it available in every key!

A lot of the discoveries that you're destined to make on the fretboard will come from your own detective work. There's a big difference between being told that something works and finding out that it does for yourself. As a teacher, I've always believed in guiding pupils towards areas where they can learn and make discoveries for themselves. Ideally, my job should only be teaching people how to learn. I was always delighted if a student came to me in a lesson and showed me something he had found by himself.

On one occasion, a pupil of mine played me an improvised solo using the Dorian mode – before I'd shown him what it actually was. I was really delighted, because it meant that his ears had told him that something sounded good, irrespective of what it was called.

So be prepared to play detective and try to track things down for yourself – ask 'why' not 'what' occasionally and you'll do fine!

CAGED Supplement

As some additional information to ponder over, here's a chart showing all of the CAGED major scale shapes converted into dominant 7th (or Mixolydian mode) scales with all the intervals in place.

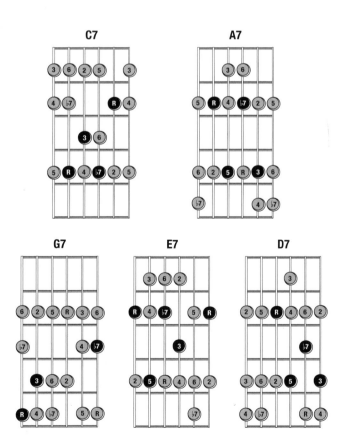

11 IMPROVISATION

I'll say straight away that I believe that improvisation is almost impossible to teach. But, having said that...

The first paradox we encounter, of course, it that improvisation is obviously not impossible to learn, and so what's missing? All of the world's greatest improvising musicians have evidently learnt their craft from somewhere – and so what gives?

We can all improvise to certain extent and do so every day of our lives. When you pop out to the newsagent's and decide on a circular route home via the park merely because it's a nice day, you're applying very similar criteria to those involved in improvisation.

Similarly, when someone asks you if you had a nice holiday and you spend a couple of minutes going over the highlights for them – that's improvisation, too. What's more, if three different people asked you exactly the same question on three separate occasions, your reply would be similar – in that it's based on the·same information – but it's extremely unlikely that it would be word for word.

Improvisation isn't making something out of nothing, neither is it 'playing exactly what you like' in the same way that, when you went out for a paper a moment ago, you weren't walking on thin air in pitch blackness; there were certain things that you took for granted – pathways, for a start – and merely worked out your improvisatory route in accordance with them. Again, you didn't walk straight across your neighbour's garden, stomping over his prize azaleas as you did so; in other words, you didn't do exactly what you liked but stuck to the accepted highways and byways.

If, when asked about your holiday, you'd replied with a set of entirely random and unconnected words without any punctuation or pauses for breath, then your answer would have been unintelligible. Instead, you would have improvised your reply operating within the accepted guidelines of grammar and an agreed mutual vocabulary. The way you described things would have been your own, but certain predictable staples would still have had to apply. You wouldn't have had to follow the rules of English to the letter, either; as long as your reply was colloquially acceptable, everything would have been fine. So sometimes it's okay to break the rules, but, as the old maxim says, ya gotta know 'em first...

So our first definition of improvisation might be 'spontaneous composition within a set of given guidelines', and this is possibly where we can find our first way in – by being made aware of what guidelines exist. But there are other factors worth considering before we find out exactly what those guidelines are.

Expression

Anyone who has observed a child's reaction to music will probably agree that it tends to be spontaneous and completely uninhibited. In my experience, no child ever has to be told to dance; the desire to let music move them physically in a quite literal sense is already there from birth. Children are great improvisers, too, in that they are natural explorers, willing to experience everything the world serves them up without too much timidity, self-cautiousness or inhibition.

Give a child an instrument like a drum or tambourine and they'll explore every sound they can make – usually continuously and for long periods of time! But the point is that they don't care; their reaction to music is instinctive and natural and, given the chance to take part or contribute, they'll do so unflinchingly.

But something happens between infancy and adulthood – or even adolescence. We become naturally inhibited and so often the desire to perform is counteracted by self-consciousness and the fear that we'll make a fool of ourselves somehow.

I read with interest a survey that said that the single thing that strikes terror into most people isn't the idea of earthquakes, volcanic eruptions or even being mugged on the street; it's public speaking. For many, the thought of standing up in public and making a speech holds nothing but unparalleled horror. This transfers into playing in public, too. I'm lucky in that I've never felt the stage to be a scary place and tend to get excited rather than nervous before gigs, but I've known people – brilliant performers whose talent, you would think, would immunise them entirely from nerves – to be violently ill before going on-stage.

So, even though it's generally acknowledged that we should practise in preparation for a performance, we can be totally unprepared for the extra pressure put upon us by the public platform's foreign environment.

Heaven knows what it is that steers us away from uninhibited childhood towards self-conscious adulthood. Maybe it's being told not to 'show off' by parents and schoolteachers. But, whatever the cause, it all adds up to a set of barriers we erect between ourselves and musical performance – and this is before we've introduced the basic ideas about becoming familiar enough with music on the one hand and our instruments on the other.

So, for many, the channels between our adult selves and our desire to improvise have been well and truly blocked, and this is why so much has been written about improvisation that borders on the metaphysical.

Where Does It Come From?

Often, at workshops and seminars, I ask the students present where they think that a musical note begins. In the fingers? On the fretboard? When the string is set in motion by the pick? I tell them that the answer is easier to fathom if you look at things from the point of view of a singer. The singing note doesn't begin with the vibration of the vocal cords or the shape of the mouth, and it certainly has nothing to do with what sort of microphone they're using – so where does it all come from?

Obviously, a singer has to send some sort of instructions to the vocal cords to ensure that the correct pitch is programmed in, and so we could say that a musical note begins with some sort of overall conception of that note somewhere within.

We've all heard talk about having a musical 'soul', or we've heard it said that a player really 'plays from the heart', and this isn't as far from the truth as it may seem. One thing is for certain: improvisation doesn't begin with the intellect...

I've often heard great improvisers asked what they think about while they're improvising and the answer is generally the same. Most will say 'nothing' and risk being condemned as being extremely unhelpful as a result. But it's true – and I think I can prove it to you.

Let's take another familiar analogy – that of driving a car. If someone said to you, 'What do you think about when you're driving?' you'd most likely have to stop and think about it because you're not really 'thinking' about anything.

You might be listening to the radio, carrying on a conversation with your passenger, telling the kids to stop fighting in the back, trying to work out how you're going to explain to your boss why you're 30 minutes late for a meeting – anything. One thing is for certain, though: you're not sitting there thinking about maintaining the correct pressure on the accelerator, calculating the exact distance between you and the car in front, trying to remember which pedal operates the clutch, whether you should be in third or fourth gear, considering what the rev counter is telling you... What you *are* doing is relying on a set of finely honed instincts that you've developed through the experience of driving. If a child ran out in front of you, you wouldn't stop to think, 'Now, which one's the brake?' You wouldn't have time, because you would have reacted purely on instinct and, hopefully, instantaneously.

So when a musician tells you he doesn't actually think about what he's playing, this is what he means. Thinking about it would mean that the process would grind to a halt.

To prove this point further – and I believe it to be a point that is vitally important to understand before the process of improvisation can be fully appreciated – I was once in a recording studio with a very well known guitarist and brilliant improviser. He had to record something very technically specific and he just couldn't get it right. It was incredibly simple to play, but every time he tried, he found himself thinking about what he was doing and he floundered. And yet, when I played it first and he was able to hear it, things must have been channelled differently in his brain, because he played it immediately. I think it was because he was able to hear it in his head, and this caused him to stop trying to intellectualise it.

Another parallel can be drawn here if we return to the idea of telling someone about your holiday. If I asked you, 'What are you thinking about while you're replying?' you'd probably have great trouble giving me an answer. In general we don't 'think' and speak at the same time in a way that everything you utter has been through some sort of intellectual process first. You definitely don't stand there worrying about whether you've conjugated your verbs correctly or ended a sentence with a pronoun. If you did so, you'd be forever faltering, hesitant and not at all pleasant to listen to.

So maybe you can see how thinking is certainly not one of the things that goes on when you're playing.

We're our own worst enemies in many other respects, too. No matter how much we've managed to lose our childlike unselfconsciousness, we still find ourselves saying, 'I can't do this' or 'I'll never be able to play this' and setting the stage for unavoidable failure.

If ever I found one of my pupils saying that he or she

thought that they'd never be either technically or musically capable enough to play a particular piece, I had to apply all the psychological knowhow that I possess (which isn't much) to get them to realise that the biggest thing preventing them from achieving what they wanted was themselves.

Head Versus Heart

I believe that when people approach improvisation they subconsciously choose between two routes: head or heart. It's possible to learn to improvise from a set of rules which, after plenty of practice, will allow you to play the correct notes over any given backing. However, this way can obscure your natural musical instincts. You want the notes you play to be more than merely correct; you want them to be inspired and heartfelt. Managing to play a successful guitar solo is very different to getting the right answer to a mathematical equation.

The other way is to obey the directions of the heart and literally play what you hear inside your head.

Music And Technique

The whole basis of improvisation comes from two different quarters: you need the ability to create melody lines spontaneously over any given harmonic backdrop and you need the technique necessary to execute those ideas. So, given that a pocket definition of improvisation would be 'the art of playing the ideas that form inside your head', a handy question at this stage of the game might be, 'Can you play the music that's already there?' By this, I mean any tune you know well enough to sing in the shower, hum idly while you do something around the house, nursery rhymes, and so on. Can you play the melodies you already know?

Do this experiment: pick a tune you know really well – and it can be absolutely anything; a nursery rhyme, folk song, the National Anthem, anything. The only rule here is that it must be something you can hum all the way through. Now, find the tune on your guitar. If you can't, then there is still some work to do in the region of ear training. If you can sing it, you should be able to play it, even if the process is a painfully slow one.

If this is still beyond you as a musician, it means that there is a part of your musicality that remains underdeveloped and needs work – *not* that you can't do it or you just don't have 'the gift'.

In a way, the discovery of this shortcoming should be welcome, because it means that you now know where to direct your energies when you practise.

If improvisation truly is playing the ideas that form in your head, then trying to play the ideas that are already there is a good place to kick-start the process.

Putting It All Together

So, what's the best way to start looking at chords and scales together? I believe the first place to start is to look at the natural hierarchy that the notes of the scale fall into when sounded against a chord.

It's a mistake, for instance, to think that improvisation – or spontaneous composition – is merely a matter of playing a given scale over a related chord. It's not. Disregarding for a moment the more spiritual side of improvisation, where all thoughts of a theoretical nature are put aside in favour of taste and experience combining together to select 'all the right notes in all the right places', the notes of any scale are by no means equal.

Let's take as an example a situation where the prevailing chord is C major and the chosen scale relative (I use that word in the familial sense of the word!) is, once again, C major.

```
Cmaj chord:  C   E   G   C
             1   3   5   1

C maj scale: C   D   E   F   G   A   B   C
             1   2   3   4   5   6   7   1
```

In any scale, the strongest notes are the chord tones, or the notes that exist within the chord. So, in C's case, these would be C, E and G; but even here things are not equal. Each of these three notes exerts a unique amount of gravitational pull on a melody.

Without a doubt, the strongest tone is the root. It's the most stable note you can choose to play over the chord and will sound like 'home' every time. The root note (or 'key centre' – whatever you want to call it) has the strongest influence and is usually present in a subliminal way throughout a piece. As an exercise, try humming a simple melody (again, a nursery rhyme will do just fine) over a single root note on the guitar and you'll hear how it 'fixes' to the root all the time, even if the chord has changed.

The other two notes within the chord are very strong, too, although not as strong as the root. If you were to play a solo and kept landing on the 3rd or 5th, everything would sound properly 'punctuated' from a musical point of view.

But this is not the case with the remaining notes of the scale. If you finished a phrase on the F, for instance, it would, at best, sound like a 'comma' rather than a 'full stop'. In other words, it's not a bad note, it's just not the best.

So, as improvising musicians who want to play effective, musically piquant solos, we have to acknowledge that the root note is supreme and the chord tones are its acolytes, first and foremost.

You may have heard the expression 'passing tones'; a general term for notes that aren't chord tones. They are employed to ease the path between chord tones – very loosely speaking – and are generally the scale tones that are currently not members of the harmonising chord. So, a chart showing the 'power' of the members of the C scale might look something like this.

C – root
D – scale tone
E – chord tone
F – scale tone
G – chord tone
A – scale tone
B – scale tone

Or, to put them in bunches:

C
E   chord tones
G

D
F   scale tones
A
B

A simple experiment will reveal that even the scale tones weren't exactly born equal, either. For this, we can revisit the sort of thing we were doing when we were adding scale tones to the triad and forming chords. Some work well and produce a sweet-sounding chord, while others clash slightly and introduce a little dissonance to the proceedings.

In fact, if you try the remaining scale tones over the triad in a melodic fashion – just sustaining the note over the chord – you're really doing exactly the same thing, except that this time it's melody combining with harmony to produce a combination of both.

You should find that the F stands out as being the least 'melody-friendly' note in the bunch, and A is arguably the nicest, in the same way that a major 6th chord (C, E, G and A) is fairly benign.

The B clashes against the root, meaning that you wouldn't want to hold it for too long over the chord, and the D sits uncomfortably between the C and E chord tones to produce a slightly unsettling effect.

Naturally, this is exactly what you're *not* thinking about when you happen to find yourself playing a solo in C over a C major chord. That would call for all sorts of cunning calculations that you simply haven't got time for when you're getting down to the business of making music. And,

of course, I shouldn't really refer to it as a business, either; it makes it sound too formal.

What you do rely upon, however, is your experience in picking the right notes to play, and that experience usually begins with trial and error – loads of it. Many students say to me that they know that they have to play a related scale over any given chord, but, no matter what they do, the end result always sounds like they are merely playing up and down the scale. I tell them that this is because their ears haven't yet got used to these 'anchor points' – the chord tones that will give their melodic expression a bit of shape and punctuation. At present, they're letting the scale play them and not the other way around.

So part of your practice routine should involve experimenting with the scales from a melodic point of view. There are some backing tracks on the CD to help you along the way – and many of them are in the key of C, so that you can use the material we've been looking at without the worry of transposing anything.

Make sure that you're aware where the chord tones lie within a given scale and practise first of all coming back to the root after every excursion. Visualise it like you're new in town and don't want to wander too far from 'home' before you're sure about your surroundings. You'll find that your sense of phrasing should improve immediately.

Next, experiment with the other chord tones, too. You'll find that ending a phrase with the 3rd of a chord sounds good, and the 5th is okay, too (although arguably not quite as good as the 3rd). I hope you'll find that there is a significant difference between landing on either, though. Just as we tried to draw up some sort of mental chart with the chords and scales that described the sound in very personal terms, that's what ought to be going on here. You'll soon begin to learn where the good, 'safe' notes are within a scale fingering and will find ways to incorporate them within your solos.

Once you've established how the chord tones sound over the chord, try using the other scale tones more liberally. Remember that you're never too far from a safe haven. In these terms, the scale would look like this:

C	D	E	F	G	A	B	C
root	scale	chord	scale	chord	scale	scale	root

So the D could easily be redirected onto a chord tone, as could the F. The A and B are only one step away from safety as well, albeit in opposite directions.

But – and I don't care how often I repeat this – don't try looking at this sort of thing scientifically to the extent that you're worrying about hitting a chord tone at strategic points during your solo and desperately searching the fretboard to find one. This sort of information has got to be absorbed by the ears, not by the eyes and hands. This intuitive playing starts to happen eventually, although it may seem a long way away at present. Just keep playing over the backing tracks and try to 'feel' your way through. Record yourself, if possible, to give you a clearer idea of how you're progressing. Keep the tapes and date-mark them so that you can track your development. Listen back every two months or so; you'll be surprised at how quickly your ear will start to lead you.

Improvising Over Chord Changes

Getting back to the idea of targeting chord tones while improvising, what happens when the chords change? The answer is that we merely extend the system we've already put in place. Most of the time the chord change will be diatonic, which essentially means 'in the same key'.

As an example, remember when we looked at the modes of the major scale? Each time we were using the notes of C major, but in a different order, so that the Ionian and Dorian modes, for example, were really just two different ways of looking at the same thing...

C Ionian: C   D   E   F   G   A   B   C
              1   2   3   4   5   6   7   1

D Dorian: D   E   F   G   A   B   C   D
              1   2   3   4   5   6   7   1

Exactly the same database, just a shift of emphasis from a C root to a D root. In practice, you'll find that all that happens is you end up playing from the same scale, but with different target areas. Let's say that you were playing over this section of music:

‖ C maj / / / | C maj / / / |
| F maj / / / | Fmaj / / / ‖

Two bars of C, followed by two bars of F. So, for the fist two bars, your 'target' chord tones would be these:

C maj: C   E   G

For the second two bars, they would be these:

F maj: F   A   C

When the change to F happens, you'll sense a shift, with C – previously the safest note in the scale that you could play – now becoming the 5th of the chord. It's still safe, but it's been relegated temporarily. However, a note that

definitely wasn't safe before – F – now becomes the safest note and A has been promoted from good-sounding scale tone to brilliant-sounding chord tone.

This all might sound like advanced maths, and the temptation on everyone's behalf, when confronted with this for the first time, is to think that they'll never get the hang of it and they would rather just try trial and error instead. All well and good, but this kind of thinking is permissible in the practice room.

If you make an exercise out of playing from one set of chord tones for two bars and a second set for the subsequent two bars, what's happening is that you're training your ears to respond intuitively to a chord change. It's hard work to begin with, but do you remember your first driving lesson? A bewildering series of movements, gear changes, mirror, signal, manoeuvre, emergency stop... These were all separate elements that had to be learned. Now, I expect, driving is entirely instinctive, and actually thinking about what you're doing impedes your progress! The minute you actually catch yourself thinking, 'Now, which one's the brake?' it's too late. And it's the same with guitar playing – there are many individual little lessons to learn, like the one we've been discussing, but eventually they all come together into a cohesive whole.

For the moment, then, you'll have to try to visualise something like this on the fretboard:

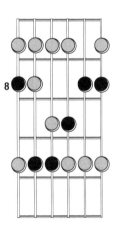 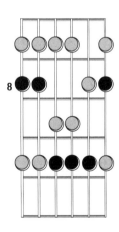

Chord shape for C major in an 'E-shape' C scale   Chord shape for F major in an 'E-shape' C scale

Here's another thing to consider, too. There's a big difference between a key change and a chord change, and we'd better settle this here and now.

In our example above, you're moving from C to F, but the key remains in C. In other words, when you play over the F chord, you're still using the notes of the C major scale; it's just that the 'points of gravity' have changed a little.

This means that, over the F, you'll be playing a B, a note that isn't really at home if played when the actual key is F. Look at this:

F Lydian mode: F G A B C D E F
                 1 2 3 4 5 6 7 1

F major scale: F G A B♭ C D E F
               1 2 3 4 5 6 7 1

In the F major scale, the 4th note is B♭; in the Lydian mode, it's B natural. So which one do we pick? In this context – that is, the key is C major – we're safe using the Lydian mode version of F. You might decide that the chord-tone/scale-tone hierarchy has to be re-evaluated a little, although, once again, this type of thing is horrendously subjective.

F Major Chord

Root: F (ultra safe)
Other chord tones: A C (very safe)
Scale tones: G D E (good)
'Visitor': B (questionable)

In practice, the only way to tell how useful the B is going to be to you personally is to experiment. I find it okay – the key of C has been established to the point where it nestles in there unnoticed. You might find that it doesn't quite make the grade.

If we now add another chord to the exercise, we should see more of a pattern of key-based scale use emerging:

‖ C maj / / / | C maj / / / | F maj / / / |
| Fmaj / / / | G7 / / / | G7 / / / | C maj ‖

Now we've got a G7 introduced into the chord arrangement. This is another diatonic chord, inasmuch as it uses only the notes of C major, and so it's perfectly at home and doesn't represent a key change or anything too drastic.

So now, we've got a new set of 'target notes' to play with...

C: C   E   G
F: F   A   C
G7: G   B   D   F

...and three modal variations of the C scale to take on board:

C Ionian: C D E F G A B C
           1 2 3 4 5 6 7 1

F Lydian: F G A B C D E F
           1 2 3 4 5 6 7 1

G Mixolydian: G A B C D E F G
               1 2 3 4 5 6 7 1

As an exercise, try playing along with the backing track that contains these three chords and try to target just the root note at the beginning of the bar, like this:

Count:

    ‖ C 2 3 4 | C 2 3 4 | F 2 3 4 |
    | F 2 3 4 | G 2 3 4 | G 2 3 4 | C ‖

At first, don't play anything else (pretend you're a bass player – easy life, right?). The change of root note is the most important thing for the ear to be introduced to, as it's the clearest possible indication that there has been a harmonic shift in the music.

Next, play only the chord tones, starting on the root, like this:

    ‖ C E G C | C E G C | F A C F |
    | F A C F | G B D F | G B D F | C ‖

Repeat this exercise as often as you get time to practise – and do it for a good couple of months. Remember, it's not a technical exercise, and so, after you've played it a couple of times, it's not going to feel difficult or in any way technically challenging. This is an aural exercise; it's for your ears and your developing sense of music. So, playing it over a couple of times every time you practise (spend only a couple of minutes on it) will do you the maximum amount of good.

The next stage is to begin to introduce other notes from the scale in with the chord tones, but always hitting the chord root at the beginning of the bar. What you should find beginning to happen is that, slowly but surely, you're beginning to phrase more musically, because your improvising will have more relevance to the harmony part.

By all means try the exercise in different keys (after reading the section on the CAGED idea, this should be fairly easy to bring about), because I know how boring hearing the same thing every day can be. I've recorded the backing track in three different keys to address this problem. Pick one at random and fire away – it will keep you fresh.

This kind of thinking extends to any piece you come across where the melody stays within a single key throughout. If you found a chord arrangement that changes through C maj, A min, D min, F maj, G7, and so on, apply the same logic every time: find the root notes and chord tones first and try your best to 'hear' them as often as you can before leaping off the deep end and trying to improvise blind (or, more accurately, deaf!).

▲ Tracks 30-2

I'll say yet again that this isn't the way improvising musicians actually think; this is merely a means of introducing your ears to some vital information while you learn. Eventually you'll be able to forget all about this and just play.

Melody

Another area that an awful lot of musicians forget about (especially guitarists, it seems) is melody. Remember that the original melody of the piece you're playing is a perfect fit for the harmony – the two were created out of each other, after all – so learning the melody to a piece is often a very safe passage into improvising over the chord changes. We saw earlier on how a scale can be derived from a melody, and so there is really no better way of finding your way through a tune than to learn the melody and try to vary it slightly as you play over the changes.

You can certainly get away with this on the bandstand, to a certain extent. Your audience will probably be quite familiar with the melody concerned, and so they will be grateful for the set of aural clues you're going to leave them throughout your solo.

Fingerings

Either try to work out the melody by ear or try to find a transcription, then sit down and make sure that you've got a logical, easy fingering available. Don't make things harder for yourself by working out awkward fingerings. The chances are that, if something seems much too difficult to be practical, there is very likely an easier alternative – it's up to you to find it.

When I studied classical guitar for a year (to brush up my reading and fingerstyle technique), my teacher – a very wise man by the name of Robert Jones – spent ages working on fingerings for the various pieces we were learning together. I very quickly saw that an awful lot of the essential flow of a piece depends on left-hand (and, in classical-guitar terms, right-hand) fingering.

We looked at preparation, which means setting the left hand up to play a section of music with the absolute minimum movement. I saw that, for instance, where it was easy to play an F on the first fret of the top E string, the music called for my left hand to be in the fifth position very soon after – so maybe we should use the F on the B string, 6th fret.

All these things were schooled into me, and it's helped me enormously since, because I know that, if I'm finding something difficult to play, there's always an alternative – and a lot of the time it's an easier alternative.

So never take the first fingering you discover as gospel; explore the fingerboard for alternatives until something

feels right. And remember that a lot of this is very subjective, too; something that you find easy to play, another player will find awkward. The important thing is that it feels right to you.

Whatever you do, don't allow yourself to become precious about playing a piece 'your way'. Keep an open mind and, if someone shows you an alternative that looks like it might work better, be grateful for what this lesson has taught you.

Arpeggios

The place where chords and scales meet is called the 'arpeggio'. The word itself just means 'harp-like', but to us it means playing the notes of a chord one at a time. So, for this...

C major

...you would play this:

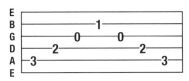

You can probably see how arpeggios tie in to what we've been talking about; by playing chords this way, you're feeding yourself chord tone information and highlighting the 'safe tones' for your ear.

Taking things a step further, I recommend that you try to sing chord tones, too. It might be painful at first, or even excruciatingly embarrassing, given the usual domestic set-up (partners can be soooo cruel!), but it will be another piece in the jigsaw, and you'll agree that anything that has even a 10 per cent chance of improving your musicianship another notch or two is worth trying.

If you want to turn this area into a practice routine, then you should follow these steps:

1 Play the chord

2 Play each note of the chord individually

3 Sing each note while playing it

4 Play the chord again

5 Try to sing the individual notes without accompaniment

To begin with, you're going to find step 5 particularly difficult. But here, as always, repetition is the key; the more you practise them, the easier things will become.

To begin with, start with basic major and minor chords like these:

C major

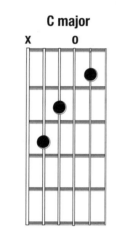

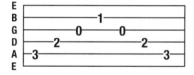

C minor

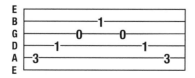

F major

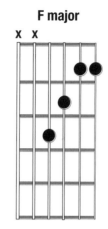

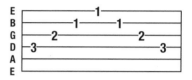

F minor

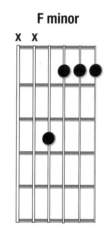

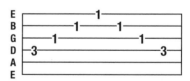

The advantage here is that both these chords trace the basic chord in order: root, 3rd, 5th. We've seen how many guitar chords tend to be inversions or 'edits' of much fuller chords, and so it's more advantageous to start out with the basics before taking on anything too despotic.

Key Changes

Another point we have to look at and understand is what happens if the piece you're playing is non-diatonic. In other words, somewhere along the course of the song, it actually changes key – which means you have to consider using another scale to base a solo upon.

Sometimes key changes are obvious – you just spot a chord that definitely doesn't belong to the key, like this:

‖ C / / / ‖ F / / / ‖ A♭maj7 / / / ‖ etc

Even if it's not particularly obvious from looking at the chord chart, you'll hear the musical equivalent of a bump in the road.

Play through the example above and you should be able to hear what I mean.

To begin with, you need to be able to assimilate what's actually happening from a melodic point of view. Ask yourself, 'Why's that chord there?' Most of the time – that's pretty much 100 per cent – it's got everything to do with the melody of the song, and so your first step is to find out what's happening melodically at the point where the harmony appears to go haywire.

If you've taken my advice and learned to play the melody first, then you're already prepared for what's going to happen and you should easily be able to put the same sort of twist into your improvisation at that point.

Your other resource is to hit the root of the new chord on the first beat of the bar – it will always work (unless something very strange indeed is going on, that is). Then, you can take your pick of the new chord's chord tones.

If the key change is of the temporary kind – say just one or two bars – then you won't have too much time to play anything more. Remember that, by knowing the chord shape inside-out, you know the chord tones as well, and so the job isn't as hard as it might sound.

Most importantly of all, don't play a guessing game in situations like these; use your new-found detective powers to find out what the musical problem is and try to solve it.

Improvising Using Pentatonic Scales

There's no doubt that you'll be spending quite a lot of the time playing in and around pentatonic scales when you're soloing. So much of today's popular rock music is derived from the blues, and the minor pentatonic, for instance, is halfway good enough to cover most of the popular music that falls within the idiom.

As we've already seen from previous examples, the pentatonic scales – both major and minor varieties – are really only abbreviated versions of the seven-note major and minor scales, and so there are no special rules for them – everything we've looked at so far in terms of improvisation holds true when dealing with them.

If you look closely at this particular shape for the minor pentatonic, you'll find that you can trace the chord within with little difficulty:

Minor pentatonic scale   **Minor 7 chord shape**

You have to admit that both of these shapes share a lot in common. But if we look at where all the chord tones lie within the scale – that is, allowing for all the repeated tones within the scales – we get the following...

This is actually very close to a minor 7th chord and contains more chord tones than scale tones! This is one of the reasons why it's considered to be an almost 'failsafe' scale – it's actually quite difficult to play a wrong note. But the rules of phrasing still apply, and it's worth remembering the idea that the root notes always represent 'home', and if you're new to the area, you don't want to wander too far to begin with.

Practise phrasing with the root as the first and last note. A simple example would be to play something like this:

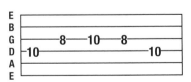

Of course, this represents nothing more than peeking around the door, in terms of regarding the root as home. But starting out with this kind of basic idea begins to school the brain into phrasing musically, right from the beginning.

Practising effective phrasing should be as much a part of your practice routine as playing scales or learning new songs. Put on a backing track and explore how far you can go away from the root before your sense of music starts calling you home. Think about musical punctuation. To oversimplify things a little, you could say that there are really only two types of phrase: those that are complete within themselves, inasmuch as they begin and end with a root, for instance; or a sort of 'question-and-answer' routine whereby two phrases complement each other. Try everything you can – study solos by players you like (there's never been an easier time to do this as just about everything you can name me is available somewhere, and a final resort is always the Internet!) and look closer than just learning the notes. Remember to ask 'Why?' rather than just repeat everything like a parrot: 'Why did he choose to play that note against that chord?' These are the questions that will stimulate you into moving towards new areas, musically speaking.

Pentatonic Chord Changes

Remember when I said that the pentatonic scales are present in just about every culture across the world at a folk level (for 'folk' read 'indigenous music')? Well, as we know, their use is not schooled, and in blues and blues-based music in particular, more rules are broken than are actually observed.

To begin with, there's this idea of playing minor scales over dominant chords. That breaks the 'keep-it-in-the-family' rule straight away, but we know how it works. If you regard the 3rd of the minor pentatonic as being neither major nor minor but an indefinite point in between, it's possible to see its relevance to the dominant chord:

```
C minor pentatonic: C  E♭/E  F  G  B♭  C
                       1     3  4  5   7  1*

               C7: C  E  G  B♭  C
                   1  3  5   7  1
```

* This number refers to the position of the note in the parent minor scale.

If we allow the 3rd in the pentatonic scale to be either major or minor, then this scale can be seen as a perfect fit for the dominant chord. In fact, if we analyse the notes in the minor pentatonic as if it was a chord rather than a scale, we would determine it to be either an 'edited' major or minor 11th:

```
      C11: C  E  G  B♭  F
           1  3  5   7  11

Cmin 11: C  E♭  G  B♭  F
         1   3  5   7  11
```

This hopefully clears up the much-asked question 'Why do we use a minor scale over a major chord?' But the minor pentatonic still has a few more rules to break.

As we've seen, with the diatonic scales, soloing over a song in a single key generally requires the use of only a single scale – the same as the key of the piece. (I say 'requires', but that's not to say that you can't get more adventurous later on…) Then, when the chord changes, you merely move to the relevant modal variation within the parent scale. (If all this still sounds like nuclear physics, you need to review pages 176-8.) Not so with the pentatonic – or, more correctly, not necessarily with the minor pentatonic.

I'll explain: it's perfectly feasible to stay within a single scale and play a good solo, but look at what happens to the scale in terms of root notes and scale tones when you do:

```
C minor pentatonic: C  E♭  F  G  B♭  C
                    1   2  3  4   5  1

            C7: C  E  G  B♭

            F7: F  A  C  E♭

            G7: G  B  D  F
```

As you can see, whereas the C7 fits the scale tolerably well (allowing for the blue third, it's practically perfect!), we lose a scale tone when we move to F7 (ie the A). In this case, we've got a root note, a 5th and a 7th (aka the blue third of the C minor pentatonic, which could be defined as being 'in between' E and E♭, and so both notes have an honorary presence in the scale), but no third – which is a shame, because the 3rd is a useful chord tone or 'target note' for soloing.

When we move on to the G7, we're immediately in trouble because the 3rd – the B in G7 – conflicts with the scale's B♭, which would be G's minor 3rd.

A lot of players who stick to the minor pentatonic for blues and rock soloing get around this problem by either merely editing out the 'wrong' note or by sticking the right one into the scale as a 'visitor'. This means that the might of the pentatonic as a sort of one-stop soloing resource is immediately brought into question. If it doesn't maintain its failsafe capability, what are we going to do?

A simple enough solution is actually to change scale along with the chord. This way, of course, you're guaranteed a perfect fit each time:

```
            C7: C  E  G  B♭

C minor pentatonic: C  E  F  G  B♭  C
                    1  2  3  4   5  1
```

F7: F A C E♭

F minor pentatonic: F A♭ B♭ C E♭ F
                    1   2   3   4   5   1

G7: G B D F

G minor pentatonic: G B♭ C D F G
                    1   2   3 4 5 1

Remember that the 3rd is that 'not major or minor' anomaly in each case and *voilà* – perfect fit every time.

You can try a simple experiment: using the C blues backing track on the CD, play only the chord tones of each chord to hear how 'right' each sounds. For the moment, it will make what you're doing look more obvious if you use these chord shapes:

G7

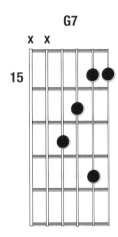

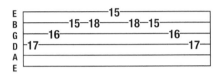

C7

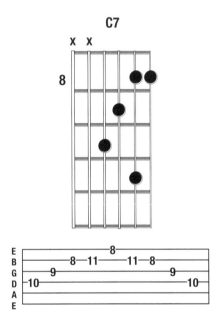

F7

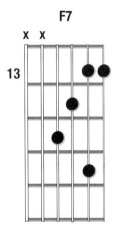

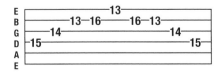

Play the C7 arpeggio over the C7 chord and repeat the process for the other two chords in the arrangement.

The most important thing that's happening here is that, once again, you're listening to the chord tones throughout one of the most popular chord arrangements in Western popular music. And don't forget, it's an exercise for the ears, not the hands, and so don't worry about speed or anything. If you've dealt with your self-consciousness, sing along as you play and tell yourself that the data you're inputting here will be extremely useful in the future.

Superimposition

Of course, the amount of hand movement necessary to perform the previous exercise is almost certainly out of the question from a practical point of view; it was really just to demonstrate a point. In practice, you'd find a way of playing your blues or rock solo with the minimum amount of movement – preferably within a couple of positions on the fretboard.

So what happens if we look at all the notes we need in order to satisfy the need for chord tones all in one place? First, we'll review what notes we need:

C7: C E G B♭

F7: F A C E♭

G7: G B D F

Put them in alphabetical order starting on C:

C D E/E♭ F G A B♭ B C

This turns out to be defined as a Mixolydian scale with a blue third and a natural 7th. I've seen it in some books referred to as the 'bebop major' scale, too.

More important than any names we want to hang on it, though, is the fact that we know already that all these notes can be found within a single position, and so we're on our way to solving the economic-blues-scale conundrum. But we're still faced with the truth that this scale doesn't sound particularly bluesy – and it won't until those 'blue notes' are added.

So, we might have solved the position problem – or proved a point, whichever way you want to look at things – but we still haven't really established a set of reference points on the fretboard that are sufficiently bluesy to be practical.

Let's take a look at the two pentatonic scales for C:

C minor pentatonic: C E♭ F G B♭ C

C major pentatonic: C D E G A C

Now let's try putting them together and see if the shoe fits...

C D E♭ E F G A B♭ C

This time, we've got the E♭/E in there, plus the other members of the Mixolydian scale – still no B, though, and where's that distinctively bluesy flat 5th?

You can see from this example that finding a single scale for the blues isn't as easy as it may sound at first. But, there's no doubt that these two pentatonic scales are very useful reference points and extremely good – as starting points.

I think that just about everyone has started out by moving between the two scales to play a solo – once they've discovered that the minor pentatonic just doesn't go far enough.

So your blues soloing overview on the fretboard might look a little like this:

C minor pentatonic

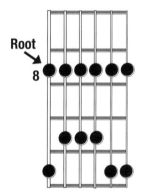

C major pentatonic

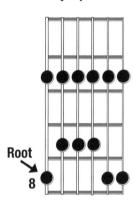

Even this is a little heavy-handed, though. You might not want to move between positions all the time, but it's a good discipline to begin with, until your ears start to pick up where all the good notes are and superimpose both major and minor scales into a single position.

For now, though, it's a good idea to work out where the various roots, chord and scale tones are within the two positions and practise using them.

In Conclusion

If I was to leave you with any advice at all on the subject of how to get out there and use the information in this book, it would this: be yourself.

I've taught a great many students who have been devoted to the styles of a certain players, and I've seen the danger signs long before they have. I've told them,

always acting the philosopher, that you can't take a photograph of a mirror and expect it to reflect. Similarly, you can't photocopy a £5 note and use it as legal currency.

The way forward is to learn from everyone, take note of what you find interesting or inspiring about another player's playing and ask the question 'Why? Why does it work? What makes it tick? Is there a way I can take the idea further and somehow make it my own?'

Another thing to be wary about is the character called Ivor Mate. He used to dog some of my pupils and his influence was generally destructive: 'Ivor Mate says you need a really expensive guitar to get a good sound...' whereas, of course, you don't. 'Ivor Mate who says you don't need to learn to play barre chords at all...' and so on.

I guess the moral of this particular story is to trust your judgement and not that of someone else – not even mine!

12 FINGERING TIPS

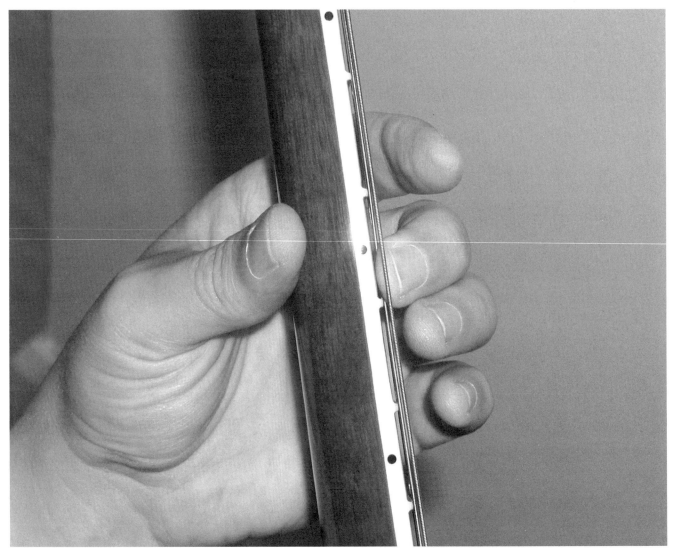

Make sure that your left hand-thumb supports the fingers – think of it as a sort of 'pivot point' around which the fingers work. Laying the thumb down along the neck horizontally is wrong because it gives no support to the fingers at all and makes the job of playing that much harder

When you're bending strings, it's perfectly okay to hook the thumb around the neck to give you something to push against with your fingers

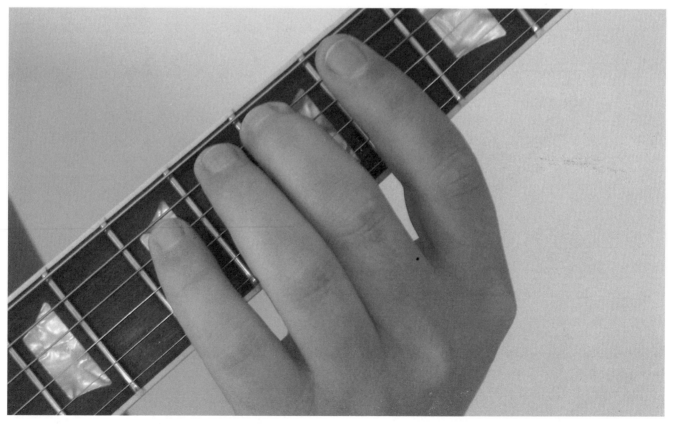

When playing scales, try to adopt a 'one finger per fret' rule, as shown here. Different scales or melody passages break this rule all the time, but if you adopt it as a sort of standard, it usually helps to solve most of the fingering riddles you might come up against

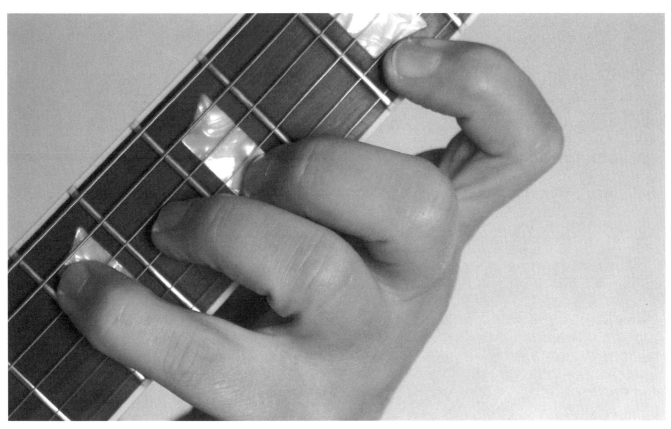

Whether you're playing chords or scales, you're going to find that a stretch like this one is sometimes necessary. The most important thing to remember is that the thumb must still support the hand's 'centre of gravity'. Try to 'reach back' with the first finger rather than distort the whole hand – and don't worry if this kind of thing feels impossible at first, it's all part of the learning process!

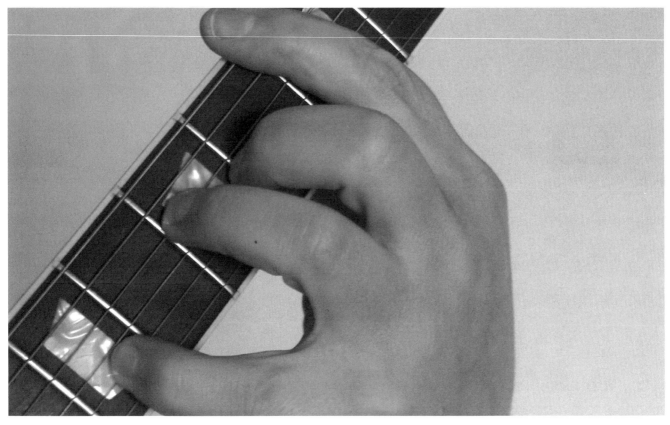

This is where the hand's other extremity is called upon to stretch. Once again, try to 'reach' with the little finger, and don't be overly concerned if you find it difficult at first. The necessary muscles take a while to become supple enough for this kind of movement

Sometimes the hand and fingers are called upon to go against nature. Here, the top joint of my third finger is bent back on itself a little to enable a partial barre, and this manoeuvre is something that was never included in the body's original blueprint! But, as with any specialised form of movement (like ballet or certain sports, for instance), this is something that comes with time, patience and practice. 'Don't rush things and let nature take its course' is the best advice here

The pick should be held firmly between the right-hand first finger and thumb. Don't be tempted to support the pick with any other right-hand fingers, as this can lead to restricted movement

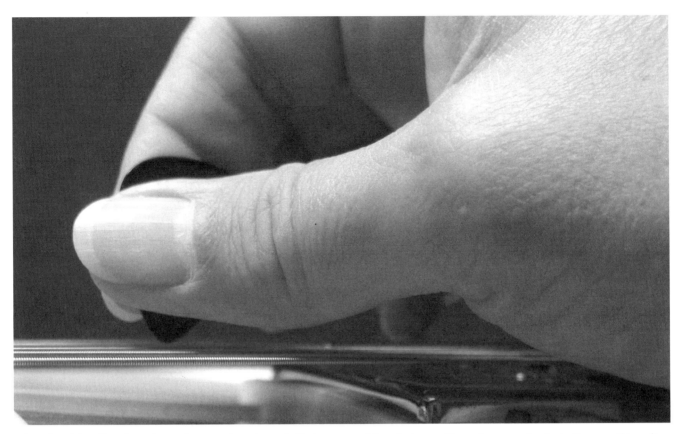

When the pick strikes the guitar strings, you're using only the top 2mm of the plectrum – it's really more of a stroke than anything else. Digging in too hard with the tip of the pick can result in a very harsh, twangy sound on chords and a lot of unnecessary movement on scale passages, because you have to keep lifting the pick to change strings – a bit like running a hurdle race!

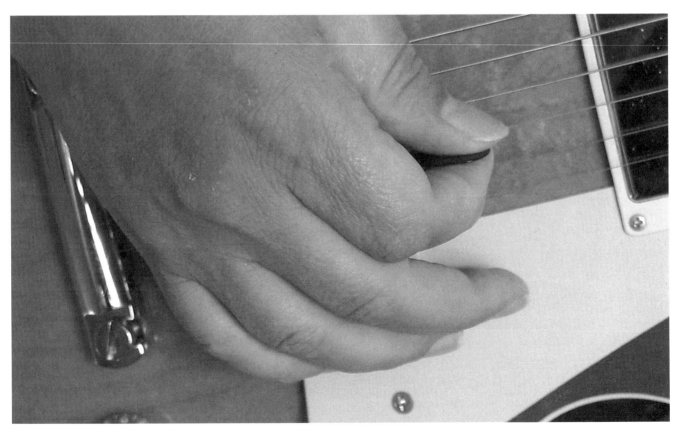

The fingers of the right hand that aren't involved in holding the pick should be allowed to relax and hang loosely. Don't clench your hand up to make a fist as this introduces a lot of unnecessary tension into the hand and forearm which will restrict freedom of movement

BIOGRAPHY

David Mead has played on radio and TV, as well as in bars and clubs all across the UK. A private teacher for longer than he cares to remember, he embarked upon a career in journalism around 1992, when he joined the staff of UK's prestigious *Guitarist* magazine, working his way up to editor three years later. From there, he joined *Guitar Techniques* magazine as editor, a post he held for six and a half years before leaving to pursue a career as a writer and musician.

He remains fully active in the field of guitar education, holding the post of director and course leader of the International Guitar Festival in Bath, UK, taking part in seminars all over the country and writing a monthly column on sight-reading for *Guitar Techniques* magazine.

David has written many guitar tutors, among them the best-selling *10 Minute Guitar Workout*, *100 Guitar Tips* and *100 Tips For Acoustic Guitar*. He has also co-written jazz guitarist Martin Taylor's autobiography, *Kiss And Tell*, and edited Doug Sundling's definitive *The Ultimate Doors Companion*. All titles are available from SMT, 8/9 Frith Street London W1D 3JB. www.musicsales.com

www.davidmead.net   info@davidmead.net

NOTES

NOTES

CD TRACK LIST

All highlighted items refer to chapter headings. Unhighlighted items refer to examples that can be found as illustrations within a given chapter.

Equipment: David Mead used a Yamaha APX7a steel-string acoustic guitar and a Paul Reed Smith signature electric guitar. Strings were Elixir .13 steel and Picato .9 electrics. Microphones were by Beyer & Rode. Effects were Lexicon, Yamaha, Roland and Rocktron. Keyboards/strings/programming/miscellaneous guitar by Phil Hilborne. CD recorded, mixed and mastered by Phil Hilborne.

Phil Hilborne uses and endorses PRS guitars, Picato strings and Cornford amplification.